M000312773

DUTY BEYOND THE BATTLEFIELD

DUTY BEYOND THE BATTLEFIELD

African American Soldiers Fight for Racial Uplift, Citizenship, and Manhood, 1870–1920

LE'TRICE D. DONALDSON

Southern Illinois University Press
Carbondale

Southern Illinois University Press
www.siupress.com

Copyright © 2020 by Le'Trice D. Donaldson
All rights reserved
Printed in the United States of America

23 22 21 20   4 3 2 1

Cover illustration: "Confidence under Pressure," by Michael L. Warren II, 2018

Library of Congress Cataloging-in-Publication Data
Names: Donaldson, Le'Trice D., [date] author.
Title: Duty beyond the battlefield : African American soldiers fight
    for racial uplift, citizenship, and manhood, 1870–1920 / Le'Trice D.
    Donaldson.
Other titles: From triumph to tragedy
Description: Carbondale : Southern Illinois University Press, [2020]
    | Revised and expanded version of the author's thesis (doctoral)—
    University of Tennessee, Knoxville, 2006, titled From triumph
    to tragedy : African American soldiers fight for citizenship and
    manhood in the Spanish-American-Cuban-Filipino War. | Includes
    bibliographical references and index.
Identifiers: LCCN 2019017718 | ISBN 9780809337590 (paperback) |
    ISBN 9780809337606 (ebook)
Subjects: LCSH: African American soldiers—History. | African
    Americans—Social conditions. | Racism—United States—History. |
    United States—Race relations.
Classification: LCC E185.63 .D66 2020 | DDC 305.800973—dc23
LC record available at https://lccn.loc.gov/2019017718

Printed on recycled paper ♻

This paper meets the requirements of ANSI/NISO Z39.48-1992
    (Permanence of Paper). ∞

To my mother, Sherran Miller, and my aunt Anna Franklin
Thank you for all your love and support.

And to my grandmother Dorothy Dorsett, my grandfather
Jesse Bryant, and my godmother Sheralyn McCartney,
who did not make it to the end with me but
are never far from my thoughts.
I miss them so very much, and I know they are watching over me.

CONTENTS

Gallery of illustrations beginning on page 95

ACKNOWLEDGMENTS

Edgar Guest wrote a poem titled "It Couldn't Be Done." I routinely read and recited this poem throughout the process of working on this manuscript because it inspired me to complete it. However, I know that I could not have finished if not for the community of friends and family surrounding me. It takes a village to help make a book possible, because writing is truly a community effort. This book is no exception. I've benefited from the support and guidance of some of the most amazing scholars.

The inspiration for this work came from a question I could not shake after reading Kristen L. Hoganson's *Fighting for American Manhood: How Gender Politics Provoked the Spanish-American and Philippine-American Wars* while I was a master's student at the University of Tennessee–Knoxville: How did African American soldiers construct their masculine identity? The more I researched the question, the more I became intrigued by the lack of scholarly sources that could answer it. With the help of Cynthia Griggs-Fleming, I began my journey into the world of African American military and gender history.

The person most responsible for my becoming a scholar and historian is my mother, Sherran Miller. From a young age, she encouraged my love of reading history and researching. My first research project in elementary school was on the presidency of John F. Kennedy. She'd take me to the library almost every weekend and listen attentively as I'd rattle on about my project. She enrolled my brother and me in a college prep TRIO program, Upward Bound, at Alabama A&M. Between her and my stepfather, Calvin Miller, they made sure I made every Saturday class, which paved the way for my studies at the University of Tennessee–Knoxville. There, I became a Ronald McNair Post-baccalaureate Achievement Scholar, thus launching my career as a historian.

Funding for this project was initially made possible by the history departments of the University of Memphis and York College/CUNY; the African American studies program at the University of Mississippi; and the U.S. Military Academy at West Point.

When I think about my academic mentors, the first person who comes to mind is my academic father, George White Jr. When reflecting on all our conversations and his words of encouragement, I cannot help but become overwhelmed with emotion. George always provided me with support, guidance, and feedback. There are no words that can express how grateful I am for him and his family, who have been my oasis during this long academic journey. I will never be able to truly repay George for all of his pep talks. I am thankful he adopted me!

Margaret Caffrey provided constant support, help, and guidance while serving as my unofficial editor and making me go beyond my comfort zone. Michael L. Warren II designed the amazing cover art for *Duty beyond the Battlefield* and allowed me to drag him along on my various research trips. And I could not have completed this project without the support of my amazing editor Sylvia Frank Rodrigue.

Earnestine Jenkins's research served as inspiration for this book. She shared her family history and helped me look at records and accounts from nontraditional sources. Stephen Stein provided valuable advice about how to navigate the world of military history.

We do not get to choose the family we are born into, but we do get to choose the extended kinships we sustain throughout our lives. Sheena Harris is my best friend and sister-scholar. We wrote this book together, and I know I would not have made it through this process without her. She encouraged me to be brave, fierce, and disciplined. Meredith Baker is one of the most thoughtful, caring, and giving persons I've ever met. I'm thankful for her friendship and for the way she proofread portions of this manuscript. The relationships I forged while a doctoral student at the University of Memphis saved my life. Christina Davis, Daleah Goodwin, K. T. Ewing, Armanthia Duncan, and Shirletta Kinchen made up an amazing support system and were always encouraging. Other fellow scholars in the struggle who deserve my thanks were James Conway, Jack Lorenzini, Troy Hassall, Jeff Jones, Reginald Ellis, Darius Young, Amanda Lee Keikialoha Savage, and Ashley Fair.

My research would not have gone as smoothly if I had not benefited from the support and help of the archivists and librarians at the Schomburg Center for Research in Black Culture, the University of Memphis Library and Special Collections, the Library of Congress, the University of Utah Special Collections, the Moorland-Spingarn Research Center at Howard University, the National Archives, the University of Tennessee–Knoxville Special Collections at Hopkins Library, the U.S. Military Academy, the U.S. Army Military History Institute, the Nebraska Historical Society, the State Archives of North Carolina, Marist College, and the Buffalo Soldiers Museum in Houston.

I am grateful to my family and friends, especially Nina Archie, Maurice Iwunze, Nadiah and Nabila Khalid, and cousins Victoria Franklin and Jacqueline Kinloch, for opening their homes to me while on my research trips. I loved bouncing my historical ideas off the scientific mind of my brilliant niece Daphne Goeway. My best friend, Chiquita Ester, with whom I've been through so much, has always been supportive and a tower of strength.

Andre Johnson organized the writing accountability group that served as a wonderful support system to help me finish this manuscript. The group was a great sounding board for ideas and provided honest feedback, helping make this a better book. Additionally, for all the advice and encouragement at times during this project when I needed it the most, I want to give a special thanks to Jennifer Williams, William Mulligan, John Morrow Jr., Shirley Joiner, Chad Williams, Derrick Lanois, Ava Purkiss, Shennette Garrett-Scott, Michelle Scott-Hillman, Deirdre Cooper-Owens, Amanda Nell Edgar, Ethel Scurlock, Shannon Eaves, Dionne Bailey, LaShawn Harris, Keisha Blain, Erin Chapman, Jennifer Ransom, Daniel Franke, Vanessa Grande, Karen Jackett, Daryl Scott, Patrick Alexander, Brigitte Billeaudeaux, Tonya Thames Taylor, Charles Ross, Karen Bradley, Naina Shahzadi, Charisse Burden-Stelly, Micki Kaufman, Cherisse Jones-Branch, Maggie Yancey, Mark Stout, Gregory Mixon, and Arwin Smallwood. I'm also grateful to W. Chris Johnson, Jayanni Webster, Dana Asbury, Courtney White, Tyron Sanders, and Jeffrey Lichtenstein for their feedback, proofreading, love, and support.

I would like to thank God, through whom all things are possible. Reverend Donald and Ms. Carolyn Ester of New Bethel Missionary Baptist Church gave me a home for the holidays and a spiritual center. Dion, Leo, Anton, and Lerone are the four best brothers a girl could ever ask for; they were each there for me with a kind and supportive word during this process. Lastly, I thank the outside readers of my manuscript for all of their suggestions and edits.

DUTY BEYOND THE BATTLEFIELD

INTRODUCTION

T he hot sun beamed down on his dark skin, forcing him to perspire so much that he was drenched in sweat, and it seemed that the longer he walked, the more the temperature increased. Eventually his legs, both wounded by gunshots, gave out under him, and he began to crawl through the Arizona desert. The shirt on his back clung to him uncomfortably as if it was a second skin, but his wool army trousers and boots protected his knees and shins from being too bruised as he stumbled and crawled to the Cotton Wood Ranch for help. The convoy he was a part of—made up of eleven buffalo soldiers and one white officer, the paymaster—had been ambushed, and almost every man in the group was wounded. As he worked his way to the ranch, he knew he had to ignore the pain and the heat because his fellow soldiers were counting on him. If he did not make it at least two miles to raise the alarm and return with wagons, all of his wounded comrades would die. The weight of their lives weighed on him, but somewhere in the deep recesses of his mind, Corporal Isaiah Mays thought, If I fail, my people fail.

Corporal Mays and Sergeant Benjamin Brown, both of the Twenty-Fourth Infantry, earned the Congressional Medal of Honor for their heroism during the Wham Paymaster Robbery of 1889. Sergeant Brown, the convoy commander, was shot in both arms and his stomach during the robbery. He kept fighting until he could no longer hold a weapon. Eight of the buffalo soldiers were wounded during the gun battle, and two were shot multiple times. The encounter lasted thirty minutes, and despite the incredible fight put up by the soldiers, the robbers successfully made off with the payroll of $28,000 (present-day equivalency of $772,030) in gold and silver coins. The actions of the black soldiers in that convoy went a long way in securing the position of African American men as soldiers in the U.S. Army.[1]

Isaiah Mays, a man born as property in Virginia, joined the army during an era when African Americans were defining and shaping their identity and autonomy in post–Civil War America. The shadow of slavery and the paternalism it fostered haunted black men while in the service of their country, but it did not prevent their fighting for economic independence, their desire for literacy, or the way they shaped their communities.

"Once you let the black man get upon his person the brass letters, 'U.S.,' let him get an eagle on his button, and a musket on his shoulder and bullets in his pocket, and there is no power on Earth which can deny that he has earned the right to citizenship in the United States," declared Frederick Douglass during the Civil War, but they could have easily been said by any number of black soldiers. Clearly, what these men needed was a chance to reaffirm their entitlement to citizenship. Indeed, many blacks believed that their rights of citizenship had been earned through their participation in the Civil War. The opportunity had finally arrived for the young men of another generation; they would have a chance to fight and prove again to the world that black soldiers were just as brave, honorable, and manly as white soldiers. A war with Spain represented an arena in which black men could exercise their citizenship. Moreover, the arena of combat was critical precisely because white laws and customs prevented blacks from exercising their citizenship in other areas.[2]

After earning his freedom by fighting in the Civil War, the black soldier redefined the status of African Americans as citizens and freedom fighters willing to claim the rights of full citizenship and manhood. Yet the African American soldier of the second half of the nineteenth century is one of the most misinterpreted figures in American military history. *Duty beyond the Battlefield* presents an analysis of African American soldiers from 1870 to 1920, of how they constructed and comported their citizenship and manhood through interconnection with the African American community, and of how they influenced and were in turn influenced by the community, something no other study has examined. This book provides a contextualized gender paradigm, revealing how black soldiers created a new identity as men and citizens and framing the service of these men as a part of the much larger civil rights movement of the nineteenth and early twentieth centuries.

The time period analyzed in this study begins with the second reorganization of the army until after World War I and highlights the transitional role black servicemen played during this politically charged era. Many of these men went on to become leaders and organizers in the fight for civil and human rights across the African diaspora. They represented a bridge between several intersecting cultures in America: European colonial/settler culture, formerly enslaved African culture, Mexican/Latinx culture, and Indigenous American culture. They fought in popular and iconic conflicts in American history such as the Indian Wars, the war to secure Cuban independence, and the First World War. They also fought in seemingly unpopular and brutal campaigns, suppressing a colonial rebellion in the Philippines and hunting for the Mexican rebel Pancho Villa. In so doing, black soldiers fought to assert, preserve, and defend their most prized possessions: their citizenship and black manhood. These soldiers evolved from simply being warriors to being symbols of racial consciousness and racial pride.

According to historian Jacquelyn Dowd Hall, "Remembrance is always a form of forgetting, and the dominant narrative of the civil rights movement—distilled from history and memory, twisted by ideology and political contestation . . . distorts and suppresses as much as it reveals." When we examine the African American military experience, it is often through distorted lenses, and when Hall discusses how the history of the long civil rights movement has been usurped by American conservatives, she thoroughly dismantles the notion that the civil rights movement should be confined to a particular decade and region. My research extends this argument by asserting that African American soldiers should be included in the long civil rights movement. The activism of black soldiers went beyond the much-discussed Double V (victory at home, victory abroad) campaign of World War II. There was a long tradition of activism by black soldiers and from the African American community surrounding black participation in the military. These men encouraged a "march of freedom" to the West, as seen in the Exoduster movement of the 1870s, and continued with the Great Migration of the early twentieth century.[3]

Thousands of African Americans headed to the western frontier to homestead and find a safe space to create independent black enclaves and communities. They followed advertisements that promised new beginnings and new opportunities. Unlike whites who joined the military as a last resort, black men enlisted and reenlisted because service provided an opportunity to start life anew.

African Americans by the end of the nineteenth century were legally reduced to the status of second-class citizens. Black men saw military service as symbiotic with participation in the hegemonic masculinity of war culture and as an opportunity to prove to white Americans that the 1896 *Plessy v. Ferguson* decision and its articulation of the "separate but equal" doctrine was a grave mistake. As historian Willard Gatewood observed of black soldiers serving in the Philippines, "Confronted with lynching, disenfranchisement, and other evidence of racial prejudice, blacks viewed the war within the context of their deteriorating status at home."[4]

The goal of *Duty beyond the Battlefield* is to reexamine the black soldier from the era of Reconstruction to the end of the First World War and to contextualize the black soldier's unique experience fighting for race and country. Black soldiers served while being viewed as domestic enemies—especially during World War I, when the Department of Justice and Military Intelligence spent years investigating and surveilling the African American community. The agency these men enacted by serving in the military was bold and both directly violent and indirectly nonviolent. Simply by wearing the uniform sent a clear message to Jim Crow America: these men rejected racist notions of black inferiority and were willing to fight as citizens and men. The black military presence on the frontier helped to reshape the American West. Black soldiers did not behave as passive victims of prejudice; they formed group cohesions centering on racial uplift that kept the men from deserting.[5]

By strengthening the gender analysis, this work demonstrates that black soldiers fought and served for two principal reasons: as a means of exercising their citizenship and as a means of demonstrating that they were real men in an era when proving one's manhood was a national obsession. American manhood is rooted in the need to prove itself. African American men needed to go beyond proving their manhood; they needed to prove their humanity. Blacks were consistently depicted in negative and inferior stereotypes. The rise of social Darwinism only fueled the rhetoric of scientific racism that claimed black men to be cowardly, sexual deviants, and incapable of military leadership. This study provides a critical window through which we can reconstruct their motivations for fighting and serving not only in times of war but also in times of supposed peace. The preservation of the black soldier's citizenship and manhood was intertwined with the fight against the Jim Crow oligarchy, which had taken hold in the South and was exported to U.S. colonies and later to Europe during the Great War.

When we think about black manhood, it is important not to view it as static or timeless. For black soldiers, their masculine identity was directly bonded to their racial identity. This meant that their military service belonged to the black community and would reflect on all those who would come after them. The fight black soldiers took to the streets to defend their honor, rights, and citizenship ties directly to their fight to assert their humanity. This is why black soldiers need to be included as active participants in the discussion about the long fight for black civil and human rights.

In *Black Regulars*, William Dobak and Thomas Phillips make the inaccurate assessment that the African American press, being solely focused on middle-class issues, paid little attention to the everyday life of the black foot soldier. The campaign to get African Americans into the military academy and commissioned as officers became a key campaign for African American civil rights. The two cannot be separated. The need for black soldiers to be led by black officers directly challenged the racist notions that blacks could fight only if under the leadership of white officers. This is why it is necessary to insert into the long civil rights movement the African American soldiers and the various forms of activism and defiance they performed on the frontier and on the border.[6]

When thinking about racial uplift and racial progress, black men understood the symbolic value of simply being mobile in America. Migrating westward and being able to flee coerced labor, intimidation, and southern tyranny gave black troops status. They were able to associate and build relationships with individuals who made their livelihood outside the traditional mainstream economy. With the exception of the chaplains in their regiments, they were judged or categorized as being from the lower class.[7]

The motivations described for the turn-of-the-century black soldier in *Duty beyond the Battlefield* differ from those found in mainstream books and other interpretations. Typically, most scholarship regarding this group of soldiers emphasizes their need to prove that they deserved to be citizens and their quest to gain economic opportunities denied them as civilians. But this study starts with the proposition that these soldiers already defined themselves as citizens and that war was perhaps one of the few areas in which they could exercise their entitlement. More importantly, this study differs from other scholarly analyses because of the critical examination of how these men constructed their masculinity and of how their military service created a racially conscious generation of soldiers and veterans who became a critical backbone of the "New Negro" movement of the 1920s. Only within the last decade have historians begun to add gender to the discussion of the black soldier. This study asserts that proving their manhood, demonstrating their citizenship, and preserving racial pride served as the primary motivations behind these soldiers' desire to serve and fight. As an African American journalist wrote in 1898, "War is a blessing in disguise for the Negro. He will get honor. He will have an opportunity of proving to the world his real bravery, worth, and manhood."[8]

One of the most striking aspects of black military history, which is often overlooked, is how black westward migration grew with the presence of African American soldiers in small rural towns and along the southwestern border. *Duty beyond the Battlefield* connects the training and deployment of black soldiers with the creation of black communities throughout America's frontier in the late nineteenth century and in the Philippines. Nearly one thousand black soldiers at the end of the Filipino rebellion remained behind in these Pacific islands to marry and take care of their families, unlike the white soldiers who took no interest in the children they fathered with the Filipino women. In her book *Racial Beachhead* (2011), Carol McKibbon touched on how the military increased racial diversity in small towns around the country after World War II. My research discusses how the buffalo soldiers continuously increased the black populations of every small and isolated military post in which they were located and even encouraged other blacks through various news articles and ad campaigns to migrate with them.

Life on the frontier was hard, violent, isolated, and dangerous. Black enlisted soldiers engaged with and often married women who worked in positions that did not align with traditional Victorian morality. The wives of these soldiers played an equally important role in how African Americans formed communities and economic stability when they settled in the West. The men frequented saloons, brothels, and gambling establishments on their furloughs. The caravans that followed black troops always included individuals who made their living through an underground economy. Veterans of the Twenty-Fourth Infantry who founded the all-black town of Blackdom, New Mexico, would go into business with Mattie/Mittie Moore Wilson—a successful brothel owner from Roswell, New Mexico—and help establish a prosperous black-owned oil enterprise, the Blackdom Oil Company.[9]

Recent scholarship on black military history, citizenship, war, and society, such as Chad Williams's *Torchbearers of Democracy*, Elizabeth Leonard's *Men of Color to Arms!*, Gerald Horne's *Black and Brown*, James Leiker's *Racial Borders*, Christian Samito's *Becoming American under Fire*, Jeffrey T. Sammons and John H. Marrow Jr.'s *Harlem's Rattlers and the Great War*, and Adriane Lentz-Smith's *Freedom Struggles*, focuses on and complicates certain previously examined notions of the black military experience, going beyond economic gains to examine citizenship and the fight for racial equality. Older studies by Willard Gatewood, such as *"Smoked Yankees" and the Struggle for Empire* and *Black Americans and the White Man's Burden*,

1898–1903, emphasized that the disillusionment and frustration African Americans experienced in the 1960s and 1970s were expressed as the feelings of the turn-of-the-nineteenth-century African American.[10]

Duty beyond the Battlefield contends that we need to look at the years directly after the Civil War to challenge this tradition. Rather than focusing on one particular war, this study examines the evolution of black soldiers during an era of constitutional crisis when the definition of citizenship was restricted. These men are the heirs to the legacy of the black founding fathers and constitutionalists of the previous generation. Racial uplift, citizenship politics, and gender identity all played significant roles in helping to transform the black soldier of the late-nineteenth and early twentieth centuries. This work makes an important scholarly intervention in the realms of military history and African American history and contributes to the growing scholarship on citizenship.

African American soldiers had a complex relationship with indigenous peoples on the frontier. Black soldiers viewed their service as not only fulfilling their duty but also securing a place for their own humanity at the unfortunate expense of the Plains Indians. James Baldwin described the African American man as an "unloved stranger" and "exile in his own land" and observed that the "cruel and totally inescapable ambivalence of his status in his country" compelled him, in Gatewood's words, "to wage a persistent battle for self-identity and self-esteem." This fueled the need for African Americans to settle west and along the Rio Grande border, creating their own enclaves throughout the western territories as a direct result of the presence of armed black soldiers. As Shona Jackson argues in *Creole Indigeneity*, black people inherited a certain level of settler power and used techniques similar to those used by white settlers.[11]

As a military history, this work adds to the relatively new arena of scholarly exploration of war and society. For instance, the migratory patterns of African Americans in places such as New Mexico, Alaska, Wyoming and Utah are directly linked to the stationing of black soldiers in those states. I contend that the caravan of African Americans who followed black soldiers helped to expand and establish black communities in the West. In towns such as El Paso, Texas, blacks enjoyed a certain level of political and economic autonomy because of the consistent presence of black soldiers. The military provided a level of protection that black communities could not get in the rest of the South, where race riots and lynching were commonplace. *Duty beyond the Battlefield* highlights how black soldiers, simply by being armed and in uniform, served as a deterrent against racial violence in certain communities. They were able to create new identities as citizens and define freedom on their own terms rather than relying on someone else to define it for them.

Duty beyond the Battlefield adds to the scholarly inquiry around the issue of masculinity and in the particular ways in which black men were able to express manhood in a society committed to circumscribing all black expressions of humanity. In this regard, I demonstrate the ways in which soldiers served as templates for the possibilities of black manhood and inspiration for racial advancement. In addition, this study shows how the lives of these soldiers—and their interaction with their communities—reinforced the notion that freedom among African Americans was generally accepted as a communal enterprise.

Catherine Squires in her work "Rethinking the Black Public Sphere" coined the terms "counter-public sphere" and "enclave public sphere" for marginalized peoples. Squires asserts, "A public can enclave itself, hiding counter-hegemonic ideas and strategies in order to survive." Black soldiers and the communities they created formed their own enclaves to insulate and protect themselves and to combat the hegemonic ideas of racism and oppression at secluded or isolated posts. In this text, then, "black enclave" refers to a loosely connected group of black migrants in one place. The enclave served as a form of protection and networking for small black communities on the isolated frontier and borderlands.[12]

Black troops, through their positions as a mobile constabulary frontier force, created highly visible and mobile counter-public spheres when they served as correspondents to the African American press. The more educated the soldiers became, the more politically engaged they became in challenging the American apartheid system. During the Filipino conflict more so than the Cuban campaign, black soldiers served as correspondents and a voice of humanity against the rhetoric of white American imperialism, demonstrated by their actions as well as by the number of black veterans who stayed and built a life in the Philippines.

With respect to citizenship studies, this work complements an existing and growing body of work that addresses how individuals and groups claim their rights as citizens, navigate varying democratic processes, and struggle with human rights dilemmas that question their legitimacy as people entitled to live in a responsive nation-state. Moreover, this study reveals that many of the greatest assertions or expressions of citizenship were simple acts that many white citizens took for granted, like learning to read and write, learning how to use a weapon, and engaging in self-defense.

It is necessary to rethink the history of how black soldiers constructed their identity from the end of the Civil War through the end of World War I. The radicalism of black chaplains and officers such as Henry Vinton Plummer, T. G. Steward, and Allen Allensworth has yet to be included in the current discourse on African American soldiers. Allensworth and Plummer supported the migration and relocation of blacks out of the South. Allensworth, after leaving the military, founded his own town in California and structured it like a military unit.

Significantly, this study also is among the rare pieces of scholarship that take seriously the role played by black chaplains in the leadership of former slaves and the development of them into racial warriors. The responsibility of the chaplain in the black units went beyond spiritual guidance. They both educated and ministered to the men of their regiments and at times even recruited, as in the case of Chaplain Garland White during the Civil War or Chaplain George Prioleau during the Spanish-American-Cuban-Filipino conflict.

Black clergymen were chosen to create a curriculum to educate enlisted black servicemen. However, this curriculum extended past teaching them simply to read and write. They also taught their men what citizenship meant to them and to the black community. This is why it is necessary to understand how militant race men such as Allensworth, Plummer, and Steward created a generation of politically active and community-centered soldiers who were not afraid to fight and defend themselves against the abuses of racist police in places such as Brownsville and Houston.

"Race man" as used in this disquisition is defined as a man who was concerned with the growth of the race and followed the uplift philosophy of progress. My research overall helps to properly contextualize how such men began to see themselves as not just soldiers but as race men and responsible for the uplift of their people.

The book is divided into two parts. The first section focuses on the transition and evolution of African American servicemen beyond that of soldiers into symbols of racial pride and leaders in the community. It begins with the buffalo soldiers and assesses how through education and acts of defiance these men evolved into race men.

The section closes with an examination of the African American participation in the unsuccessful search for Pancho Villa in the Mexican Punitive Expedition (1916–17) and of how African American soldiers viewed their military participation in this tumultuous time in American and world history. The transition from an embarrassing and unsuccessful hunt for Villa left the American military unprepared for entry into the First World War. Rather than conceptualize black soldiers and officers who served in the Great War as a single military campaign, we must widen our gaze and view the soldiers who served in this conflict as fully evolved from a generation of black men seeking vindication for their race. World War I provided a different experience for these race warriors who were exposed to European military culture on a global stage. These two conflicts provided a springboard for a racially conscious generation of veterans, who became the backbone of the "New Negro" movement of the 1920s and laid the framework of the Double V campaign of World War II.[13]

The second section constructs what it meant to be a military race man. Analyzing and contrasting the military careers of Henry Ossian Flipper (1856–1940), the first black officer to graduate from West Point, and Charles Young (1864–1922), the third black officer to graduate from West Point, will demonstrate the political significance of military service to racial consciousness. Flipper, upon his graduation, rejected the correlative nature of military service and racial uplift and embarked on an escapist type of ideology, which steered him away from racial leadership and down a path where he joined in criticizing black soldiers who committed acts of violence to defend themselves. Charles Young, however, embraced the role of carrying the mantle of his race and encouraged racial uplift, essentially becoming a race man. Flipper, not Young, became the model for the black officer that men such as Benjamin Davis Sr. and Colin Powell fashioned themselves.

PART 1

1.
BULLETS AND TORCHES

The Making of the Race Warrior on the Western Frontier, 1870–96

> We will never be able to get what we want in this country until we are willing to organize and stand together as one man on things essential to the welfare of our people as a whole.
>
> —Sergeant Vance Hunter Marchbanks, Tenth Cavalry

In the spring of 1893 in the wild and dusty "tent city" of Crawford, Nebraska, tensions ran high between the small white population and the black soldiers stationed two miles away at Fort Robinson. At one point, the white civilians of Crawford attempted to lynch former buffalo soldier Charles Diggs, but he escaped the mob and found safety and protection at the fort with his former comrades of the Ninth Cavalry regiment. Diggs understood that the white civilians would not dare cross these soldiers and essentially attack the U.S. Army.

After the incident with Charles Diggs, a letter surfaced on the post written by the "Yellow Cape" that boldly called for the soldiers to boycott racist establishments. The anonymous author issued a warning to the white citizens of Crawford: the soldiers of the Ninth would burn their town to the ground if necessary. The letter stated,

> You lynch, you torture, and you burn Negroes in the south, but we swear by all that is good and holy that you shall not outrage us and our people right here under the shadow of "Old Glory," while we have shot and shell, and if you persist we will repeat the horrors of San Domingo—we will reduce your homes and firesides to ashes and send your guilty souls to hell.

The broadside of the letter was signed "500 men with the bullet or the torch."[1]

Although the anger and defiance expressed in this letter were widely shared among the soldiers, its authorship was initially attributed to Chaplain Henry V. Plummer of the regiment. However, only Sergeant Barney McKay of the Ninth's Troop G received any punishment, a court-martial for "conduct to the prejudice of good order and discipline." McKay, no stranger to standing up for racial pride, had been involved with shooting up the town of Suggs, Wyoming, when fellow soldiers experienced racial abuse at a local establishment. Through their willingness to resist and defend themselves against white violence with violence of their own in such an affirmative manner, the soldiers of the Ninth demonstrated their racial pride.[2]

In the second half of the nineteenth century, black regulars evolved from simply being soldiers into race warriors. Not only did the four black regular regiments secure the U.S.–Mexico border and engage in various campaigns in the Indian Wars, but these soldiers also participated in community development for African Americans and helped encourage black migration to the western frontier. Additionally, they served as "vanguards of the race," as Chad Williams labels them, and actively contributed to the ideology of racial uplift. By exercising their rights as citizens and men and displaying skill and leadership, the buffalo soldiers strengthened African Americans overall. The uniform offered a promise—a promise of status, citizenship, manhood, and full partnership in the grand American destiny.[3]

After emancipation black men redefined their manhood to center on power and autonomy over their families and political rights. Military service laid the foundations for their citizenship. Black men who served in the military held the belief that "the man who risks his life for his country has the right to vote in it." The men who chose to serve in the military after the Civil War were men of conscious agency who were complex and paradoxical characters, not easily defined as villainous enforcers of white domestic authority (in the way they forcibly removed Plains Indians from their lands and killed all those who opposed the U.S. government's Indian removal policy) or heroic martyrs of injustice. Rather, these men represented themselves and their race to the best of their abilities. They understood that in their pursuit to better themselves, they were also uplifting their community but at the same time sacrificing Indigenous Americans. Black troopers and settlers juxtaposed their livelihood against that of Indigenous Americans, who in their eyes sided with the Confederacy; black soldiers and settlers chose their people and the benefits of living in a community where they were not the most despised people. The concept of the professional black soldier was a direct challenge to the white masculine hierarchy because such men were educated, disciplined, self-motivated, and militarily trained to properly defend themselves with a rifle, saber, and revolver.[4]

THE GOLDEN AGE

The era of Reconstruction has been labeled the "Golden Age" for African American political and civil rights. Reconstruction in the eyes of many signaled the possibility of America becoming a racially egalitarian society. After Reconstruction black people became systematically and legally oppressed and disenfranchised during what has been called the nadir of African American history.

Frederick Douglass, the father of two Civil War veterans and longtime advocate for black military service, stepped to the podium on June 14, 1876, at the Republican National Convention, weary and worried, and made an impassioned plea to his audience:

> You say you have emancipated us. You have; and I thank you for it. You say you have enfranchised us; and I thank you for it. But what is your emancipation?—What is your enfranchisement? What does it all amount to if the black man, . . . after having been freed from the slaveholder's lash, he is to be subjected to the slaverholder's shotgun?

Yet, despite these harsh conditions and evolving status of African Americans during this time, African American soldiers continued to make strides to break the barriers of racism that permeated the army and the western frontier. African Americans never surrendered to white supremacy. They resisted, and their resistance and service is their legacy.[5]

At the end of the Civil War over 13 percent of the Union army comprised African Americans. These soldiers were utilized as the representatives of the victorious Union government. The men of the U.S. Colored Volunteers were mostly ex-slaves, and their presence in the South had a profound effect upon the newly freed men and women of that region. The black soldiers stationed throughout the former Confederacy represented a living testament that slavery was over and that black people were no longer required to obey their former masters. A white southerner observed, "The effect of Negro soldiers on the freedmen was cited by many southerners as another cause for their discontent with the Negro troops. To a great extent, they incite the freedmen to deeds of violence and encourage them in indolence."[6]

In the months and years directly following the end of the Civil War, the Union blue uniform symbolized for many the victory over centuries of

American chattel slavery. The black man in Union blues stationed throughout the conquered South represented a direct challenge to the white paternalistic hierarchy. There were several instances in cities such as Memphis and New Orleans where black soldiers openly clashed with white civilians. In his 1865 report about the conditions in the South for President Andrew Johnson, General Carl Schurz highlighted the plight of black people. Because "some in the South did not realize that the Negroes were free," Schurz recommended "the bodily presence of a Negro with a musket on his shoulder." Schurz went on to state, "To protect the Negro and punish the still rebellious individuals it will be necessary to have this part of the country pretty thickly settled with soldiers."[7]

Schurz reported that the dead bodies of black men and women could be found along the roads throughout the former Confederacy, illustrating why the presence of black soldiers mattered so much to the newly liberated black community. They helped to police the former masters and Confederates and kept them from attacking and exploiting freedmen. The successes and failures of black soldiers s mattered far beyond the realm of the battlefield. The visibility of the black male body in uniform, especially during Reconstruction, was a stark contrast to what white America was accustomed to in previous decades.[8]

The army uniform represented the authority and autonomy black men had been denied before the Civil War. Male power during this era was directly connected to one's race. This belief was directly related to the rise of social Darwinism during the late nineteenth century. The ability of black soldiers to defend themselves, their families, and their communities from acts of racial violence and attempted control conflicted with how white people tried to demean black manhood. The agency to be mobile and occupy various spaces throughout the western frontier provided a level of autonomy over one's life that these men may not have been able to enact if they had remained in the Jim Crow South.

Slavery stultified black manhood and prevented black men from protecting and providing for their families. They were not officially allowed to be soldiers/warriors, and this helped to perpetuate the image of the black man as nervous, weak, childlike, and scared. This white paternalistic view of black men evolved in the post–Civil War era into black men becoming hypersexualized, violent animals that needed the chains of bondage to keep them in their place. Black men in uniforms with muskets, intelligence, and discipline directly challenged these racist views. Biased white policy makers thus saw it as necessary to keep black soldiers out of the gaze of whites and blacks in the North and South. Despite Schurz's report, it became the policy of the U.S. Army not only to have segregated units in the regular army but also to keep these newly organized units west of the Mississippi River.[9]

NO MORE FIELDS AND MULES

The black enlisted soldier was not your typical Victorian male, dressed in a three-piece suit. Rather, he was a different iteration of black masculinity, rooted in violence and service. He fought, protected, and policed whites, Chicanos, and Native Americans along the frontier and the northern and southern borders. Between 1866 and 1917, twenty-five thousand black men served in the army. Henry McComb of the Tenth Cavalry boldly asserted, "We made the West!"[10]

The year 1866 became a milestone for many black men living in the racist South. They had decisions to make about their future after slavery. The desire to reject fieldwork and experience adventure motivated many young men and former Civil War veterans to join the regular army. Charles Creek decided he was fed up with his life as a farm laborer. He stated that he joined the army because "he got tired of looking at mules from sunrise to sunset." Emmanuel Stance and Jacob Wilks were both young, scrappy, volatile men when they enlisted in the army. They were both from New Orleans and would rise to the rank of sergeant in less than four years. Stance was just nineteen when he enlisted in 1866. He would become the first buffalo soldier in the post–Civil War army to earn the Medal of Honor. Samuel Harris believed that after he completed his military service he would be equipped with the proper tools and training to get a federal job. Each of these men decided to enlist in the regular army for various reasons, but what their service meant to the African American community would go beyond a paycheck or adventure.[11]

In the same year, in April, the Civil Rights Act of 1866 conferred American citizenship on blacks. Citizenship, education, and the right to vote were the cornerstones of Reconstruction. Additionally, on July 28, the Republican-controlled Congress enacted legislation to restructure and reorganize the army. One of the key components of the Army Reorganization Act authorized the creation of six permanent black regiments. The July 1866 act revolutionized the American army and rewarded the African American men who helped defeat the Confederates during the Civil War. The decision to create these permanent regiments and, further, to nominate young men to the U.S. Military Academy at West Point served as victories for African American men and for the movement led by Frederick Douglass during the Civil War to guarantee these men had the right to claim their civil and political privileges.[12]

The six new units—the Thirty-Eighth, Thirty-Ninth, Fortieth, and Forty-First Infantries and the Ninth and Tenth Cavalries—would be made up of black enlisted men under white officers. Three thousand former members of the U.S. Colored Volunteers joined the new regular army. Some of these men served in the roles of noncommissioned officers and believed that continued military service would provide future opportunities beyond sharecropping. Their ability to serve in the military signified the value of the black man as soldier and citizen. Advocates for black military service during the Civil War such as Martin Delaney, Frederick Douglass, and Charles Sumner continued to campaign for blacks in the regular army and acceptance to West Point. The black regiments honored Charles Sumner, an ardent supporter of equal rights and citizenship for African Americans, with a resolution upon his death in the *Army and Navy Journal*.[13]

Army reorganization occurred again in 1869, including a reduction in troop and unit size. The four infantry units were now combined into the Twenty-Fourth and Twenty-Fifth Infantries. The two new black infantry units completely replaced the previous Twenty-Fourth and Twenty-Fifth Infantries, giving them new unit emblems and new regimental histories.[14] Regimental identities were important in how each regiment developed a reputation for being brave, rowdy, fearless, reliable, and so on. The history of the Twenty-Fifth Infantry, a unit that famously served nine years in Texas, included participation in twenty-six expeditions without a single death or major injury. The history of this unit, with its reputation as comprising "splendid fighters and brave scouts," plays a prominent role in why it was involved in the Brownsville affair at the start of the twentieth century. The same thing can be said about the Twenty-Fourth Infantry and why it was involved in the Houston uprising in 1917. A discussion of the Brownsville and Houston incidents will be explored in chapter 3, but it is important to understand how each of the four buffalo soldier regiments perceived itself.[15]

Military life on the western frontier, as journalist Deb. Randolph Keim observed, was "isolation within desolation." The men lived in overcrowded, vermin-infested barracks, sometimes sharing straw-filled mattresses with a bunkmate and eating badly prepared food. Those who were not officers were subjected to long hours of menial labor and faced harsh and strict punishments for not following orders. General William T. Sherman declared, "Some of what are called military posts, are mere collections of huts made of logs, adobes, or mere holes in the ground, and are about as much forts as prairie dog villages might be called forts."[16]

Title DUTY BEYOND THE BATTLEFIELD: AFR

Condition Good

Location Walden Aisle Q Bay 09 Item 9673

Description May have some shelf-wear due to normal use. Your purchase funds free job training and education in the greater Seattle area. Thank you for supporting Goodwill's nonprofit mission!

Source Prescanned

SKU 0KVOFV00EAY3

ASIN 0809337592

Code 9780809337590

Employee 1dboufnar

Date Added 11/19/2023 8:58:28 AM

The military brought men together from all walks of life, and they all suffered together in the harshness of frontier living. For some buffalo soldiers, living the rough life of the frontier was more appealing than sharecropping or being a field hand. The fact is, men joined the army to get a skill and learn how to read.

It is not surprising that the cavalry units, which stir up imagery of knights wielding sabers, received more attention and are glorified more often than the infantry units. The infantry units received less press attention and less scholarly analysis. They did the grunt work and within the military caste system were perceived as less glamorous than cavalry units. Yet, the foot soldiers in both cavalry and infantry had to do hard, laborious tasks.

The army's primary occupations were bakers, clerks, and telegraphers, and thus basic literacy was needed by most of the black soldiers. The model of education developed by Allen Allensworth for the Twenty-Fourth Infantry became the standard model for the entire U.S. Army. He developed his own aptitude test that would suggest the abilities and talents of his soldiers.[17]

In contrast to the infantry units, the historiography of African American soldiers is dominated by the histories of the Ninth and Tenth Cavalries. Additionally, all three of the black West Point graduates at this time—Henry Ossian Flipper, John Hanks Alexander, and Charles Young—chose cavalry units over infantry. Still, despite the popularity of the Ninth and Tenth Cavalries, each regiment, whether infantry or cavalry, left its mark on the history of the western frontier.

THE CREATION OF A BLACK FRONTIER

The mobility of black soldiers helped to provide avenues for community building for African Americans relocating to the frontier. They created their own enclaves, which helped to insulate them from overt acts of prejudice at various army posts and rural western towns. "The Negro troops were particularly important in the region surrounding El Paso," notes historian Gerald Horne, "where the Negro community was largely a product of the railway industry and the military. They enjoyed a degree of political and economic success unmatched elsewhere in Texas."[18]

Following the conclusion of the Civil War, black troops were stationed in ten out of the eleven Confederate states. Shortly after the 1866 Reorganization Act, the black regulars were moved to the Mexican border and to the western frontier to suppress the various rebelling Native American groups. Black troops then became directly engaged in the diplomatic crisis with

Mexico. A real security dilemma occurred along the Mexican border after Napoleon III of France installed a puppet leader in 1864. The installation of Maximilian was a direct violation of the Monroe Doctrine and perceived as a serious threat to the U.S. government. The U.S. Armed Forces immediately began to fortify posts all along the Rio Grande and to actively recruit the Spanish-speaking black Seminoles to serve as scouts for the buffalo soldier units. One of the new and unintentional roles these buffalo soldiers assumed was that of race ambassadors.[19]

These soldiers often ventured into territories and towns where they would be that community's first introduction to African Americans. The cross-cultural interactions and combinations resulted in African American community enclaves in places such as Salt Lake City, Utah; Polk County, Iowa; Brownsville, Texas; Wyoming; Montana; Blackdom, New Mexico; and the black Seminole scout community located in Mexico. Sergeant Caleb Benson, who served in both the Ninth and Tenth Cavalries, recalled the somewhat unspoken relationship between Plains Indians and blacks: "Two white men lost their lives going to the river to make coffee, something Colored cooks did without loss of life. People may think it isn't true, but Indians never shot a Colored man unless it was necessary. They always wanted to win the friendship of the Negro race and obtain their aid in the campaign against the white man."[20]

Yet despite the various cross-cultural interactions, historian James Leiker dutifully notes that there was little evidence of a "rainbow coalition" or a fraternity of color, in which people of color cooperated in interracial camaraderie. Black regulars understood themselves to be first and foremost U.S. soldiers and citizens. "Some may have recognized the irony and approached their country's racial and imperialistic policies differently," observes Leiker. These men, therefore, should not be cast "villainous or heroic" for their role in the suppression and policing of Indigenous Americans on the western frontier. The cross-cultural interactions black soldiers had while performing their duties is reflected in the relationships they formed and maintained beyond the battlefield.[21]

One of the ways black troops helped change the landscape and community makeup of isolated frontier and border towns was through the families and caravans of people who followed the black troops. The army's regulations during this period prohibited soldiers from marrying, with the exception of some enlisted men whose wives agreed to become servants for officers or washerwomen for several officers.[22]

Unfortunately for the buffalo soldiers, they were scattered in some of the most isolated and volatile areas in the west. Various units, for example, were stationed in Utah territory, which was also known as "America's Siberia," starting in 1866. The regular army's primary responsibilities on the frontier, besides securing the borders and keeping watch over Native Americans, included laying telegraph lines, exploring, and mapping uncharted terrain. The Twenty-Fourth Infantry and Ninth Cavalry were stationed at Fort Douglas and Fort Duchesne. In 1894, the *Salt Lake Tribune* announced the arrival of the Twenty-Fourth on the front page of the paper by describing how over five hundred people arrived a week before the black troops did. The African American population in Salt Lake City between 1890 and 1900 doubled due to the presence of the black regulars. Such soldiers as Sergeant Alfred Rucker, Thornton Jackson, and George Dorsey, as noncommissioned officers, were able to wed, and they all chose to marry and settle there because of the culture and community these men were able to create for themselves.

Black soldiers established strong community enclaves in which the families of the soldiers interacted and supported one another. Viola Rucker Dorsey, the daughter of Alfred Rucker, was born at the Fort Douglas hospital in 1896. She recalled the close-knit community on the post at Fort Douglas: "The children went to the Waith School along with the kids from the Lee, Irvine, Jackson, and Acheson families." Viola Rucker eventually married George Dorsey, a man whose father was stationed with the Ninth Cavalry at Fort Duchesne. While posted near one another, the Twenty-Fourth Infantry and Ninth Cavalry would compete in baseball games in Salt Lake, and regimental bands would routinely put on concerts in the city. These types of activities encouraged a strong sense of community among African Americans and helped to forge a positive relationship with the white civilian population of Salt Lake, so much so that after the Spanish-American-Cuban-Filipino conflict, the men of the Twenty-Fourth returned to Fort Douglas as heroes with the streets of the city lined with citizens eager to welcome the buffalo soldier regiment back.[23]

A soldier of the Ninth Cavalry described life in "America's Siberia" as being filled with routine: "Reveille . . . fatigue . . . school . . . drills." The men worked twelve-hour days, seven days a week, and had only two holidays off, the Fourth of July and Christmas. The monotony of post life helped to encourage participation in male leisure and saloon culture. The men from both forts would gather at Bottle Hollow, a masculine space where blacks, whites, and Native Americans could drink and play cards.[24]

There were not many incidents of violence or racial conflict between the black and white regiments stationed together. Because of their isolation from the surrounding towns, they relied heavily on one another. The desertion rate, though, was much higher in the white regiments than in the black regiments, a fact in which each of the buffalo soldier regiments took pride. At times it almost seemed like a competition between the regiments as to which would maintain the lowest desertion rate.[25]

Despite the harsh reality of life on the frontier and Mexican border, the black regulars not only rarely deserted but often reenlisted, serving multiple terms of service. Parker Buford served thirty years with the Twenty-Fourth Infantry and was discharged in 1898; he decided to remain in Salt Lake. His son, James Buford, likewise joined the Twenty-Fourth Infantry. Another soldier, Solomon Black ("Black Sol"), completed six enlistments with the Twenty-Fourth. He claimed to be "the youngest soldier in the Civil War and . . . was still wearing knee pants when he went in as a drummer boy." Black Sol retired to Texas and married a woman twenty-five years his junior. Sergeant Jacob Wilks of the Ninth Cavalry was court-martialed four times and demoted but was able to earn his stripes back and serve multiple terms with the Ninth Cavalry. He eventually retired in New Mexico with his family.[26]

When the Ninth Cavalry arrived in Wyoming and did not receive a cordial welcome in Laden, it was not just because the unit was made up of black soldiers. The anger of the white civilians also stemmed from the caravan of black people who followed the regiment. Black prostitutes, washerwomen, and liquor salesmen tended to travel with the regiments to small towns such as Laden; they were not truly welcome. Frankie Campbell was one such woman who accompanied troops. During the Wham Paymaster Robbery, she was with the paymaster caravan on its journey from Fort Thomas to Fort Grant because she felt most comfortable traveling with a convoy of black soldiers rather than with an all-white caravan. She was married to a soldier stationed at Fort Grant and knew the best time to collect on the gambling debts owed her and her husband was on payday. Campbell moonlighted as a prostitute on occasion and had a gambling side business with her husband.

However, in the city of Cheyenne, which already possessed a small black community, the presence of the black troops and their entourage was perceived as less of an invasion by the white civilian population. Cheyenne was also near an Indian reservation, just like Salt Lake City was, and this allowed for less tension and more intermingling of these three cultures. The exposure of black troops to European immigrants brought more friendly and welcoming receptions in certain parts of the rural West, mostly because seeing black men in uniform was a novelty to many. Even though the white press in many places consistently portrayed African Americans with racist stereotypes, when some of these communities and newly arrived immigrants encountered the buffalo soldiers on the frontier, they often formulated their own more positive opinions of these men and rejected the traditional stereotypes.

The generosity of a German farm family toward the men of the Twenty-Fifth serves as an example. The Twenty-Fifth spent over two years in Montana (directly challenging the racist belief that blacks could not survive in the cold for long periods) and was eventually chosen to participate in the army's experiment to test the utility of the bicycle as a replacement for the horse. Lieutenant James Moss, the officer who lobbied to have the Twenty-Fifth embark on the bicycle expedition from Missoula, Montana, to St. Louis, Missouri, recounted how an "ignorant Swede had given them directions and how a German family insisted that the entire troop eat dinner and break bread with them on their farm." The bicycle corps expedition of 1896 represented how black soldiers served as ambassadors because of their consistent interactions with groups of people such as newly arrived European immigrants and Native Americans on the western frontier who normally never interacted with African Americans.[27]

The black soldiers also visited spaces such as Yellowstone National Park, which was traditionally viewed as nonblack. The men traveled through parts of Nebraska that were friendly, but when they reached rural Missouri the white civilians were outright hostile to the presence of these armed black men on bicycles. In Moss's trip logs, he described how astonished most people were at the sight of the black men in their worn uniforms riding bicycles. Historian Alexandra Koelle, in her examination of the bicycle corps, notes that farmers and ranchers who saw the soldiers marked them with curiosity. Lieutenant Moss in his trip log observed, "We attracted a great deal of attention all along the route. Horses and cows ran away from us and dogs ran after us, while the inhabitants stopped their work and gazed at us with astonishment."[28]

The presence of the black troops on bicycles riding through newly conquered Native American territory must have provoked a certain kind of feeling among the Native Americans forced onto their reservations, while white civilians more than likely had a very different type of astonishment at the sight. A reporter from the *Daily Missoulian*, Edward Boos, joined the bicycle expedition and wrote several stories about the trip. Yet, the depictions of the troops both in Boos's stories and Moss's reports present the men as childlike characters, no different from the minstrel presentations seen throughout the white press. The men of the Twenty-Fifth Infantry had a proud history of defending themselves against civilian and officer abuse, so the description of them as docile is somewhat surprising. After all, following the lynching of one their own by a mob in Sturgis City, Dakota Territory, in 1885, they had marched single file from Fort Meade, halted in front of a brothel-saloon, and fired several volleys inside. They then marched down the street to the home of a Mr. Dolan, fired several volleys into his home, and, in the words of historian Arlen Fowler, "marching in perfect cadence, retreated down the street and out of sight." The businesses and homes targeted by the soldiers were owned by people who had disrespected the men of the Twenty-Fifth and who may have been involved with the lynch mob that had killed their brother-in-arms.[29]

The description of childlike behavior is also questionable because of the mandatory army education the men received. Education was of the utmost importance to the African American community, one of the cornerstones of the racial uplift ideology. Education was a key component in shaping black soldiers into race men/race warriors.

ELEVATION THROUGH EDUCATION

To inspire and elevate the race, in 1867 black army chaplain Theophilus Gould Steward wrote,

> What can elevate us? To elevate the blacks and place them beyond the reach of foul wrong, power, force, must be put in their hands. . . . The strength must be infused in the man. He must be made strong. This will come only from labor, study, and thought. The only way to elevate is to increase the intrinsic worth.[30]

Steward was the chaplain for the Twenty-Fifth Infantry and one of the most prominent thinkers of his time. He was a contemporary of W. E. B. Du Bois, Charles Young, Frederick Douglass, and Bishop Henry McNeal Turner. Steward used his position as army chaplain to continue his goal of uplift and empowerment of the African American community. Therefore, because Steward was responsible for the education of the men of the Twenty-Fifth Infantry, it adds further doubt to the claims made by Lieutenant Moss in 1896 that depicted the men as speaking in a slave-like dialect, since Steward had been teaching the men since 1894. Once Steward retired from the army in 1904, he would go on to be a professor of history, logic, and French and to serve as vice president at Wilberforce University. In his biography of Steward, Albert Miller described him as a "race man, one who had a strong sense of racial identity and who constantly fought for racial pride, elevation, and self-determination." The students of T. G. Steward would surely have been taught to adhere to the ideology of racial uplift and elevation.[31]

One of the key differences between the buffalo soldier regiments and the all-white regiments was in the duties of the chaplain. During the Civil War, chaplains in the black volunteer regiments were responsible not only for their spiritual guidance but also for teaching the men to read and write. This tradition was carried over into the black regular regiments, where chaplains traveled with the men. In 1863, a chaplain with the Fifty-Ninth U.S. Colored Volunteers wrote to his son about how eager the men were to learn to read and write and noted that he and his wife taught them.

Each regiment had a unique experience with its regimental chaplain. The Ninth Cavalry, for example, had two chaplains, Joseph C. Jacobi and Marcel J. Gonzales, who served in this capacity for fifteen years. However, because they were either physically unfit or on disability, they could not perform their duties consistently. Charles C. Pierce, appointed in 1882 to the Ninth, resigned two years later in 1884, because he felt he had failed at changing and bettering the men's wayward behavior. In 1884, Henry V. Plummer became the first black army chaplain in the regular army and was appointed to the Ninth Cavalry. He successfully served and educated the men of his unit until 1894, when he was court-martialed for intemperance.[32]

Army regulations specifically outlined one of the duties of the regimental chaplain as "the instruction of enlisted men in common English." The four black regiments were the only ones required to set up post schools, the primary reason being that most of the African American soldiers joining the army after the Civil War were former slaves. The ethnic composition of the white units were mostly foreign-born emigrants from Ireland, England, Germany, and Canada who had different reasons and motivations for getting an education and joining the military. In fact, the white men who enlisted often were drifters, petty criminals, murderers, the unemployable, and those who had fallen on hard times. The average white soldier enlisted with reluctance and dread because for them, military service was the last resort for a desperate man. The white officers in these regiments often felt these men unworthy of an education and refused to provide the necessary funds, buildings, or personnel to teach them.[33]

The Twenty-Fourth had a totally different chaplain experience. Its first chaplain was Reverend John N. Schultz, who served in this position from 1869 to 1875. He maintained a stable system of education with the regiment until he was forced to resign after an affair with an enlisted soldier's wife. Schultz was then court-martialed for conduct unbecoming an officer. The

Twenty-Fifth Infantry also had a relatively stable educational structure with its chaplains. The first was Ellington Barr, who served until 1871. The system he established—which included classes for children and men—easily transferred to the next chaplain. Barr had to hold classes in his quarters because the army post at Fort Clark, Texas, did not possess a schoolroom.[34]

The Tenth Cavalry's first chaplain was W. M. Grimes, who served until 1890 and was replaced by F. H. Weaver. The Tenth did not get a black chaplain until 1897, when William T. Anderson was appointed. Anderson, born a slave and liberated by his mother, who moved them to Galveston, Texas, was both a doctor and a minister. In fact, during the War of 1898, Anderson became the first African American officer to be in command of a post. From April 19 to June 28, 1898, Anderson commanded Fort Assiniboine, located in the Department of Montana. He kept a much lower profile than his contemporaries, yet his impact was no less important. (The racial problems of the Tenth Cavalry are explored in more detail in chapter 4.)[35]

The importance of the regimental chaplains is often overlooked when discussing how black soldiers thought about themselves as members both of an oppressed group and of an imperialist army. The morale and reenlistment in the black regiments remained higher than in the white regiments because of the positive benefits the troops received while in service. When historians view these men, it is often through the clouded lens of their devout loyalty to the flag and proving they deserved citizenship. But these men already thought of themselves as citizens. It was the chaplains—in particular the black chaplains Allen Allensworth, George W. Prioleau, T. G. Steward, and Henry V. Plummer—who incorporated the uplift ideology within their teaching methods and taught these soldiers how to be productive and disciplined race men.

Education became (unenforced) army policy in 1878 when the War Department issued a command requiring all posts, garrisons, and camps to establish and build schools for enlisted men. One of the key reformers behind the new policy was Chaplain George Mullins of the Twenty-Fifth Infantry. In 1877, Mullins observed,

> The ambition to be all that soldiers should be is not confined to a few of these sons of an unfortunate race. They are possessed of the notion that the colored people of the whole country are more or less affected by their conduct in the army. The chaplain is sometimes touched by evidence of their manly anxiety to be well thought of at Army HQ and throughout the states. This is the bottom secret

of their patient toil and surprising progress in the effort to get at least an elementary education.[36]

Inspired, Mullins worked diligently to formulate an educational program that benefited the eager young men of his unit. In 1881, Mullins was appointed chief of education, a reward for his success and advocacy for reform in army education. His major goal was achieved and enforced in 1889, when all enlisted men were mandated to attend school if they did not possess an elementary education.[37]

Mullins was not the only chaplain to push for educational reform within the army; Allen Allensworth and Henry Plummer also found a way to leave their mark on their units' educational programs. Plummer, the first black army chaplain appointed in the regular army, held strong beliefs about education, military service, and racial uplift. He was a close friend with race leaders Frederick Douglass and Bishop Henry McNeal Turner.

Plummer, a former slave, was appointed the chaplain to the Ninth on July 1, 1884. He was a veteran of the Civil War, where he learned to read and write while serving in the Union navy. He made a name for himself in the D.C. area, and with the ardent support of Frederick Douglass, he was appointed chaplain in the regular army with the rank of captain. Chaplains did not have direct command in the field, so Plummer's appointment as a black officer did not directly challenge the white supremacist hierarchy within the military the way black line officers John H. Alexander, Henry O. Flipper, and Charles Young did once they joined the army.[38]

Henry Plummer's background in politics differed from that of the other black chaplains and officers. He had worked at hiring "Dollar Niggers," as he called them, during the election season, paying each person one dollar for his vote for a particular candidate. Plummer, unlike his white predecessors, made progress with the post schools and getting the men to attend church services. The post schools Plummer oversaw taught both soldiers and their children. He advocated the ideology of racial uplift and adhered to the belief that the key to being a successful and productive citizen was education. He pushed for a commonsense approach to the uses of education, wanting the men to be able to sign their names on the payroll and understand the international ramifications and representations of their uniform. He encouraged all men lacking an elementary education to attend school in the day and in the evenings.[39]

Plummer became actively involved not only in his ministry and education but also in establishing a post newsletter called the *Fort Robinson*

Weekly Bulletin, and he was a regular correspondent for the black newspaper the *Omaha Press*. The weekly newsletter served as an organ for Plummer to discuss gossip and social issues. He wrote under the pseudonym "The Owl." He committed himself to the temperance movement, and to the chagrin of his commander, Colonel Biddle, he joined the "Chaplains' Movement." One of the cornerstones of the "Chaplains' Movement" was opposition to post canteens selling beer and wine. In his March 1892 report to the adjutant general, Plummer wrote about the "menacing evils" of alcohol and got a temporary ban on alcohol at Fort Robinson:[40]

> No one is benefited by its existence. . . . Many of the most promising young men of the service are being made confirmed drunkards, mendicants, and gluttons by the inducements of this system . . . being entrapped and enticed by the apparent legality . . . and are on the high way to moral, mental, and physical ruin.[41]

Henry Plummer's way of being overly social and relaxed with the enlisted men upset some of the white officers of the Ninth. The real issue with the white officers of the Ninth Cavalry was the presence of the three black officers in their unit—Plummer, Second Lieutenant John Alexander, and Second Lieutenant Charles Young—who between 1884 and 1886 were the *only* black officers in the entire army. Alexander and Young, who were line officers, and Plummer, who was in charge of the troops' education, raised the old fears, similar to those of the days of slavery, of an uprising. The racist white officers feared that the black officers and soldiers plotted against them and needed to be separated. So, Alexander and Young were sent to Fort Duchesne. Alexander "knew his racist colleagues wanted nothing to do with him," which is why when he mentored Charles Young he encouraged Young to keep to himself. Alexander and Young's relationship will be discussed in more detail in chapter 5.[42]

During the Charles Diggs incident mentioned at the beginning of the chapter, whites suspected the chaplain as leader of the protest. Lieutenant Colonel Reuben Bernard was the temporary post commander and claimed that Sergeant Barney McKay was responsible for distributing the letter on base. He was court-martialed, reduced in rank, and sentenced to two years in prison for violating Article of War 62—conduct "to the prejudice of good order and military discipline." However, Colonel Bernard never believed that McKay was the author of the letter. He wrote General John R. Brooks that he as well as all of the other officers and citizens of Crawford believed that it was Plummer who was behind the letter. He even claimed that Lieutenant Alexander told him Plummer was a bad seed and needed to be removed. This claim by Bernard that Alexander spoke to him personally about Plummer was highly unlikely, given Alexander's belief that all of his fellow white officers hated him.[43] Still, Plummer and Bernard did not get along, and it was established among the enlisted men that Bernard was a racist. Plummer filed three letters of discrimination against him while Bernard was the temporary post commander.

In April 1894, Plummer wrote the secretary of war requesting permission to lead an expedition into Central Africa with several volunteers from the four buffalo soldier regiments. He wanted to introduce American civilization and to create "a colony of our own people." Plummer had the backing of leaders such as Bishop Henry McNeal Turner and J. R. McMullan of the International Migration Society, who wrote letters of support to the War Department. Plummer stated in the letter to the secretary of war that "under the glorious stars and stripes would be the climax upon all the laws enacted looking towards the elevation of the Negro race." Plummer's request to go to Africa gained a lot of press attention, essentially forcing the Cleveland administration to address the issue. The secretary of war wrote Plummer back informing him the U.S. had no legal authority to detail soldiers for such a mission.[44]

Chaplain Plummer, because of his brash style and willingness to challenge authority, made enemies. A Jamaican immigrant named Robert Benjamin resented Plummer for over a decade. Sergeant Benjamin never forgave Plummer for reporting him for failing to attend his duties properly or for refusing to lend him money. The sergeant enacted his revenge when one night Plummer showed up to Benjamin's house after having a few drinks with two other NCOs. Benjamin's wife and daughter were home and Plummer came in to get some milk for an upset stomach. Instead of leaving after getting the milk, Plummer decided to sit and play with Benjamin's little girl. When the sergeant arrived home, there was a huge argument, and the next day Benjamin filed a complaint of intemperance against Plummer. The judge advocate's investigation concluded that the charges of drunkenness should be dropped, but Colonel Biddle insisted that Plummer be charged with conduct unbecoming because he was seen wearing the jacket of a noncommissioned officer and drinking with these same noncommissioned officers.[45]

During the court-martial of Plummer in June 1894, two other NCOs, Sergeant David Dillon and Sergeant Jones, contradicted Benjamin's claims and testified how Benjamin was a vengeful man who held a grudge against Plummer. The *Kansas City Times* reported how the black community rallied behind Plummer and that the "color line had been drawn by Plummer's friends . . . who were exerting every available influence to prevent testimony." D. F. Jeffers, a black enlisted man stationed in California, wrote to the wife of Sergeant Benjamin, appealing to her as a black woman:

> Unless it is a matter where your personal honor is at stake, I would advise you as a matter of race pride to avoid being a witness against the chaplain, you know the general feeling against the few colored officers we have and that there are always those who are ever ready to take any advantage of the leaders of the race.[46]

Despite the contradictory testimony of even Benjamin's own wife, Plummer was found guilty of conduct unbecoming. His need to socialize with the enlisted men was a part of his teaching and ministry style. All of this was explained in the various affidavits sent to President Grover Cleveland, asking him to pardon and not discharge Henry Plummer. As a chaplain, he bucked the system and did not "keep his place" as a black man. One week before Plummer's official dismissal, Sergeant Benjamin was promoted. When Sergeant Dillon, one of the NCOs who testified against Benjamin, got into a heated altercation with Benjamin over his wife, he too was court-martialed and discharged.

Henry Plummer stated not long after his dismissal that "patriotism and devotion to duty counts for naught against falsehood and prejudice under the present regime." Plummer remained active in Republican politics and did not cease fighting to clear his name. He died in 1904. Although Henry Plummer's ordeal with the Ninth ended on a negative note, he did leave behind a positive legacy of leadership within the Ninth Cavalry and black community. His activism served as an inspiration to his men, as did the activism of Allen Allensworth, the first black officer and chaplain to the Twenty-Fourth Infantry.[47]

Allensworth, a former slave from Kentucky, managed to serve in the Union navy during the Civil War and to elevate himself to a position of political influence during the era of Reconstruction. After Chaplain J. C. Livety retired in 1886, leaving the Twenty-Fourth Infantry, Allensworth found out that the unit had never had a black chaplain and immediately started the process to become the regiment's next chaplain. One of the hurdles Allensworth overcame was the Democratic president Grover Cleveland.

Allensworth was active in the Republican Party and learned to navigate the politics of the Gilded Age like a pro. He knew that he had to appeal to

President Cleveland within a political narrative in order to gain his support and nomination. He actively worked to build connections with other black leaders and went to the Black Leadership Conference in Nashville in 1879. Allensworth wrote to Cleveland's personal secretary,

> A number of my democratic friends in KY and Ohio, [who] desire to strengthen the administration and party among my people, encouraged me to apply to the President for appointment. . . . I want to show my people that a Democratic administration can appoint a colored Chaplain as well as a Republican administration which appointed Mr. Plummer to the 9th Cavalry.[48]

Allensworth possessed qualifications to be an army chaplain beyond his being friends with some Democratic politicians. He was a graduate of Roger Williams University and had taught at various schools for the Freedmen's Bureau, and he served as the only black Republican delegate at the Republican National Convention in 1880 and 1884. Allensworth viewed living in the South as stifling and wanted to do something to change or alter the future of the masses of African Americans residing in the Jim Crow South. He viewed military service as an escape. In 1882, a soldier from the Twenty-Fourth Infantry informed him that all the chaplains for the black regiments were white and urged him to consider joining one of the black regular units.[49]

Allen Allensworth received his appointment to the Twenty-Fourth Infantry in the spring of 1886. The moment he received his commission he ordered his uniform; he could not contain his excitement. When Allensworth arrived at Fort Bayard, New Mexico, the men of the white Fifth Cavalry, which was stationed there as well, had already decided they would not salute the new black captain. This was upsetting to the men of the Twenty-Fourth Infantry. Allensworth was their first black officer and chaplain. Each day as Allensworth would walk by the barracks bakery, the men of the Fifth Cavalry would run inside the bakery to avoid saluting him. The chaplain had a decision to make: he could bring the men up on charges and have them sent to the guardhouse, or he could find another way for the men to pay him the respect due his rank.[50]

So, he delivered a sermon titled "An Officer Hung for the Want of a Salute." Allensworth's sermon highlighted the story of Haman and Mordecai in the Old Testament book of Esther and pointed out that despite their differences and disagreements, Mordecai should have saluted Haman. The point of the lesson was to stress the fact that each man in the army took a sworn oath to obey the rules and regulations of the army. The following day the men of the Fifth Cavalry stood and saluted Allensworth instead of running inside the bakery. The men of the Twenty-Fourth likewise stood up and applauded their chaplain for accomplishing this victory.[51]

Allensworth's education policies differed from those of previous chaplains. Instead of handling the teaching load alone, he selected a group of men and trained them as teachers. Allensworth's strategy for successfully implementing an educational policy would revolutionize the military educational program. When the War Department made elementary education compulsory for all soldiers, he already had a fully trained staff to handle the new influx of students. Allensworth completed a training manual in 1889 based on the course structure he created while at Fort Bayard; the manual became the model for post education in the U.S. Army. Allensworth's program included classes for both children and adults. He earned the respect of the black community because of his efforts in education.

In 1887, the *Washington Bee* included Allensworth on a panel with the editor of the *Richmond Planet*, John Mitchell Jr., to discuss the future of the "Negro." The *St. Paul Appeal* regularly covered Allensworth's career and his various activities. He went to the National Education Association meeting in Toronto in 1891 with his own money, and his participation at the conference was covered by the *Appeal*. The *Cleveland Gazette* followed the life of Allen Allensworth closely. The paper's motto was "We shall endure to present a newspaper, knowing as we do, the power of the Press as a civilizer and educator. We advocate education, equality, and progression." Allensworth, Plummer, Steward, Young, and almost every other black chaplain in the regular army advocated this ideology.

Allensworth despised the industrial education model. He sent correspondence and the official bulletin from the conference to the newspaper the *Appeal*. Once again, an African American soldier served as a race ambassador on an international platform. Allensworth was specifically invited to give a paper titled "Education in the United States Army" at the annual meeting. Allensworth, like Steward and other race leaders, believed that education in the military provided black men with a more nuanced understanding of their citizenship and would make them more effective, active, and responsible citizens. He emphasized this point in the paper he delivered in 1891: "In the earlier history of the Army it was considered sufficient for a soldier to be able to march and handle a gun. This view has changed and it is now a recognized fact to be a good soldier a man must be a good citizen."[52]

Allen Allensworth served with such distinction as the chaplain of the Twenty-Fourth that when army regulations allowed for the promotion of chaplains to the rank of major, he was one of the first to be promoted. Yet it took an act of Congress for him to get his promotion. He wrote articles about race and remained politically active throughout his military career. He wrote one article for the *New York Age* titled "Social Status of the Race." In this article, he argued that in order to change the laws of oppression in the U.S., public opinion needed to be changed, because the laws were a reflection of public opinion.[53]

The activism of Allen Allensworth with the Twenty-Fourth Infantry served as a model for T. G. Steward when he assumed the chaplaincy of the Twenty-Fifth Infantry. Steward's appointment in 1894 had the support of Blanche K. Bruce (the first African American to serve a full term in the Senate) and Francis Grimké (one of the leading African American clergymen of his day). He wrote an article in 1894 titled "The Colored American as a Soldier" to dispel the myths and stereotypes about black men being somehow less honorable and efficient as soldiers than white men. When he arrived at his post, he did not expect as warm a welcome as he received, and this played a major role in his continued support of the army during the Spanish-American-Cuban-Filipino War.[54]

The educational programs of Steward resembled Plummer's and Allensworth's, but he also had classes for the women of the post, teaching them European history on Sundays. The desire to provide a complete education to the men of their regiments supports the idea that chaplains such as Steward, Plummer, and Allensworth helped inspire the troops to be racially conscious and prompted some to become focused on formulating supportive communities outside of the Jim Crow South.

DEFIANCE ON THE FRONTIER

Defiance by black soldiers against abuse can be traced back to the volunteers of the Civil War. On the frontier, acts of violence committed by the black regulars demonstrate their rejection of white supremacy and assertion of their manhood. On March 10, 1871, four black soldiers were fined for fighting with the police in Texas. The men threw bricks, knives, and sabers at the police because they refused to be bullied by the local white authority. A soldier from the Ninth Cavalry in 1867 protested barbaric treatment and poor leadership. In addition, an act of defiance at San Pedro Springs, Texas, was described by historian Frank Schubert as a protest rather than a mutiny, which was what the War Department called it.[55]

Sergeant Harrison Bradford, twenty-four years old and a Civil War veteran, decided he had had enough of the racist and barbaric treatment of him and his men by their commander Lieutenant Edward Heyl. Heyl had directed that certain soldiers be suspended by their thumbs from a tree because they did not move quickly enough in completing his orders. Bradford witnessed Heyl beat with a saber one of the soldiers who freed himself from the tree and attempted to stop Heyl and another white officer, Lieutenant Seth Griffin, who in turn tried to restrain Bradford and ended up in a brawl with the enlisted men and was stabbed. Bradford was shot in the head by one of the officers involved in the brawl.

The turmoil among the white officers and black enlisted men came to a head that day in April 1867. Harrison Bradford had protested the continued mistreatment of his men because he knew that Heyl was wrong. Despite Bradford being killed, the men still gave statements supporting Sergeant Bradford's decision to openly object to Heyl's treatment. The post commander, Lieutenant Colonel Merritt, had the incident fully investigated, and Lieutenant Heyl was ultimately found guilty of mistreating the black enlisted men of the Ninth and dismissed from the army.[56]

The relationship between the black enlisted men and the white officers who commanded them varied among the regiments. The racial complexity of the frontier forced white and black soldiers to build bonds and trust with one another because their lives depended upon it. The Tenth Cavalry did not have the same kind of tumultuous beginnings as the Ninth; the regimental commander Benjamin Grierson played a major role in the reason the dynamics of the Tenth differed from the Ninth. The two infantry regiments were a bit more active than the cavalry in their acts of defiance and assertion of their manhood against white racists, both officers and civilians. The infantry was more likely to shoot up a town than the cavalry, one reason the Twenty-Fourth and Twenty-Fifth Infantries developed contentious identities.

When we think about the racial and ethnic communities of the western frontier during the Gilded Age, images of white cowboys fighting Indigenous Americans in order to tame the West still permeate. The individual, cultural, and ethnic makeup of the western frontier was far more racially mixed than Hollywood has imagined. The battles and campaigns in the Indian Wars and along the border of the Rio Grande were not viewed as traditional warfare. Native Americans rarely met on the open field of battle, so the Indian Wars of the late nineteenth century were more a series of smaller incursions than the large, open-field battles of the Civil War. In fact, much of the work of black soldiers on the frontier and border was police duty. They stood between whites and Chicanos in El Paso during the Salt War of 1879. Most of the work the black regulars did in the West centered on helping to transform a desolate frontier into one with established borders and provide infrastructure to poorly inhabited and explored territories.

When these black troopers, rejected and rebelled against racist behavior, it could be seen as them fighting for their humanity. One of the duties of the infantry on the frontier was to guard stagecoach lines and stations. While the Twenty-Fifth Infantry was posted in Texas guarding the El Muerto Station, a black sergeant refused to accept the insults and abuse from the manager of the station. He arrested the manager and reported to his post commander for further instructions. The jail facilities at Fort Davis were not adequate to keep the station manager, but the post commander approved of the manager's arrest and issued a stern warning to ensure that the soldiers did not receive any more harassment from the employees of that station. The commander stated, "We will be careful hereafter not to come in conflict with the stage men if it can be avoided, but at the same time you will see that the soldiers are properly treated. . . . The escorts and station guards furnished by the government are hereby ordered not to put up with any abuse from the stage men." The stage company because of the arrest of the stationmaster was forced to reexamine its policies and take corrective actions to ensure its employees did not have another confrontation or arrest by the men of the Twenty-Fifth.[57]

The mobility of the black regulars allowed them to assert more autonomy over their lives than the average African American of the second half of the nineteenth century. The experience of the Ninth Cavalry in Johnson County, Wyoming, highlights the assertion of black manhood in the way the soldiers openly defied white civilian prejudice as well as found a way to ease blatant hostility toward African Americans.

There were times, in fact, when white civilian leadership wanted to capitalize on the open hostility between white civilians and black soldiers. During the Johnson County War (1889–93), in which large ranchers and cattle companies were pitted against smaller settlers and rustlers, six members of the Wyoming Stock Growers Association cabled U.S. senator Joseph Carey requesting black troopers to come to their state to replace the white soldiers sent by the president and acting governor. The cable stated, "We want cool level-headed men whose sympathy is with us. . . . The colored troops will have no sympathy for Texan thieves, and these are the troops we want."[58]

The soldiers soon arrived in Suggs—as did several white prostitutes who followed the men to their new post—which did not sit well with the townsfolk of Suggs. The dispute between the stockmen and the homesteaders intensified with the arrival of the black troopers of the Ninth Cavalry. The residents followed the soldiers and their officers throughout the town spewing insults and verbally harassing the men.

Therefore, it should come as no surprise that on the afternoon of June 16, 1892, the men of the Ninth shot up Johnson, Wyoming, after a white civilian yelled at Private Abraham Champ of G Troop as he entered a local saloon, "Ain't your mother a black bitch?" and then proceeded to point a gun in Champ's face. Private Emile Smith, who was with Champ, drew his pistol on the white man, which in turn caused several other whites in the saloon to pull their guns on Smith and Champ. The bartender defused the situation and got the two soldiers out of the saloon unharmed.[59]

However, Smith and Champ could not let the matter rest and returned to camp to inform the men there what happened. This resulted in at least twenty men from the Ninth returning to Suggs the following night, when they proceeded to fire into a couple of saloons; additionally, they killed at least two horses, they exchanged gunfire with some townsfolk, and at least one soldier died. The men were later arrested and confined to camp. General Schofield ordered the men of the Ninth to stay away from Suggs. The men left the area two months later and returned to Fort Robinson. The people of Cheyenne were more welcoming to the men of the Ninth, who were praised in the white press.[60]

Not all acts of defiance by black soldiers resulted in violence. Writer and former first lieutenant George Schuyler, while still a seventeen-year-old private in the Twenty-Fifth Infantry, engaged in what he called the first "stand-in" at a bar in Seattle, Washington. Schuyler in his autobiography, *Black and Conservative*, describes the racial climate of Seattle as no "Negro Haven" but better than most places on the Pacific Coast. The white establishments in Seattle that did not want to serve black patrons tended to break the glasses or dishes of the African American customers in front of their faces right after they were done eating or drinking, indicating that it was time for them to leave. One day Schuyler and his compatriots decided that they could not accept this treatment, so they went to one bar and ordered several drinks. After each drink, the bartender smashed their glasses. The group decided that they would leave, round up more members of the First Battalion, and return to that establishment. When they showed back up, the bartender weakly asked, "What do people want?" Schuyler bellowed,

"Beers all around!" waving a five-dollar gold piece in the air. The bartender scratched his head and sheepishly smiled, "You boys win, have one on the house!" In the mind of the young private, they won a small victory. "We staged the first stand-in and won."[61]

These examples of defiance and public acts of violence and retaliation against racist treatment from white officers and civilians demonstrated that the black regulars were going to continue the legacy of the black Civil War soldiers of organized and vocal resistance to racism. The irony of all these acts of rebellion and assertions of manhood by these men is that the primary reason they were sent to the western frontier was to ease racial tensions. The *Cleveland Gazette* reported in 1884 that "race men train in the U.S. Army." The article went on to report that the service of the nearly 200,000 black troops who fought with the Union army helped to elevate and raise the self-respect and discipline of those who served. Military service among the black community meant more than they were just as willing to die for the flag; it meant the opportunity to learn how to read and write, to learn self-defense, and to escape the oppressive Jim Crow south.[62]

It was during the Spanish-American-Cuban-Filipino War when the world saw the evidence of the level of intellect of black soldiers as they served as war correspondents for African American newspapers. The black regulars through acts of defiance and assertions of their manhood on the frontier directly challenged the white racist beliefs that blacks belonged only under the thumb of a southern master. These men were educated and aware that they carried the mantle of the race when they put on that uniform. In the mind of the young, such as future soldier George Schuyler, soldiers represented people of authority. He never forgot the first time he saw black soldiers and the impression it made upon him.

> I never saw any colored person in any position of authority in Syracuse until the U.S. Army held maneuvers in the area around 1909. The black infantrymen and cavalrymen were something else again. We were impressed by their superb order and discipline, their haughty and immaculate noncommissioned officers, and their obvious authority.[63]

The buffalo soldiers of the nineteenth century evolved from men who just wanted to escape the plow to racially conscious ambassadors domestically and internationally.

2.
MY HOME, MY COUNTRY

The colored soldier has fought bravely in the Revolutionary War, the Civil War, the Spanish-American War, and the World War. But the Negro will not be given justice through the valor and bravery he displays in war.

—Sergeant Vance Hunter Marchbanks, Tenth Cavalry

Former second lieutenant James M. Trotter arrived in Louisville, Kentucky, to welcome the largest gathering of African American veterans of the Civil War. Trotter was one of the few blacks to be commissioned as an officer during the Civil War, and when he stood before the crowd on that sweltering August day in 1887, many things had gone terribly wrong for African American men in the army. But now, in front of thousands of black veterans and civilians, Trotter would not dwell on the issues of Henry Flipper and Johnson C. Whittaker. He stood in front of his people with pride and full racial consciousness. He declared, "I see before me today men from all over . . . who were determined to never give up; men who were bound to fight until death."[1]

James Monroe Trotter, the father of twentieth-century civil rights activist William Monroe Trotter, viewed his military service through the lens of racial consciousness and uplift. He taught his son these same values, which helped to shape him into a vocal advocate of civil and human rights for the African American community. Yet, at the end of the Plains Wars and the official closing of the frontier, the status of African American soldiers and officers was tarnished. In 1882, Second Lieutenant Henry Flipper was dismissed from the army for conduct unbecoming an officer. Cadet Johnson C. Whittaker, in 1881, was court-martialed and expelled from West Point for allegedly assaulting himself. President Chester A. Arthur in 1883 overturned his conviction, but the academy expelled him again, claiming he would have failed his exams. The Whittaker and Flipper cases were still headline news in 1892. This is why it is not surprising that Trotter began his speech with the need to encourage the African American community to never give up and to keep fighting, even unto death, to serve their country and race.[2]

The mood in America was shifting. America's gaze turned away from the now closed frontier and to the Caribbean and the Pacific in hopes of expanding American power overseas. The Panic of 1893 helped fuel figures such as Theodore Roosevelt, Henry Cabot Lodge, and Captain Alfred Thayer Mahan to push for the expansion of America's naval and military capabilities. Roosevelt in fact spent an entire weekend, May 10–11, 1890, devouring Mahan's *Influence of Sea Power upon History.* This book changed Roosevelt's life and arguably helped alter the course of global history. The leaders of Germany, Japan, and Great Britain all read and adhered to the strategic philosophy of political power intertwining with sea power.[3] This is why when war fever took hold of the majority of America at the end of the nineteenth century, African Americans eagerly joined in the cause to liberate the oppressed Cubans from the cruel and brutal clutches of Spain.

SINKING A SHIP AND STARTING A SPLENDID LITTLE WAR

In the late hours of the night on Tuesday, February 15, 1898, the battleship USS *Maine* exploded in the Havana harbor. Two hundred and sixty-six sailors were killed, twenty-two of them African American. Most Americans immediately assumed that the cowardly Spaniards caused this deadly explosion. The destruction of the *Maine* was labeled "Spanish treachery" in the jingoist newspapers. The United States had been at odds with the Spanish since the Cubans started their fight for independence in 1896. America saw the repressive treatment of Cuba by the Spaniards as an opportunity to prove to the rest of the Western world that America's manly character would not allow injustice or cruelty of any kind against a country fighting for democratic independence. The four black regiments stationed in the West anticipated this opportunity to fight. Close to sixteen thousand American soldiers, both black and white, moved to the Florida coast and prepared for a summer invasion of the last colonial possessions of the once mighty Spanish Empire.[4]

With the ending of the Indian Wars in 1890, black soldiers were occupied performing constabulary duty on the Native American reservations and protecting newly arrived frontiersmen and their families in the West. According to historian Willard Gatewood, "A majority of blacks seemed to consider participation in the military struggle an obligation of citizenship which they would gladly fulfill, if they could do so in a way that would enhance rather than degrade their manhood." The destruction of the *Maine* outraged most African Americans, because with the destruction of the ship, twenty-two black sailors lost their lives. The black soldiers were equally anxious for the opportunity to perform their duties as citizens, soldiers, and men.[5]

They envisioned a war with Spain as an opportunity to fight for their country in a more public arena and as a chance to regain some of their recently lost rights. The U.S. Supreme Court had issued its "separate but equal" ruling in *Plessy v. Ferguson* just two years earlier. The editor of the *Cleveland Gazette*, H. C. Smith, described the emotional position of the black community: "The colored men of America have immense interests at stake. As citizen and patriot, let him again prove himself an element of strength and power in vindicating the honor of his country." It was after the *Plessy* decision that Chaplains Allen Allensworth, T. G. Steward, and George Prioleau became more critical and vocal in their criticisms of both political parties over the American apartheid system. Allensworth voiced frustration with the legality of Jim Crow racism and bluntly observed to the *New York Age*, "Laws are merely public opinion in legal form. To change these laws we must change public opinion." Yet in spite of his frustration, Allensworth delivered a speech to the Twenty-Fourth Infantry encouraging his men to win when waging the small battles of life. This is why it became increasingly important for African American soldiers to utilize their military service to change public opinion. Citizenship and manhood were very much connected in the minds of black men, and the adoption of the "Mississippi Plan" throughout the South only intensified the alarm among African Americans in the rest of the country.[6]

The "Mississippi Plan" was used by southern Democrats to rid their states of "Black Republican Rule." It was a terrorists' plan that prevented most black and white Republicans from voting and returned the "right" men to political office by 1898. Complete "home rule" by then had reached every southern state except North Carolina, the home of George H. White, the only black congressman left.[7]

In this chapter, we examine how black soldiers utilized military service to work to advance the civil rights of African Americans. The men who volunteered for the Spanish-American-Cuban-Filipino War did so knowing that they would be representing the entirety of the race. These soldiers epitomized the race men of the era and were committed to the racial uplift of their community. Those who decided to stay in the Philippines after the conflict was declared resolved did so because of how they understood their manly duty to the women they married there and the families they were committed to and their desire to exercise their economic rights as American citizens in this new territory.

DEATH OF A POSTMASTER

A few days after the destruction of the *Maine*, another event that was equally shocking to the black community occurred: a race riot erupted in the rural town of Lake City, South Carolina. President William McKinley, after his narrow victory over William Jennings Bryan in 1896, owed a great deal to the African American community for its pivotal electoral support. As a result, McKinley sought to reward the black community by appointing African Americans to various government positions, including Frances Baker as the new postmaster in a predominantly black part of South Carolina. One night while Baker and his family prepared for dinner, the post office, which also served as their home, was set ablaze. Baker and his infant son, whom he had grabbed in his attempt to flee the fire, were bombarded by gunfire and died. His wife and four other children were also wounded but survived this vicious terrorist attack. The racial violence that erupted in Lake City was meant to convey a message to all black South Carolinians about what would happen if they attempted to step into the world of politics.[8]

The black community was outraged that this injustice happened and that white Americans did not feel the same sort of kinship with black Americans as they did with the Cubans. The crimes against the Baker family were compounded by the fact that no one would be punished for the deaths, injuries, and destruction. Although this lack of accountability was common practice in the South, many blacks refused to simply acquiesce to the lack of justice. The rampant disenfranchisement, lynching, and subsequent emasculation of black men throughout the South were becoming increasingly more difficult for African Americans. This type of racial violence needed to change, which is one reason the black soldier became so important to the black community. The black soldier was a tangible figure who had decided to exercise his right to fight and die for his country; he was an unsung hero. He represented the ultimate symbol of manhood in the black community. Black soldiers' ability to participate in a war, which was typically seen as a manly act, solidified their successful masculine image. They were able to carry a weapon, receive military discipline, and, most importantly, wear the uniform of the U.S. Army.[9]

BLACK REGULARS RETURN FROM THE FRONTIER

"The American Negro is always ready and willing to take up arms, to fight and lay down his life in defense of his country. All the way from northwest Nebraska this regiment was greeted with cheers and hurrahs." Chaplain George Prioleau of Ninth Cavalry described the sentiment of his seasoned troopers as they made their way to Port Tampa, Florida, to prepare for war. The opportunity had finally arrived for another generation; they would have a chance to fight and prove again to the world that black soldiers were just as brave, honorable, and manly as white soldiers. A war with Spain represented an arena in which black men could exercise their citizenship. Moreover, the arena of combat was critical precisely because white laws and customs prevented blacks from exercising their citizenship in other areas.[10]

The Twenty-Fifth Infantry was the first regiment to mobilize for war against Spain, ordered to Key West in early March 1898. T. G. Steward observed in a letter to the *Christian Recorder* that the men were not welcomed by crowds there: "The 25th colored regiment was the first regular soldiers to appear in the South. . . . They appeared as splendid specimens of picked fighting men. The white citizens of Key West did not look upon them in that way." The soldiers looked forward to their departure from the Jim Crow South.[11]

President McKinley did not want to declare war until all the facts had come back from the formal naval inquiry investigating the cause of the *Maine*'s explosion. The jingoist press, however, was livid that McKinley did not immediately declare war on Spain for the destruction of a U.S. warship. McKinley's manhood was constantly being challenged throughout his presidency. The president was not as bellicose as some members of his party, proceeding to slowly mobilize the army for war, as he wanted to be sure that the destruction of the *Maine* was an act of war and not an accident. In fact, the other black regulars did not get their orders for mobilization until April, but by the time Congress formally declared war on April 25, all the black troops were transferred from their western positions in Montana, Utah, and Nebraska.[12]

With the formal declaration of war on Spain, black soldiers were able to receive the type of appreciation and support from the country that they had so desired. Wherever they stopped on their train ride from the West, they were met with cheering crowds and glowing admiration. Sergeant Horace Bivins of the Tenth Cavalry described their arrival in Nashville on their way to Chickamauga Park: "At Nashville, Tennessee, we were met by thousands of people, both white and colored. Our band played in response to the cheers that went up from the great multitude." The prevailing attitude among black soldiers was that of intense manly pride. Their reception was in striking contrast to the reception the Twenty-Fifth had received in Key West. These soldiers felt they would finally be able to gain the honor and respect their fathers had earned in the Civil War. Charles Young, the only black line officer in the army, had been greatly influenced by his father, a Civil War veteran. He stated that it was one of the reasons he wanted to join the military. He remembered his father very proudly as a man "whose heart glowed with love of country, liberty, and civic duty . . . who taught me my patriotism, which with us was no fair weather word. Achieving full manhood rights was one of his core convictions."[13]

The Spanish-American-Cuban-Filipino War and the spirit of militarism it inspired were widely celebrated as the true saviors of American manhood. Many in the black community saw the war with Spain as a blessing. The manliest from their race would finally show white America that they were willing to die and prove to the world that they were proud to be American citizens. When these soldiers fought and served, they did so knowing they would be carrying the race on their back. They knew that every valiant act would be a credit not just to a man but to the race. These men epitomized the definition of race men and galvanized the community behind them in their desire to uplift the race. The *Indianapolis Freeman* commented, "It is a blessing in disguise for the Negro. He will if for no other reason, be possessed of arms, which in the south, in [the] face of threatened mob violence he is not allowed to have. He will get much honor. He will have an opportunity of proving to the world his real bravery, worth, and manhood."[14]

The war with Spain was seen not only as a chance for black men to prove their manhood but also as an opportunity for *all* men to demonstrate their manly abilities. A national crisis of manhood, whether real or imagined, permeated America. The war with Spain was, therefore, not perceived as just another war but as a chance for the redemption of all men in America, because as T. G. Steward declared, "soft men cannot carry on a hard fight." American men in their minds apparently had become soft and they needed a war.[15]

THE GENTLEMAN SOLDIER

Black men took pride in their performance as soldiers because, in part, they were able to be role models in the black community, serving as leaders and providing racial and social uplift. Such a man was Christian Fleetwood, born a free man in Baltimore, Maryland. He went on to serve in the Civil War, where he was awarded the Congressional Medal of Honor and promoted to the rank of sergeant major. In fact, a unique component to Fleetwood's military service during the Civil War is that there was a petition started by all the white officers of his regiment to get Fleetwood promoted to the rank of lieutenant. The petition stated, "Sergeant Major C. A. Fleetwood has so proved himself as a gentleman and a soldier in every way, during daily intercourses extending over considerably more than a year." There were several vacancies in the line officer corps, but Secretary of War Edwin Stanton denied the request of the white officers because "there was no law under which a colored man could be commissioned to a rank carrying command at the time."[16]

Despite not being able to move up in the ranks, Fleetwood's military service did not end when he was discharged. Fleetwood wanted to do his duty to his community and not only served as a clerk with the War Department but went on to establish and promote various military groups in Washington, D.C. Fleetwood and Charles Fisher developed a tradition of military service for young black men in D.C. by establishing the Colored High School Cadet Corps in 1880. Fleetwood also pushed for cadet corps to be adopted by the black high schools in the District of Columbia. The young men who formed this unit would eventually organize the first African American National Guard unit in Washington, D.C. Fleetwood, after being appointed by Grover Cleveland, served as the commander of the unit, which would eventually join another unit and become the Sixth Battalion of Washington, D.C.

In 1898, at the start of the war, Daniel Murray made an emphatic plea in several black newspapers across the country to have Major Christian Fleetwood serve as a commander of the Fiftieth Volunteer Infantry. He was willing to lead the regiment, but the unit was blocked from serving and Fleetwood never saw action during the Spanish-American-Cuban War. [17]

Fleetwood, despite not being able to serve in the war, was still successful in recruiting other young black men and getting them to serve as soldiers and possible role models. The *Baltimore Ledger* reported the story of a soldier who also acted in this way. During the summer of 1898, Sergeant J. P. Smith of the Tenth Cavalry was walking down a street in Chattanooga when a bedraggled twelve-year-old black boy drew his attention. He took the boy into a clothing store, where he bought him a completely new outfit, including a hat and shoes, which came to a total of ten dollars. When the boy emerged from the store, he was completely unrecognizable to his friends.[18]

Why did Sergeant Smith purchase clothing for a youngster who was a stranger to him? Smith did his charitable deed because he was a soldier who felt a certain responsibility for this boy. There is a possibility he may have seen something of himself in the twelve-year-old and sought to help him in a way that no one ever had. Smith may have also wanted him to understand that to be a good man and have self-respect, he had to present himself in a respectable way, and in order to do that he had to wear certain kinds of clothes. Sergeant Smith helped that boy because, as a soldier, he could. It may have been a simple act, yet not every soldier had ten dollars to spare, which made it a grand gesture worthy of note in the press.

Men like Smith and Fleetwood knew that they were symbols of hope and pride for their race, which afforded them a certain economic status in the community. They received both a consistent and steady salary from the army and an education from the chaplains assigned to their regiment. Thus, their performance in Cuba had to be nothing short of perfect: they were fighting not only for their own manhood but for the manhood of all black men and the uplift of the entire race. The editor of the *Illinois Record* of Springfield noted,

> I want the black man to show the world that he is a nobler and better type of citizen than the ignorant and colorblind white man. I want the black man of this country to show pride that if the white man cannot protect the colored man when in peril that the black man can and will protect him in his helplessness.[19]

The chance to defend the honor of all African Americans was an opportunity that these soldiers could not refuse. It is important to understand that these men went to Cuba because they wanted to help free the Cuban people from the tyranny of Spain, but they also wanted to demonstrate their patriotism and to protect black America's honor.

THE FIGHT FOR HONOR

Private John E. Lewis of the Tenth Cavalry wrote to the *Illinois Record* requesting all young black men come and defend America's honor. "It is time that every patriotic young colored man should come to the front, defend its honor, and show that we are truly American citizens and that we will protect our homes and government," he declared. Despite the opinions of many white Americans, Private Lewis believed that blacks were already citizens. He wanted to show white America and the world that it was because blacks were true citizens that they would be willing to fight and die right along with their white brothers in the protection of the United States. Given the conservative retrenchment cross-country and the academic explanation of black inferiority, where else could black men show themselves to be "true American citizens"?[20]

Black soldiers yearned to establish a stronger bond with their white comrades. While fighting in Cuba, they had a certain opportunity to establish that bond. At the famous charge of San Juan Hill, the Ninth and Tenth Cavalries were on the front line. Both regiments were a part of the First Brigade, which was commanded by Major General "Fighting" Joe Wheeler of Alabama. In the introduction to Henry V. Cashin's book *Under Fire with the U.S. Cavalry*, Wheeler asserts that "those who see in the future of the colored race in America a difficult and perplexing problem will find encouragement in this book." He then goes on to state that because these men were disciplined soldiers, they would be able to train others in the race to be like them. Wheeler, a former Confederate general turned Democratic congressman, gave up his seat in Congress so he could fight in Cuba. It is also worth mentioning that it was at the battle of San Juan Hill that Theodore Roosevelt and the Rough Riders became legends in American history.[21]

African Americans considered the battle at San Juan Hill to be one of the defining moments in black military history. It was there that black soldiers proved that they could withstand shot and shell while singing "It will be a hot time in the city tonight." The battle, which started at 6:30 a.m. on July 1 and lasted until the afternoon of July 3, saw the death and wounding of twelve officers from both the Ninth and Tenth Cavalries, so most of the orders came from the noncommissioned officers. The men of the Tenth Cavalry, held in reserve when the fight started, ultimately moved to the front line and maneuvered themselves in a position where they could penetrate the Spanish line at a vulnerable point, allowing the First Battalion to surround the Spanish.[22]

It was because of their display of courage under fire that twenty-five noncommissioned officers from the four black regular regiments would be commissioned as lieutenants in the four black "immune" volunteer regiments. The "immune" regiments, composed of three thousand black troops, were called such because of the belief that blacks were supposedly immune to yellow fever. African Americans had been very vociferous in their objections to there being only one black line officer in the military, and the appointment of the twenty-five NCOs to the position of lieutenant in the volunteer regiments was a way for Republicans to satisfy the black community.[23]

At the same time that the Battle of San Juan Hill took place, the Twenty-Fifth Infantry participated as part of the First Brigade in another battle.

The Battle at El Caney was an attempt to capture a heavily guarded Spanish blockhouse. The first regiment to the line was the Seventy-First Volunteers from New York. They were brigaded with two regular regiments. When the men of the Seventy-First, under the command of Brigadier General Hamilton S. Hawkins, made their initial charge, their line faltered under fire. They became panic-stricken and either froze or ran to the rear. The men were a part of the larger Fifth Corps division under the command of General Jacob Ford Kent, who reported to General William Shafter. General Kent became disgusted by the poor performance of the men of the Seventy-First. Kent made this emotional appeal to the men: "For the love of country, liberty, honor, and dignity, in the name of freedom, in the name of God, for the sake of your dear mothers and fathers, . . . stand up like men and fight." In response, the Twenty-Fifth Infantry of the Second Regiment took the place of the Seventy-First Volunteers. This incident, as shocking as it was, was not reported in any of the black newspapers, although it would have been an excellent opportunity for the black press to demonstrate that black soldiers were more manly than white soldiers and that they never faltered under fire in the way the men of this unit did. Yet when black regular infantrymen were falsely accused of cowardice under fire by Theodore Roosevelt, the white press jumped at the chance to question and attack African American soldiers' military performance.[24]

One explanation for the reluctance of the black newspapers to report on the incident with the Seventy-First Volunteers is that they were trying to help black soldiers establish and strengthen their bond with white soldiers. They did not want to characterize African American men as great soldiers by denigrating white troops. Another explanation is that the black press did not want to upset white America. Newspaper and journal editors and reporters were hoping that because black soldiers performed heroically in battle, white America would not support the further disenfranchisement of African Americans in the South. Stephen Bonsal, a war correspondent who sympathized with the plight of the black soldier, attempted to demonstrate to white America that black soldiers had gained the respect of some of their white brothers in uniform.

Bonsal reported on one story in which a corporal from the Twenty-Fourth Infantry was walking to a watering hole. He carried no cup or canteen and was so weary that he just threw himself on the ground and drank the muddy water. A white cavalry man saw this and rushed to him shouting, "Hold on Bunkie; here's my cup." The soldier looked dazed for a moment, and a few spectators stared in amazement. The black corporal stated that such a thing rarely happened in the army. "Thank you," said the corporal; "we are all fighting under the same flag now." Bonsal reported that he was glad to see that he was not the only man who had come to recognize the justice of constitutional amendments, in light of the gallant behavior of the colored troops throughout the battle. His response reflected what these soldiers hoped to achieve. They wanted respect and recognition for their actions, and in a small way they accomplished this goal.[25]

THE TRIALS AND TRIUMPHS OF THE "MUTINOUS SIXTH"

In Knoxville, Tennessee, at Camp Poland, the all-black Sixth Volunteer Regiment from Virginia was disarmed after an assault on the regiment from the First Georgia Volunteers resulted in four of the Georgians disappearing. After the incident, the camp moved farther away from the city and orders came from the headquarters of the First Army in Lexington, Kentucky, that several of the regiment's officers needed to be reviewed. Shortly after their review, all the black officers in the unit were dismissed, declared unfit. When the soldiers realized that the white regiment commander was not going to replace the black officers with men from their ranks, the soldiers decided not to obey orders from the new officers. The men were ordered to stack their arms, but they refused. The ammunition was then removed and stored in another camp.[26]

This incident made headlines across America and served as a motivation for whites to attack black soldiers. The Sixth Virginia Infantry was also credited with destroying a "hanging tree" in Macon, Georgia, where a black man, Will Singleton, had been hung. The men then went on to open fire and destroy a sign at a public park that stated "No Dogs and No Niggers Allowed." This regiment was portrayed in the black press as made up of heroes who would not stand for racist treatment, as they were willing to fight and die for their country.

The Sixth Volunteer Infantry had a long, defiant history. Organized in 1876, it was able to exist because of help from the African American community. The black militiamen of Virginia depended on the private contributions of black citizens for equipment and uniforms. This unit reported directly to and received orders from the office of the adjutant general, which afforded it a special status. The unit had all black officers and a sizable contingent of soldiers from Hampton who participated with the militia. When war erupted with Spain, the men of the Sixth were ready to demonstrate their manhood and patriotism. However, they made it very clear that they would serve only with black officers.[27]

John Mitchell Jr., the editor of the *Richmond Planet*, initiated and led the "No officers, no fight" campaign in the press and the community. The governor of Virginia, J. Hoge Tyler, compromised with the Sixth and agreed for the unit to have black officers, but it had to have a white battalion commander. Tyler chose Lieutenant Richard Clayborne Croxton to be the commander. The unit reluctantly agreed, but it was not long before the men had problems with their white commander, who was young and a recent West Point graduate. Croxton had poor health, but he was soon promoted to the rank of lieutenant colonel.[28]

On September 12, 1898, the Sixth Virginia was transferred to Camp Poland in Knoxville, Tennessee. Another black regiment, the Third North Carolina Infantry, was already there. However, the white soldiers at the camp did not approve of these units being housed together, so they were separated. Once the Sixth was settled, Colonel Croxton ordered his soldiers to keep away from the white soldiers while in camp and to avoid establishments in town. The men of complied with Croxton's orders despite having rocks thrown at them by white soldiers from Georgia and the hostile environment at the camp. Their obedience notwithstanding, Croxton wanted to remove the black officers and replace them with white officers, which upset the men greatly. He claimed that the black officers lacked any formal education and did not possess the kind of authority needed to lead men. Croxton espoused the common racist musings about blacks being incapable of serving as officers, even though all of the Sixth Virginia's officers had attended the Hampton Institute and Major William Johnson was a school principal. Still, Croxton ordered all African American officers of the Sixth to be formally reviewed as a way to remove them from their positions. However, these men informed the adjutant general that they would not submit to the review. The entire unit rallied behind its officers and had the support of the black community and press. The officers resigned rather than submit to the authority of Colonel Croxton. Willard Gatewood noted, "Black civilians in Virginia were searching for a way to ensure that the War Department would be apprised of what they described as the disgraceful treatment of the Negro officers. A mass meeting in Richmond resulted in the appointment of a committee to call upon Secretary of War Alger." Croxton replaced the officers with white men and one black soldier from the Twenty-Fourth infantry, yet when these men attempted to command the black militiamen, no one responded to their authority. Similar committees were organized during World War I and World War II to advocate on behalf of African American soldiers while they were deployed.[29]

The soldiers had an organized community behind them using the press and letter writing to put pressure on the governor and War Department. These men were protesting for their rights as citizens and soldiers. In their acts of defiance, whether destroying a lynching tree or tearing down Jim Crow signs in Georgia, they were heroes to the black community and did not have to fight in Cuba to be viewed as such. They resumed their duties only after Major Johnson came and spoke with them and Croxton promised to replace the white officers with black ones. To the men of the Sixth, this was a small victory, but to the rest of white America, they earned the nickname the "Mutinous Sixth." Morale in the unit never fully returned, despite the men destroying the signs of Jim Crow and beating up a racist barkeep. Men in the unit were arrested for their behavior at Camp Haskell; they were severely criticized in the media for their "mutiny" at Camp Poland; and in the town of Macon they were discriminated against only until they stopped spending money, and then the local press and business owners attempted to change their tune and treatment of these soldiers.

Nevertheless, the unit suffered both good and bad press after the Camp Poland uprising. It was enough ammunition for the enemies of the black militia in Virginia to get the unit disbanded, and the men were mustered out of National Guard service on January 26, 1899. This upset the African American community of Virginia and contributed to the growing disillusionment among black civilians and the black press with "McKinley imperialism." It did not help that black soldiers were being attacked and killed for simply wearing the uniform of the U.S. Army. For example, on Thanksgiving Day in 1898, a member of the Tenth Cavalry, Corporal David Garret, was killed by a black man named "Horse" Douglass. Douglass had been bragging about how he was paid by several white men to kill members of the Tenth. He was never punished. The murder of David Garret and other black men angered and frustrated the men of the Sixth and contributed to the feeling that there was very little "to inspire a patriotic thrill in the breast of the Negro."[30]

The Sixth Virginia's tumultuous existence ended in 1899, yet not all black militias had the same experience as the Sixth. The Third North Carolina, which was organized by James Young, had a different experience. Historian Helen Edmonds in her groundbreaking study *The Negro and Fusion Politics in North Carolina* described James Young as being "easily the most outstanding Negro in the state." James Young was born a slave on October 26, 1858, in Raleigh. His father and owner was Captain D. E. Young, whose life as a career soldier greatly influenced Young's desire to participate in military service. Young's father made sure that his son was properly educated and helped to get him a job once he graduated from Shaw University. Young worked as an internal revenue collector and became heavily involved with the Republican Party of North Carolina. By the 1890s Young was focused on education and the plight of African Americans. He strongly believed in racial uplift, and while he was the owner and editor of the *Raleigh Gazette* he ran stories and wrote editorials that focused on providing a political voice for the black community of North Carolina.[31]

Young's story and life are important not only because he played an important role in North Carolina's politics but because he was the organizer and driving force behind the Third North Carolina Volunteer Infantry. In 1898, similar to what John Mitchell, the editor of the *Richmond Planet*, did in his campaign for the Sixth of Virginia, Young called for black officers to serve in North Carolina's all-black regiment. However, unlike Mitchell, Young wanted to serve in the regiment he was promoting in his newspaper. Young, despite his belief in pacifism, put the needs of the race above his own, went out and encouraged black men to serve in the military, helped in getting large numbers of black men to enlist, and garnered black support for the war. He was so dedicated to serving that he gave up being editor of the *Raleigh Gazette* and focused all of his attention on the regiment and getting all black officers to fill the ranks. Young was successful despite the protests of many whites in North Carolina, at least partly because he helped the governor of North Carolina, Daniel Russell, get elected in 1896 on the Fusion ticket. Russell then rewarded Young for his help by appointing him the colonel and regimental commander of the Third.

Initially, when the Third was called to serve, it was designated the Russell Black Battalion Army Corps. It comprised new recruits who were members of the state guard, and Young fought relentlessly to get enough men to make up an entire regiment. He traveled all over the state recruiting young men and was successful in raising an entire regiment. The Third became a great source of pride not only for the African American community in North Carolina but also for blacks across the country.

The Third trained at forts in Macon, Georgia, and Knoxville, Tennessee, with the Sixth, but because of who its regimental commander was, James Young, it was able to escape some of the negative press that followed the Sixth. In fact, while in Knoxville, the Third was singled out for a special commendation. Both regiments did communicate with one another, despite being separated in the camps. And both regiments faced similar hostility from their fellow white soldiers, evident from the regimental records of the Third after the murder of one of its own, Robert Thomas of Wilson, North Carolina, in Macon. After his death, a couple of white soldiers from an all-white regiment stationed with the Third went missing and were feared dead. Following these events, several members of the Third were discharged without explanation in the regimental records. Customarily when a soldier was discharged a reason was provided, but this was not the case on the day following Robert Thomas's death. Black soldiers have a history of responding to or retaliating against the murder of one of their fellow brothers-in-arms, so it is not surprising that those white soldiers went missing the day that Thomas was killed and that those black soldiers were discharged in such a rapid manner.[32]

Still, James Young and the Third North Carolina were able to be a source of pride for the black community differently than the Sixth of Virginia was. The Third was reviewed by President McKinley on December 21, 1898, and received a special commendation from Secretary of War Russell Alger. Yet despite being a source of great pride for blacks, the Third was not received at home with an enthusiastic welcome by the whites of North Carolina. In fact, while Young and the Third were gone, the state legislature had enacted laws that would not allow blacks to serve in the state guard. However, this did not prevent members of the Third from continuing their military service. After the Third was mustered out, at least five officers from the unit were commissioned to serve in the two all-black volunteer regiments that fought in the Philippines. James Young continued to support military service; during World War I he was called upon by the Selective Service to help with the recruitment of black men into the armed forces.[33]

Young organized and served in the military because he believed that it would benefit African Americans. Young's dedication to racial uplift motivated him to fight not only for blacks politically and militarily but also for black education. Young's historical legacy focuses on his political and educational platforms, yet there was more to him than just a politician, an educator, and an editor; he was a soldier. Young did not have to serve; he *chose* to serve and be an example for his men. He was able to bring pride and racial uplift to the black community by putting on a uniform inspired young men to serve and fight not only for their country but for their community.

BLACK HEROES UNWELCOME AT HOME

On August 12, 1898, a cease-fire was ordered. The United States had defeated Spain in Cuba. Because of their heroic performances at San Juan Hill and El

Caney, black soldiers became heroes. The editor of the *Indianapolis Freeman* published a letter from a white officer that stated, "I think the Negro soldiers can be thanked for the greater part of that glorious work. All honor to the Negro soldiers! No white man no matter his ancestry may be ashamed to greet any of those Negro cavalrymen with an outstretched hand." Black soldiers returned home to America triumphantly and were greeted by parades and dinners thrown in their honor. One newspaper declared, "All honor to these gallant nineteenth-century knights! They are typical Americans and their noble conduct should bring a blush of shame to the snobs who disgrace Uncle Sam's uniform by sneering at their dark-skinned brethren and compatriots."[34]

This triumphant return did not last for long, though, and the hopes for the recognition of the black soldier's citizenship and manhood were about to be dashed. E. E. Cooper, the editor of the *Colored American*, stated that "when the colored soldier returns he will bring with him an accumulation of manhood, patriotism, military prowess, and a stronger determination to be a full-fledged citizen." Yet shortly after the return of black troops, violence broke out in Wilmington, North Carolina, the home state of the only black representative in Congress, George H. White, and one of the few states that allowed for an all-black regiment to be staffed completely by African American officers. In November 1898, the city of Wilmington erupted in a horribly violent race riot that drove thousands of blacks from their homes and killed dozens.[35]

The Wilmington riot occurred because of an article written by Alexander Manly. In it, Manly boldly and bluntly observed that many of the alleged rapes blamed on black men by white women were more likely to have been consensual encounters. This article also fueled the fire for the "respectable" white citizens of Wilmington preventing African Americans from voting in the upcoming elections. Thousands of blacks fled and many appealed to McKinley to intervene, but he did nothing.[36]

The race riot was not the only incident of racial violence after the war. In Huntsville, Alabama, as soon as black troops arrived, they were met with problems with white soldiers, so it was no surprise that white soldiers killed Private John R. Brooks of the Tenth. Brooks worked as an employee of the *Richmond Planet*, of which John Mitchell was the editor. Brooks was unarmed.[37]

Violence committed against black soldiers took place throughout the South after the war. The "era of good feeling" that the war with Spain was supposed to usher in between whites and blacks never came to fruition. The African American soldier stationed in the South was forced to stay at his fort because away from the base he ran the risk of being attacked or shot by an angry mob. The reason such violence occurred is simple: white men hated what the black soldier represented—a positive symbol of manhood for the African American community. Black soldiers constantly challenged the Jim Crow system, and this unsettled whites. These men were armed and militarily trained; the white mob could not use the normal forms of terror against them. Instead, they attacked them in the press. For example, in 1899, Theodore Roosevelt, in an interview with *Scribner's Magazine*, claimed he stopped a group of black infantrymen from retreating at the Battle of San Juan Hill by pulling his pistol. The goal of Roosevelt to tarnish the reputation of the buffalo soldiers in the press was part of a political strategy of appeasement of the racist white voters of the South.[38]

Chaplain George Prioleau of the Ninth Cavalry recounted an experience in Jim Crow America he had while traveling through the South on a leave of absence during the summer of 1899. Prioleau, a graduate of Wilberforce University and the former pastor of several Ohio congregations, regularly corresponded with the *Cleveland Gazette*, sharing his experiences in his service to "God, Race, and Country." In this particular report, he recounted the prejudice he encountered once he was forced to leave the mixed railroad coach he traveled in from the frontier and entered Texas. Prioleau disdainfully recalled the event:

> I entered the coach set aside for Negroes, but it was full of greasy and dirty Mexicans. I deliberately wended my way to the coach for white people, took seat and settled myself, but my seat was hardly warmed before the porter informed me that I could not ride in that car, that I must go forward. I refused; he called the conductor and I still refused, I said to the conductor so that everyone could hear, that I only ride with the two leading races of this country through Texas—the white man and the Negro. . . . They hustled me to rear and I entered a coach all to myself.[39]

Prioleau's defiance did not end there; his classist and prejudiced stance led to confrontations with "Mexicans and poor whites" trying to ride in his private car. He felt that as an officer in uniform, he should be treated as a gentleman and not be forced to deal with the riffraff of the lower classes. His act of defiance, despite being steeped in bourgeois prejudice, was widely read and demonstrated to blacks even after the *Plessy* case: a single soldier could stand up and live against Jim Crow.[40]

FIGHTING IN AN UNHOLY WAR

Roosevelt's negative comments did not sit well in the black community. For example, the *Broad Ax* of Salt Lake City called him "Teddy Roosevelt the paper soldier, who denies that he slandered Negro soldiers." Yet, the *Broad Ax* went on to quote Roosevelt's own words about the dependency of black troops on their white officers and their retreat from the line. Roosevelt's words hurt many black soldiers because they respected him. He had at first praised them for their heroic deeds in Cuba, and now he was calling them cowards. The negative reactions that black soldiers endured truly harmed the African American community. They had believed that if they fought bravely in the war, there could be no doubt about the abilities of blacks to perform as citizens and as men. But "mob law, mob violence, now reigns supreme throughout the South and in many parts of the North. The brave deeds of the black man in all the wars of this country and especially in our most recent struggle are either forgotten or are ignored." On February 4, 1899, Filipino rebels fired on white soldiers in Manila. The Filipino Rebellion had begun, and black soldiers, unlike the black press, looked forward to going to the Philippines. For many soldiers, the reason was simple: it would be better for them to fight a colonial war in the Philippines than to fight a race war in America.[41]

The Filipino Insurrection started near Santa Messa, northeast of Manila. The tension had been mounting in the Philippines since shortly after the armistice had been signed in Cuba. With the Treaty of Paris on December 10, 1898, the United States decided that for the good of the Filipino people, the Philippines would not become an independent nation. Instead, it would stop being a Spanish colony and, for the price of $20 million, it would become an American colony, along with Puerto Rico and Guam. The moment the treaty was signed, the Filipinos attacked American troops. The Filipinos were enraged and offended because not only were they not signers of the treaty, but also they were completely left out of the peace negotiations. The Aguinaldo-led rebellion should not have been a surprise; the Filipinos had revolted against the Spanish thirty-four times.[42]

The United States had finally become an imperialist nation with Pacific colonies. The McKinley administration felt that the Filipinos were not capable of self-government and that it was America's responsibility to help educate and Christianize them. Imperialists believed that only white men possessed the unique capacity of self-government and encouraged America to take up the "White Man's Burden" and join the rest of the major Western nations as an imperialist power. However, the imperialist ideology that was driving the McKinley administration was not popular with all Americans, especially African Americans. The black community, reflecting the outrage expressed in the black press and by African American leaders such as Booker T. Washington, felt that it was wrong for America to give Cuba its independence but not the Philippines. America, in the minds of those in the black community, went to war not to become a colonial power but to provide freedom and independence to the people Spain had so brutally oppressed. In spite of the overwhelming disapproval of African Americans regarding the war in the Philippines, they were ever supportive of black troops. John Mitchell of the *Richmond Planet* stated, "Much as we detest this Filipino War, we will always uphold the honor of American soldiers, to whom mutiny is a stranger, wherever we may be, whether shooting Cuban bandits or suppressing patriotic Filipinos."[43]

The first black regiments, the Twenty-Fourth and the Twenty-Fifth, did not arrive at Manila until July 1899. By December 1900, over six thousand African American troops would be in the Philippines, the largest number of African Americans in the army at one time since the end of the Civil War. Two additional volunteer regiments were added to the four black regular regiments stationed in the Philippines, the Forty-Eighth and Forty-Ninth Infantries. Both of these new regiments had both black and white officers. The black officers of these volunteer regiments had all been officers in the volunteer units from the previous war with Spain.[44]

The reactions of the black press to the Filipino War were different from those expressed when America was fighting Spain. Therefore, the rhetoric about what constituted manly behavior changed. One reason for this change is that many prominent black leaders such as Bishop Henry McNeal Turner and Booker T. Washington spoke out against America's war with the Filipino rebels. Washington stated, "My opinion is that the Philippine Islands should be given the opportunity to govern themselves. They will make mistakes but will learn from their errors. Until our nation has settled the Negro and Indian problems, I do not think we have a right to assume more social problems."[45] Ralph W. Tyler, one of the only black civilian correspondents, took his opposition to the war a step further when he asserted, "What spark of manhood and race pride could approve American military action in the Philippines, much less take part as a soldier?" The war to save humanity had turned in the eyes of most of the black press into a war of greed and oppression.[46]

Yet there were those in the black press who supported America's involvement in the Philippines. They saw this war as a chance for the black soldier to do his manly duty and demonstrate to the Filipino how to be a man. Chaplain James M. Guthrie stated, "The black soldier will shed a light of radiance which will not only shine across the wide Pacific to make brighter the hopes of their own race in their native land, but they will illuminate the islanders towards what it means to be a part of the American republic."[47]

The other papers that supported the soldiers but not the war took a stance similar to that of the Kansas City newspaper the *American Citizen*:

> For the black, there is no glory in this war, nothing save carnage, death, and injustice. No; there is no honor, and but slight reward; and since the brave black soldier must fight in this unholy war in the Philippines. Let him fight like he can, in such furious onslaughts that nothing but the walls of hell can withstand him; and prove, to those vile creatures who robbed him of his glory and prowess, the soldier that he is, the most courageous, the most enduring, and the finest soldier the world has known.[48]

The African American soldier had already demonstrated his manly prowess on the battlefield in Cuba, and his involvement in the Philippines was not as noble a cause as that previous war with Spain. The black soldier simply saw the task in the Philippines as a duty that had to be performed, no matter how unjust. Black troops serving as correspondents for black newspapers wrote home expressing both the frustration and humanity in their service to American imperialism. However, there existed some black soldiers who gave little thought to the morality of the conflict.

M. W. Saddler of the Twenty-Fifth, in a letter to the *Indianapolis Freeman*, described the soldiers' understanding as to why they had to fight against the Filipinos: "Our greatest aim is to maintain our standing among American soldiers and add another star to the already brilliant crown of the Afro-American soldier. Our oath of allegiance knows neither race, color nor nation." The soldiers held a certain level of respect for the Filipinos that was not equally shared by the white soldiers, yet they did not let their respect for the Filipinos prevent them from doing their duties. Captain W. H. Jackson of the Forty-Ninth Infantry stated very plainly, "All enemies of the U.S. Government look alike to us hence we go along with the killing in the Philippines." Captain F. H. Crumbley in his letter to the *Savannah*

Tribune was more enthusiastic about the value of the islands to America and thought nothing of the Filipino cause: "The Americans should, and would if they knew the extent of the value of these islands, feel great pride in our national acquisition." The public sentiment at home in the U.S. against the war was very disappointing to the men fighting. Michael Robinson of the Twenty-Fifth Infantry in a letter to the *Colored American* described his disappointment: "I will say that we of the Twenty-fifth feel rather discouraged over the fact that the sacrifice of life and health has to be made for a cause so unpopular among our people. Yet the fact we are American soldiers instills within us the feeling and resolve to perform our duty."[49]

The respectable treatment that the black soldiers gave the Filipinos was a result of their definition and understanding of what constituted manly behavior. These soldiers in their correspondence to the press also demonstrated their nuanced education and empathy in interacting with a fellow oppressed people. Corporal C. W. Cordin wrote in his letter to the *Cleveland Gazette* nothing but praise for the intelligence of the Filipinos: "As far as I can note from casual observance, I should class the Filipinos with the Cubans. They are intelligent and industrious, they are friendly and hospitable." The respect and admiration black soldiers had for both Filipinos and Cubans were demonstrated in the way they treated them. These soldiers did not see the Filipinos or Cubans as inhuman or inferior but simply as men. Black soldiers did not believe abusing, robbing, or torturing the Filipinos just because they were people of color was justifiable, having experienced that same treatment themselves in America.[50]

The negative and racist attitudes that white soldiers directed at the Filipinos greatly influenced the way black soldiers treated the indigenous population. Sergeant Major John Galloway of the Twenty-Fourth Infantry interviewed a Filipino physician for the *Richmond Planet*. Señor Tordorico Santos described the difference in treatment between black soldiers and white soldiers: "The colored soldiers do not push them off the streets, spit at them, call them damned 'niggers,' abuse them in all manner of ways, and connect race hatred with duty." Galloway then went on to state, "No one white has any scruples as regards respecting the rights of a Filipino." Patrick Mason of the Twenty-Fourth Infantry further described the racist attitudes of white soldiers to the *Cleveland Gazette*: "The first thing in the morning is the 'Nigger' and the last thing at night is the 'Nigger.' You have no idea the way these people are treated by Americans here." The black soldiers also did not rob and abuse the Filipinos, because such was simply a violation of general orders given by the U.S. military governor of the Philippines

General E. S. Otis. Thus, black soldiers were demonstrating their manhood both through respect for Filipino humanity and through obedience to military commands.[51]

THE BLACK SOLDIER: A LOVER AND A FIGHTER

The relationships that developed between African American soldiers and Filipino women also influenced the behavior of black soldiers toward the Filipino population in general. Black soldiers were more welcomed than white soldiers by Filipino women. Filipino women preferred black men because they were more likely than white soldiers to marry them and be a husband and father to their children. These men could provide economic stability and status that Filipino men could not and white men would not. The Filipino woman offered a chance to the black man to do something he often could not do for black women: he could protect her. He could physically protect her in ways he could not defend black women in the U.S. because of the racial situation in America. In addition, the black soldier could provide for his Filipino wife in ways often unimaginable in the U.S. because the soldier's salary went a long way in the Philippines. George W. Prioleau, the chaplain from the Ninth Cavalry, ecstatically described in a letter to the *Colored American* that he was about to perform his third marriage between a corporal and a Filipino woman: "The soldiers of the old Ninth Cavalry are on very friendly terms with the natives; in fact, I believe it so wherever Negro soldiers are stationed on the island."[52]

Unfortunately, the relationships between black soldiers and Filipino women eventually contributed to the persistent questioning by whites of black soldiers' loyalty. Filipino insurgents started a propaganda campaign solely directed at black soldiers, which did not help their situation. The insurgents constantly bombarded African American soldiers with pamphlets questioning their purpose in fighting against them in this war when black people were being raped, murdered, and lynched in America. However, when these soldiers received such propaganda from the insurgents, they ignored it. After the battle at Fort O'Donnell in November 1899, P. C. Pogue of the Twenty-Fifth Infantry described how they burned most of the pamphlets written as an appeal to the "Colored American Soldier." Pogue stated, "The proclamations were burned except a few which were kept as souvenirs. Colored Americans are just as loyal to the old flag as white Americans." There were very few desertions by black soldiers. They insisted upon performing their duties as soldiers and they performed these duties, whether they agreed with them or not.[53]

Yet Philippine governor William Howard Taft felt that the black soldiers got along too well with the Filipinos. In fact, when white and black troops were stationed in the same town, there was a color line drawn against the white soldiers. This gave Taft great concern, and he was instrumental in getting most of the black troops out of the Philippines once the war was over in 1902 because the white soldiers resented the close relationships between blacks and Filipinos.[54]

The empathy of the black soldiers serving in the Philippines helped them create bonds and relationships with the civilian population, which the racist white soldiers could not fathom. The white soldiers possibly felt an inherent disconnect from the Filipino population because of their participation in the slaughtering of thousands of rebel soldiers. African American soldiers vocally opposed the inhumane treatment of the Filipino civilian population but did not disobey their officers' orders. The paradoxical nature of their military service allowed for them to fight in an unjust war yet still feel empathy and sympathy for the very people they were fighting against. The Filipinos understood this and maintained a positive relationship with the black soldiers, one that was often envied by their white brothers-in-arms.

The Filipinos themselves described black troops as being "much more kindly and manly in dealing with us than whites." White soldiers resented the mutual respect that the Filipinos and blacks shared. They resented even more that the Filipinos considered black troops more manly; this can be seen in the Filipino women's preference for African American soldiers and the rhetoric coming from the rebels, which was directed toward black soldiers. The African American soldier's manly behavior was something these men took pride in reporting to the press because they wanted to demonstrate that they were not the "unmanly brutes by nature" that whites constantly accused them of being. After a series of interviews with the well-educated Filipinos, a black infantry-man reported that whites had told them that African Americans were brutes and rapists, and they were glad to see that their assumptions were wrong.[55]

The war in the Philippines was vastly different from the war in Cuba. The army was forced to fight a guerrilla war and spend a lot of time chasing the rebels all over the various islands. Because this Asian conflict was un-conventional, many soldiers feared that there were not going to be the same opportunities for heroic deeds as there had been in Cuba. The Filipino War allowed for few heroes and very little glory. The most famous battle of the war was the raid at O'Donnell, which resulted in high casualties on both sides. It involved four hundred troops from the Twenty-Fifth Infantry and the capture of over one hundred insurgents. Yet, because the majority of the black press was anti-imperialist, the deeds of the Twenty-Fifth received little coverage. Even though some 250,000 Filipino civilians and soldiers died in the Filipino War, the imperialist nature of the conflict made it impossible for the black press to embrace and support it.[56]

The fight for manhood and citizenship took on a different tone in the war in the Philippines. Instead of demonstrating their manly abilities on the battlefield, black soldiers demonstrated their manhood through their treatment of the Filipinos. The racist and extremely violent treatment of the Filipinos by white soldiers stood in stark contrast to the respectful treatment of Filipinos by black soldiers. This is why they were able to establish a better relationship with the Filipinos; the Filipinos appreciated the respect they received from black soldiers and considered black troops to be manly and kind. White soldiers resented this mutual respect and admiration. The positive relationship between the Filipinos and African Americans led many black soldiers to stay after the war was over in 1902.[57]

THE DAVID FAGEN EFFECT

When David Fagen abandoned his unit to join the Filipino cause, he did so not realizing the prolonged effect his desertion would have on all black soldiers in the eyes of military authority. Fagen's legacy among black soldiers and the black community was not as a hero but as a traitor. When he was killed, the black press reported simply, "Fagen died a traitor's death." The Fagen effect strengthened the distrust of black soldiers and led to the persecution and dishonorable discharge of Sergeant Major John Calloway of the Twenty-Fourth Infantry. Calloway was accused of being sympathetic to the Filipino cause after a letter he wrote was discovered in the home of a prominent Filipino planter suspected of being a nationalist.[58]

John Calloway was born in 1872. He grew up in Bristol, Tennessee, and was a printer by trade. In 1891 he enlisted in the army; he reenlisted in 1894 and 1899. He served in Company H, the same unit as David Fagen. In all of Calloway's evaluations, he was described by his superiors as having excellent character. Calloway, a highly intelligent and talented writer, also served as a war correspondent; he even conducted an informal survey of the Filipino civilian population to gauge how civilians felt about the war there and about American soldiers. Calloway's informal survey was printed in both Filipino and black American newspapers. What he determined was that Filipino civilians preferred black soldiers to white soldiers, simply because they did not treat them in the same racist way that most white soldiers did. Calloway gained social status among blacks and Filipinos by demonstrating both his patriotism in service of America's suppression of Filipino independence and also a certain level of sympathy for the Filipinos.

However, despite his longtime service in the U.S. Army, Calloway was reduced in rank and dishonorably discharged because he wrote a letter to his friend Thomas Consigi that was interpreted as being sympathetic to the rebels. Despite the fact that Consigi was a U.S. government employee and was able to keep his job, Calloway's letter was viewed as too intelligent and demonstrated the type of complex discussions occurring between black soldiers and Filipino civilians. Calloway was described by one white official as being "one of those half-baked mulattos whose education has fostered his self-conceit to an abnormal degree." Calloway at his trial was found innocent of being a traitor, yet he was guilty in the eyes of the U.S. military and was forced to leave the Philippines. On January 12, 1901, Calloway was cast into the hold of a ship and brought home in disgrace.[59]

However, for Calloway, the fight was not over. He had saved up $5,000 and was hoping to open a business in the Philippines. He returned to the islands in 1904 and tried to reenlist but was not allowed to join the army again. Fagen's legacy continued to prevent Calloway's efforts to clear his name; the fact that both Fagen and Calloway served in the same unit was too much for him to overcome. Calloway petitioned the president and the Supreme Court in order to get reinstated and honorably discharged. He had support in both the Philippines and the United States; his friend T. Thomas Fortune wrote to President Roosevelt on his behalf.[60]

Yet Calloway, despite all of his efforts, was not able to get an honorable discharge. He remained in the Philippines and worked first for the American civilian government and then gained employment with the Quapo Pacific Commercial Company, an American hardware company. He worked there for over twenty years. He married a Filipino woman and had fourteen children. Calloway for the remainder of his life remained adamant about his military service, saying that "my country has never suffered as a result of my duty." Despite being imprisoned twice, Calloway did not abandon his desire to make the Philippines his home and to raise a family there. He was able to have a successful civilian life and was not seen by the African American community as a disgraced soldier. He had strong support for all of his petitions. He fought tirelessly to clear his name, and when he died in 1934, his death certificate in the Philippines did not describe him as a printer or an engineer but as a former soldier of the U.S. Army.[61]

Historians have portrayed Fagen's desertion as a symbol of African American solidarity with the Filipino cause. Scholar Scot Ngozi-Brown said, "The most well-known expression of African American solidarity to the Filipino came from David Fagen of the Twenty-fourth." Fagen's desertion was an anomaly, yet the prevailing ideology among scholars who discuss black soldiers of this era is that they were reluctant to do their duty and were more sympathetic to the Filipino independence movement. However, John Calloway did his duty and fought the Filipino rebels; he was proud of his service. Such men did not have reservations about their service in the Philippines: "Our oath of allegiance knows neither race nor color." These men who joined and fought did so with the understanding that they would not discuss their personal feelings about the army's policies in public. They viewed their service in the Philippines in the same way they did their service in the West when they had fought Native Americans.[62]

IN THE END: THEY DID THEIR DUTY

Marcus Garvey in the early twentieth century asserted, "Man is the individual who is able to shape his own character, master his own will, direct his own life and shape his own ends." The black soldier at the turn of the twentieth century was the ultimate Garveyite self-made man. At the end of the Filipino War, nearly one thousand black soldiers decided to remain in the Philippines instead of returning to America. They created a community and public enclave that survives even today. Black soldiers were very aware that the conflict in the Philippines was not popular. The men felt "discouraged" by "the sacrifice of life and health for a war so unpopular." Despite the unpopularity of the war, many soldiers saw the Philippines as an opportunity to change their status as men.[63]

The black soldier of the Spanish-American-Cuban-Filipino War fought because he needed to prove to America and the world that black Americans were just as manly as whites and deserved to be able to exercise their rights in every arena available to true American citizens. Blacks felt that their "fathers" had earned their citizenship by fighting and dying in the Civil War. These soldiers took pride in doing their duty, whether the war was popular or not among the African American community. They recognized that they represented the entirety of the race. They understood that as soldiers, they could not allow politics to affect their duty because they were representing not just their own interests but their country and their race.

They were able to gain economic opportunities in the Philippines that were inaccessible to them in the U.S. The soldiers who decided to stay once the conflict was over could be the men they felt they could not be in America. They were able to provide for and protect their families and achieve economic prosperity. T. Clay Smith of the Twenty-Fourth Infantry best explains the opportunities for black men in America's newly subdued colony: "Several of our young men are now in business in the Philippines and are doing nicely, indeed, along with such lines as express men, numerous clerks in the civil government, several school teachers, one lawyer, and one doctor. I think that the Philippines offer our people the best opportunities of the century."[64]

For the black men who stayed in the Philippines, the crucial incentive was the opportunity to become economically successful and to provide a stable environment for their Filipino families. That it was the soldiers who were the biggest supporters of the immigration of blacks to the Philippines and even Cuba is significant because it would be these same soldiers who would be leaders within the Black Nationalist migration movement.

No matter where he was, the black soldier never forgot the dire position blacks were placed in by racist white Americans. This is why African American soldiers continued to serve in unpopular wars. It is also one reason they wrote to the black newspapers describing Cuba and the Philippines as a black man's paradise. They did this because they believed "to free his race should be the dream of every colored man on earth, to see our future paths gleam, with a true progressive light of a new era." Black soldiers rarely fought for only selfish motives: they fought for every black man's manhood and citizenship and for all African Americans to have a better chance to achieve the American dream.[65]

At the end of the Filipino War, the black regulars returned to the San Francisco Presidio, and for a few years these war-weary soldiers served as de facto park rangers for Yosemite National Park. These men under the command of Charles Young, the first African American superintendent of Yosemite National Park, helped to protect and preserve the giant sequoias and wildlife. They also built trails and protected the parks before the National Park Service was established. These men, after the difficult fighting in the Philippines, welcomed such service in Yosemite because it was a reprieve from the daily battles they were fighting both internationally and domestically. Service in the parks allowed soldiers such as Charles Young to reflect on the duty they were performing, and he viewed his service as an honor. These men did not feel that being in the woods was a kind of punishment or that they were in exile; rather, they saw this as duty as usual. The work they were doing was not unlike the work they had performed when they were protecting the frontier.

African American soldiers and volunteers during the Spanish-American-Cuban-Filipino conflict demonstrated their manhood and their race consciousness through their military and community service. Men such as James Young, John Calloway, and Chaplain T. G. Steward grappled with fulfilling their duty to their race and country but also struggled with the complexities of serving in an imperialist and racist Army. The nearly one thousand black soldiers who chose to remain in the Philippines to make a new life for themselves did so because some found wives and others found economic opportunities to better themselves—and they did not have to face Jim Crow apartheid.

3.
FOR RACE AND COUNTRY, WE NEVER FORGET

There is a New Negro to be reckoned with in our political and social
life.   —Major J. E. Cutler

In 1919, Delilah Beasley compiled and published an exhaustive history
of African Americans pioneers in California. She was just one of many
authors extolling the "progress of the race." The book, *Negro Trail Blazers
of California*, includes poems and photographs, even addresses of the black
subjects. In the chapter titled "The Negro Soldier," Beasley shared an es-
say from a young boy named McKinley Anderson, who attended school in
rural South Carolina. Young McKinley was asked by his teacher to write
an article concerning the war. He chose to write about what it was like to
see young black men heading off to Europe to fight. He observed, "Some
how we've a feeling that those boys, if properly trained and given a square
deal, are going to make a record not only for themselves but for the race."[1]

Over the last few years, because of the centennial, World War I has re-
gained the attention of scholars as we witness challenges by nations and
non-state actors to the traditional doctrine of the causes and effects of the
Great War. One such effect was the way the white American desk generals
during World War I expended so much time and energy trying to destroy
the character and fighting abilities of black servicemen that they unknowingly and equally harmed themselves. Their resistance to African American
participation in the military only galvanized the black community to mount
more pressure on the government to allow and expand the role of black
soldiers and officers in World War I and beyond.

The fight and the continued presence of black men in the military demonstrated the determination of African American men's resistance to exclusion

from participation in full citizenship rights. The campaign to establish the officer training school for black officers and the campaign to reinstate Colonel Charles Young in a time famously labeled by historian and World War I veteran Rayford Logan as the nadir of African American civil rights highlight the black community's commitment to fully participate in the war as citizens and men.

The standard explanation and examination of the outbreak of the war deny any racial element to the conflict, but African Americans knew better. Epitomizing W. E. B. Du Bois's colonial thesis regarding American forces, the black community was living through some dark moments, yet fighting and uniting behind the black soldier. The campaign to get black commissioned officers to command black troops led to more black colleges and universities making military science courses mandatory. Despite the way the Wilson administration began overtly segregating federal jobs based on race, he conceded in appointing Emmett Scott as special assistant to the secretary of war. In addition, Walter Loving, Charles Williams, and George Haynes were appointed to federal positions to help appease the frustrated black community. Thus, for many African Americans, the Great War was about more than just a way to save democracy. Du Bois would later go on to describe World War I as a revolution. He stated, "This was not simply another war, it was a revolution which marked the beginning of the freeing of darker peoples from European control." African American leaders saw the war as an opportunity for black men to exercise their rights as citizens through the heroism and bravery of black servicemen. The hatred of Jim Crow America only strengthened racial pride and the resolve of African American men to participate in the hegemonic masculinity shaping the American military.[2]

These black soldiers returned home after the war more militant and determined to advocate for the human rights of African Americans. The "New Negro" of the 1920s had roots firmly entrenched in many of the returning Great War vets. This chapter illuminates the ways in which black servicemen used military service as a tool for the advancement of the entire race. Moreover, the white responses, whether official or private, to black military service, and by extension to black claims on citizenship, will be examined. Finally, we will consider the impact and the legacy of the black soldier of the early twentieth century. African American soldiers during World War II reflected on World War I and clearly defined at the beginning of the Second World War the Double V campaign, which is connected to the persistent campaign of the long civil rights movement.

TROUBLE ALONG THE BORDER

When historians discuss American involvement in World War I, there is very little examination of the impact of consistently tumultuous relations between Mexico and the United States along the border. The context of the famous Zimmermann telegram, which was used as one of the reasons the U.S. entered the war against Germany, highlights the necessity to examine the Mexican border crisis before U.S. involvement in World War I.

This crisis in the early part of the twentieth century was both volatile and complex. It should always be remembered that war is an extension of politics and is inherently volatile and complex. The primary goal of the military along the Mexican border in the nineteenth century was to push the French completely out of Mexico, eliminate cross-border Indian raids, and force the Mexican government to take responsibility for maintaining order on its side of the border.[3]

The black regulars such as the Twenty-Fourth Infantry played a major role in helping to maintain order and balance along the Rio Grande. During the second half of the nineteenth century, Mexican president/dictator Porfirio Diaz allowed over 85 percent of all mining operations in Mexico to be American-owned, which caused a great amount of tension and resentment toward Diaz and the United States by the impoverished Mexican population. According to combat studies historian Matt Matthews, "Mexican-Anglo relations were inconsistent and contradictory but pointed to the formation of a race situation where ethnic or national prejudice provided a basis for separation and control. In the late 19th century, these race sentiments, which drew heavily from the legacy of the Alamo and the Mexican War, were maintained and sharpened by market competitions and property disputes."[4]

The U.S. constantly maintained a strong presence and showing of force along the border of Mexico. In fact, in 1914 the U.S. Navy briefly occupied Veracruz, Mexico's principal port, in order to block German weapons and, the government hoped, force a powerful dictator out of office. President Woodrow Wilson believed in exporting democracy abroad. Therefore, it is not surprising that, based on the horrific racial climate of turn-of-the-century Jim Crow America and the ongoing hostilities along the Mexican border, a plan developed that called for an alliance of blacks, Indians, and Japanese Americans in a race war against white male Anglos. It was called the Plan of San Diego.[5]

A Texan deputy sheriff discovered the Plan of San Diego in 1915. The goal of the plan was to bring about a race war between whites and nonwhites.

Basilio Ramos Jr. was arrested with documents calling for a Mexican-American insurrection and race war along the border, which caused the Texas authorities even more concern. The plan supposedly originated in San Diego, Texas, and called for the killing of all male Anglos above the age of sixteen. This sent white Texans panicking and calling for increased border security from the federal and state governments. The targeting of African Americans with propaganda by the Mexican rebels increased suspicion among whites over the presence of black soldiers. Handbills were found all over calling for Mexicans on both sides of the border to rise up and join the guerrilla movement and to carry out the Plan of San Diego.[6]

The governor of Texas sent Texas Rangers to the border and the army increased its patrols, while the Mexican newspapers inflamed the situation by supporting the guerrillas in their headlines. The white Texas Rangers were brutal in their attacks upon innocent Mexicans. The rebels retaliated against the Rangers by destroying railroad bridges, stores, and property. The cycle of violence continued with the Rangers then systematically killing over a hundred Mexicans, and some soldiers claimed to have seen more than three hundred bullet-riddled Mexican men and boys whom the Rangers claimed to be bandits. The guerrilla movement had between twenty-five and one hundred followers initially, but after the cruelty committed by the white Rangers, the Mexican government, led by Venustiano Carranza, started supplying some guerrillas with weapons. Thousands of Mexican refugees fled back across the border after Anglo confiscators illegally seized their land. The army arrived in Brownsville and Laredo, Texas, to try to bring order and stability to the border crisis, but the troops' presence did not deter the guerrillas from crossing and attacking.

Wilson decided that one way to control the situation, without it turning into a full-on massacre, was to recognize the Carranza regime. When Carranza initially seized power, Wilson had refused to support or recognize his administration, but with the deteriorating situation at the border and the Mexican government's unwillingness to pursue the guerrillas, Wilson decided it would be best to recognize the Carranza government and lay the majority of the burden to capture the rebels on an official Mexican government. The raids ceased from the guerrillas supporting the Plan of San Diego, but the Mexican general Pancho Villa opposed Carranza, who had recently defeated him in battle in 1915. Villa, with his numbers reduced, created an alternative, nontraditional course of action to retaliate against the United States for supporting Carranza. One of Villa's men justified the raids across the border, confessing, "My master, Don Pancho Villa was continually telling us that since the gringos had given him the double cross he meant not only to get back at them but to try and waken our country to the danger that was very close to it."[7]

On January 9, 1916, Villa's guerrillas attacked a train carrying American miners and engineers near Chihuahua City, Mexico. It was reported that as the sixteen Americans were being executed, a *villista* officer shouted, "Tell Wilson to come and save you and tell Carranza to give you protection." Villa's attacks and the Plan of San Diego alarmed the white southwestern communities so much that they demanded Wilson take action. Villa's goal was to destabilize relations between the U.S. and Mexico. According to some scholars, the German government promised Villa $20 million if he could draw the United States into war with Mexico. On March 11, 1916, the newly appointed secretary of war, Newton Baker, designated Brigadier General John "Black Jack" Pershing to take command of an expedition to capture Pancho Villa and his soldiers (they were called bandits by the U.S. government).[8]

However, those orders did not provide enough information or guidance on how to proceed in chasing Villa. Namely, it did not state whether or not the U.S. Army could pursue Villa onto Mexican soil. President Wilson issued another order to General Frederick Funston on March 13, 1916: "The President desires that your attention be especially and earnestly called to his determination that the expedition into Mexico is limited to the purposes originally stated, namely the pursuit and dispensation of the band or bands that attacked Columbia, New Mexico." The U.S. Army then mobilized 12,000 troops along the southern border.[9]

The Tenth Cavalry had two companies directly involved with the reconnaissance missions into Mexico; the Eighth Illinois National Guard also participated in this "Punitive Expedition." The army's mission to capture Villa forced it to pursue him several hundred miles into Mexico. The campaign took almost a year, and the expedition disrupted Villa's operations and prevented any future attacks in the U.S. The buffalo soldiers gained national attention because of their participation in the mission and because of the media attention surrounding the Plan of San Diego. Several black political groups volunteered to mobilize their communities and join the campaign to demonstrate that they wanted no part in a race war with white Americans. The climate of mistrust and war fever had its grip on America, and the thought that African Americans would join Mexican rebels in a war against the United States stoked real fear of a violent revolution.

The climate in the U.S. in 1917 was hostile toward Mexico. The Punitive Expedition ended in January 1917 without the capture of Villa. January happened to be the same month British cryptographers deciphered the infamous telegraph from the German foreign minister, Arthur Zimmermann, to the German minister to Mexico, Heinrich von Eckhardt, attempting to find a way to make Mexico a German ally and to "make war together, make peace together," by offering "generous financial support and an understanding on our part that Mexico is to reconquer the lost territory in Texas, New Mexico, and Arizona." The British gave the decoded message to the U.S. in February, not long after Germany ended the Sussex pledge of limited submarine warfare. It did not take long for Mexican-American relations to deteriorate after the Zimmermann telegram. When the U.S. mobilized to enter World War I, some of the black regular units were ordered to remain along the Mexican border rather than be a part of the American Expeditionary Force (AEF). The Twenty-Fourth Infantry was one of the units that stayed behind—and found itself involved in the infamous 1917 Houston race uprising.[10]

THE HOUSTON UPRISING OF 1917

On May 15, 1916, Jesse Washington stood in front of a crowd of 15,000 people in Waco, Texas, and was lynched and castrated. His body was then tied to a car and dragged through the streets. Jesse Washington's death resonated with black soldiers stationed in Texas protecting the border. These men donated to the NAACP's anti-lynching campaign regularly. The murder of Jesse Washington was covered nationwide in the black press, and the fact that no one was punished stayed with the men of the Twenty-Fourth Infantry. The following summer of 1917 served as a period of racial violence and unrest. In 1917, Houston experienced a racial uprising involving nearly one hundred members of the Twenty-Fourth Infantry.[11]

The Houston police had repeatedly clashed with soldiers in the weeks leading up to the rebellion. Upon their original arrival in Houston, to provide security detail at Camp Logan, the soldiers of the Third Battalion of the Twenty-Fourth Infantry were immediately at odds with the police because they did not appreciate the disrespect that they endured in this city divided by Jim Crow. Black soldiers felt they deserved a certain amount of respect from the police and white citizens, which their uniform should have afforded them, but that respect was not forthcoming.

On the day of the rebellion, the police pursued a young man into the home of Mrs. Sarah Traeu. The officer proceeded to drag the African American woman out of her home and into the street half naked, calling for a paddy wagon. As the neighbors of the women tried to intervene, Private

Alonzo Edwards stepped forward to defuse the situation and pay the fine for the woman in custody.

Texas law enforcement officers all over the state were acting more like vigilantes, so when Private Edwards came to the black woman's defense, it only added fuel to the fire of a tense situation. Edwards was beaten and arrested. Corporal Charles Baltimore, an MP, went to check on Private Edwards, and he too was beaten and arrested. Word reached Camp Logan that Baltimore died, and despite the efforts of Sergeant Henry Vida to calm his fellow troopers earlier in the day, Vida eventually led the attack against the Houston police.[12]

Some of the men involved with the Houston uprising were former members of the Twenty-Fifth Infantry, and their anger still boiled over what had happened to their brothers-in-arms in Brownsville in August 1906. The incident involved the death of a white bartender and the wounding of one white police officer—and 167 black soldiers blamed. The racist white community accused the black troopers stationed nearby of shooting up the town, without any corroborating evidence to prove the soldiers were even in the town that night. The men of the Twenty-Fifth never broke their silence regarding whether or not they were involved, so Roosevelt ordered his secretary of war, William Howard Taft, to dishonorably discharge all three companies stationed in Brownsville. The Brownsville soldiers never had the opportunity to address the accusations made against them by an all-white commission. They would not receive justice until 1973, when the last surviving member of the Twenty-Fifth was awarded $25,000 in back pension and given an honorable discharge.[13]

The motives of the soldiers of the Twenty-Fourth who participated in the clash with the Houston police clearly stemmed from the frustrations these men felt over such oppression and violence being inflicted upon their race and from the fact that the country they had sworn to give their lives to protect did nothing to protect them. Over a hundred men of the Twenty-Fourth thus armed themselves and marched on that hot August day in 1917. At the end of the skirmish with the Houston police, four soldiers lay dead as well as fifteen whites, four of whom were police officers. (A fifth officer died later.)[14]

The men of the Twenty-Fourth would not face immediate discharge like the men of the Twenty-Fifth Infantry had in 1906, but after two trials and the largest court-martial in U.S. military history, nineteen men of the Twenty-Fourth were executed for their participation in the uprising and another fifty-four sent to jail. Private Thomas Hawkins sent a final message to his family about his situation: "When this letter reaches you I will be beyond the veil of sorrow. I am sentenced to be hanged for the trouble in Houston, Texas. Although I am not guilty of the crime I am accused of." One of the soldiers assigned to the hanging detail described the final moments of the thirteen men executed on December 11, 1917, as emotional and somber. The men silently marched to the gallows, and Private Frank Johnson, as the noose was placed around his neck, broke out in song and sang, "Lord I'm coming home."[15]

The African American community stood in solidarity with the black troopers on trial for mutiny. In fact, the family of one of the executed soldiers planned to use his funeral as a platform to protest Wilson and the war, but Major Walter H. Loving, in the role of a military intelligence officer, persuaded them to have a private ceremony instead.[16] Du Bois publicly agonized over the situation by stating, "It is difficult for one of Negro blood to write of Houston." He knew he had to walk a fine line between open support and condemnation. The soldiers rebelled against racial oppression and violated the law and military authority. Yet the black community did not shun these soldiers. In fact, the only case of a black editor being jailed and convicted for violating the notorious Espionage Act of World War I came as a result of editor John H. Murphy of the *Baltimore Afro-American* calling the soldiers executed for the rebellion "martyrs." The editor of the *San Antonio Inquirer*, G. W. Bouldin, took the support a step further and published a letter from a black woman from Austin, Texas, and one from C. L. Threadgill giving voice to the population of African Americans who appreciated the men coming to the defense of a black woman's honor. Threadgill wrote:

> Rest assured that every (Negro) woman in this land of ours . . . reveres you, she honors you. . . . We would rather see you shot by the highest tribunal of the United States Army because you dared protect a Negro Woman from the insult of a southern brute in the form of a policeman than to have you forced to go to Europe to fight for a liberty you can not enjoy. Negro women regret you mutinied, and we are sorry you spilled innocent blood, but we are not sorry that five southern policemen's bones now bleach the graves of Houston, Tex. It is far better that you be shot for having tried to protect a Negro woman, than to have you die a natural death in the trenches of Europe, fighting to make the world safe for a democracy that you can't enjoy.[17]

The Wilson administration acted swiftly in the executions of the first men because the country was at war, but this upset not only members of the black community but also some army officials. Brigadier General Samuel Ansell, the acting judge advocate general, was livid at the swiftness of these executions. Ansell stated, "The men were executed immediately upon the termination of the trial and before their records could be forwarded to Washington or examined by anybody, and without, so far as I can see, any one of them having had the time or opportunity to seek clemency." To prevent anything like what happened in the Houston case from happening again, Ansell issued General Orders No. 7, which prohibited the execution of a sentence in any case involving death before a review and a determination of the legality could be done by the judge advocate general. The NAACP and the black community did not sit silently as the other defendants were tried and another six men executed. No white civilians were charged, and the two white police officers indicted were released.[18]

Yet the Wilson administration, on the advice of Secretary of War Newton Baker, knew that it had to calm the African American community, and so Wilson commuted ten of the death sentences to life in prison, and the sentences of all who were convicted were commuted by 1927 after a vigorous and successful campaign led by the NAACP. The NAACP began the drive to have the sentences commuted in 1923 during its convention in Kansas City, Kansas, only twenty miles from Fort Leavenworth penitentiary. The five hundred delegates met and decided to make a pilgrimage to Leavenworth to visit the "Houston Martyrs." "These men are not murderers. They are not criminals. I know them," proclaimed the warden of the prison, W. I. Biddles. The NAACP, by transforming the optics of the Houston rebellion, successfully turned mutineers into martyrs and won clemency for the soldiers. The commuting of these sentences by Presidents Wilson, Harding, and Roosevelt indicates the consistent pressure by the African American community to free these men, and their eventual release stands as a testament to the black community's commitment to achieve justice for them. The narrative of the men of the Twenty-Fourth never changed: they had no choice but to stand up to and defend themselves against racial violence. Despite the efforts of Henry Ossian Flipper, who wrote a letter to *The Crisis* that completely placed the blame on the black soldiers and showed no sympathy with racially conscious soldiers, the African American media across the country expressed support and solidarity with the men of the Twenty-Fourth.[19]

The "Houston Trouble" also played a role in how black regulars were used in World War I. The fears white southerners had of combat-trained

African American servicemen returning to the U.S. was enough to spark the resurgence of the Ku Klux Klan's terrorist tactics. Nevertheless, despite the protests of white southern senators, the Wilson administration caved to the demands of the black community and allowed for two combat divisions and the creation of an officer training school for black officers.

Du Bois's editorial about the Houston uprising provides a perfect description of the sentiment of those soldiers:

> Always WE pay; always WE die; always, whether right or wrong, it is SO MANY NEGROES killed, so many NEGROES wounded. But here, at last, at Houston is a change.... We did not have to have Houston in order to know that black men will not always be mere victims. But we did have Houston in order to ask, Why? Why must this all be? At Waco, at Memphis, at East St. Louis, at Chester, at Houston, at Lexington, and all along that crimsoned list of death and slaughter and orgy and torture.[20]

The Houston uprising, therefore, should not be viewed as an isolated incident but rather through the lens of asserting manhood and rebelling against the racist oligarchy of the Jim Crow South. Chad Williams, in *Torchbearers of Democracy*, points out, "More than any other factor, southern white supremacists feared that by fighting in the military black soldiers would see themselves as true American citizens worthy of social equality with whites and inevitably encourage other African Americans to think and act likewise." These men understood that they were seen as race leaders. Williams goes on to state, "In many instances, the black press constructed black soldiers as saviors and would-be martyrs for the benefit of the race."[21]

THE RACE ON TRIAL, AGAIN

Roscoe Conklin Simmons, a black orator, at the direction of Major Walter Loving, gave a speech in Hampton, Virginia, in 1917 to prevent a riot of angry African Americans. He said,

> The American Negro knows but one government, speaks but one language, and claims but one flag. The flag that set him free.... The Negro, with no voice in his government, has but one request. He asks for the guns of war, for the uniform of his country and for the command from officers who fear neither life nor death.

His impassioned plea worked, and the angry mob dispersed. But why did his appeal for blacks to serve in the military work to disband an angry mob? Why would Major Loving, the chief black military intelligence investigator, recommend that Simmons tour the country giving this same speech to calm the rising tensions and anger of African Americans? The answer to both these questions is the belief in the black soldier.[22]

The African American community, despite all the racial violence, still viewed black military service as a way to directly challenge racial prejudice. In his unpublished World War I manuscript "The Black Man in the Wounded World," W. E. B. Du Bois argued that these men bore the responsibility of the race by performing admirably and valiantly to further the cause of civil rights at home. These soldiers were both individuals and symbols that understood that the eyes of the world were watching. Colonel Charles Ballou, the commander of the Fort Des Moines Colored Officers' Training Camp, stated as much at the opening ceremonies of the camp in 1917: "I would impress upon each and every one of you the serious reflection on your race that will necessarily follow your failure in this crucial test and the far-reaching results that will flow from your success. . . . Your race will be on trial with you as its representatives during the existence of this camp."[23]

The origin of the campaign for the creation of this type of training school can be traced back to the Civil War and was expanded further in the "no officers, no fight" campaign during the Spanish-American War. The crusade to establish an officer training school was a consistent movement within the black community and was seen as directly intertwined with the campaign for the full recognition of black male citizenship. The three-month training camp started with 1,250 candidates. At least 250 of those candidates were noncommissioned officers from the black regulars.[24]

The standing army in 1917 consisted of 126,000 men, of whom 10,000 were African American. The U.S. was ill prepared for the war in Europe and lacked the proper number of trained officers needed to fight in the type of trench warfare seen on the western front. So the establishment of a camp to train blacks as officers positively demonstrates the results of successful campaigns by the black press, Howard University undergraduates, and the NAACP in the push to continue full citizenship rights of black men.

Joel E. Spingarn, the chairman of the NAACP, helped initiate the movement to create an officer training school in 1916. One of the major obstacles to the universal training of African American soldiers as officers came from racist southern politicians such as Senator James K. Vardaman, a Democrat from Mississippi. During this era, the four-week officer training summer camp became increasingly popular among white leaders and politicians, and Spingarn wanted a training camp for African American men. However, in 1916, the debate on universal military training got heated in Congress; Vardaman openly opposed the idea solely on race. He stated, "Universal military service means that millions of Negroes who will come under this measure will be armed. I know of no greater menace to the South than this." Yet despite Vardaman's racist opposition, Spingarn successfully organized and issued the call for applicants in black newspapers nationwide.[25]

The creation of an officer training school for black officers demonstrates the progress and success of the continual efforts from various groups, leaders, and the soldiers themselves. In the March 1917 *Branch Bulletin* of the NAACP, Du Bois addressed the critics of Spingarn's push for a segregated training camp. Du Bois plainly stated the perpetual dilemma African Americans faced every day during this tumultuous era: "We Negroes ever face it. We cannot escape it. We must continually choose between insult and injury; no schools or separate schools; no travel or Jim Crow travel. We must choose between the insult of a separate camp and the irreparable injury of strengthening the present custom of putting no black men in positions of authority."[26]

The army was filled with bigoted generals who did not want the camp to be a success, so when Spingarn issued his call to "Educated Colored Men," he did so knowing that the army did not believe he could find even two hundred qualified candidates. Aware of the successful military science programs at the various black colleges and universities, though, Spingarn directed his appeal to college-educated black men. Yet he still faced criticism in the black press because he advocated for a separate camp.[27]

The critics of Spingarn's plea felt he ignored the fact that officers should be chosen from the four black regular units, which Spingarn knew would be difficult. He defended his position in an open letter published in *The Crisis*:

> Those who think that a large number of officers could be obtained from the colored regulars simply show their ignorance of the Army and the enormous amount of paperwork an officer has to do. A good officer is a man who has military training, ability to lead, and a good education; few men who have had at least a high school education can hope to pass the written examination to become an officer.

Both Du Bois and Spingarn saw the officer training school as a way to fight discrimination in the army. Charles Young joined the debate in support of

Du Bois and Spingarn and wrote a letter to Harry Smith, the editor of the *Cleveland Gazette*: "Yes we may want the whole loaf of bread, better to at least eat half. Then we Negroes must have a part a glorious one in the destiny of this country, our country." By June 18, 1917, more than 1,200 men had been admitted to the officer training school and attended the Fort Des Moines training camp until October 15, 1917; 644 men earned commissions.[28]

The NAACP's involvement in the creation of an officer training school specifically for blacks was a major part of the organization's early platform. The initiative behind this campaign involved more than just Spingarn and Du Bois. The Washington, D.C., branch president, Archibald Grimké, and branch secretary, Ray Nash, applied a tremendous amount of pressure on the Wilson administration, specifically Secretary of War Newton Baker. Secretary Baker and President Wilson received letters and visits from John Milton Waldron, the chairman of the Council of 100 Colored Citizens on the War, pushing for the creation of an officer training school for blacks. Baker wrote Wilson expressing his support for the camp after several visits from Waldron: "I was called upon many times by Mr. Waldron and representatives of his committee of one hundred. After considering their request I came to the conclusion that a training camp for colored people ought to be established, and took up with representative colored men the location of such a camp." There were also several organizations run by undergraduates from Howard University, including future NAACP lawyer and civil rights leader Charles Hamilton Houston, which put the necessary pressure on the Wilson administration to create this camp. The black press demonstrated its support for the creation of the camp by including it in the "Bill of Particulars" that also stressed the reinstatement of Colonel Charles Young (see chapter 6). The campaign to allow black men not only to serve but also to lead other black men demonstrates the symbiotic connection between the fight for military progress and the fight for civil rights.[29]

The choice of Des Moines, Iowa, by the army for the training camp was crucial to the creation and survival of the camp. The War Department figured the racial tension in Des Moines, with a population of 6,000 blacks and 110,000 whites, would be minimal since African Americans would not seem such a novelty to this community. On May 23, 1917, the War Department announced the official location for the training camp, which served as the nation's solitary training facility for African American officers during World War I, and it was assumed by many in the African American community that Lieutenant Colonel Charles Young, the highest ranking black officer in the army, would be chosen to train these future leaders.[30]

The officers commissioned from the Des Moines training camp were assigned to the Ninety-Second Division, one of two black combat divisions. The camp lasted longer than initially planned because of the resistance from the army chief of engineers and the quartermaster general. Nevertheless, after several delays, 106 captains, 329 first lieutenants, and 209 second lieutenants were commissioned and dispersed over seven training camps to take charge of their men.[31]

The African American officers of the Ninety-Third (Provisional) Division had a different training experience. All of the officers were from the all-black National Guard units, which came from the states of New York, Illinois, Connecticut, Maryland, Massachusetts, Ohio, Tennessee, and the District of Columbia. The Eighth Illinois was completely officered and commanded by African Americans and had been since the Spanish-American War, when the unit had been involved in the pursuit of Pancho Villa. This gave the men of the Eighth a unique perspective because they had the distinction of being the only unit completely staffed by blacks who had combat experience. Colonel Frank Denison served as the commander of the Eighth until it was redesignated the 370th, and at Camp Grant, the soldiers of the 370th proudly defended themselves against racist white soldiers. The *Chicago Broad Ax* reported on these men who served as symbols of racial and manly pride. Harry Haywood of the 370th observed, "I didn't regard it [his unit] as a part of the U.S. Army unit, but as some sound club of fellow race men."[32]

OUR COUNTRY, OUR WAR

"First, This is Our Country: We have worked for it, we have suffered for it, we have fought for it; nothing, humanly speaking, can prevent us from eventually reaching here the full stature of our manhood." This editorial from *The Crisis* in 1918 coincided with the rising tide of frustration within the African American community as the country readied for war. America's entry was swift, but mobilization was slow. The United States did not have enough manpower or equipment to be a fully functioning force in the war. The Wilson administration wanted an army of citizen soldiers, and to accomplish that the military would need volunteers and the draft. The U.S. Army, upon entry into the war in 1917, was not prepared, and the Wilson administration needed the morale of the nation, including the African American community, to be supportive of the American war effort.[33]

The mobilization of the American population for participation in the global conflict between the European powers was a revolutionary event in American and African American history. The U.S. was accustomed to fighting wars on a much smaller scale, which had not prepared the armed forces for maneuvering with the larger units being used across the Atlantic.[34]

According to historian John Morrow Jr., World War I started in Africa and the Balkans because of the competition over colonies and the steady decline of the Ottoman Empire. African Americans were very aware of the tensions and disputes over colonization in Africa. The presence and use of soldiers from the African colonies in the British and French armies not only played a crucial role in helping the Allies defeat the Central Powers but also exposed African American soldiers to other troops from the African diaspora. This helped expand their understanding of the necessity for a global campaign for human rights. Benton Johnson wrote that blacks did voice their concerns over America's foreign policy. The formation of the National Race Congress and the International League of Darker Peoples highlights the importance of a global movement within the diaspora to create a coherent set of demands. The International League of Darker Peoples was greatly influenced by soldiers' accounts of black and white relations on the battlefield. The soldiers who fought and bled in the trenches with white Americans and white Europeans forever changed their perceptions of race relations such that they no longer accepted unequal treatment in America.[35]

This war created a new platform for African Americans to demand basic civil and human rights. African American servicemen played an influential role in making these demands heard in the global arena. Such action caused great concern for the U.S. military and created another excuse for paranoid, racist desk generals such as Leonard Wood to question the loyalty of African American soldiers.[36]

The Wilson administration's record of accomplishment on race was poor. Despite the victory by the African American community in getting the black officer training school, the appointment of the white segregationist Lieutenant Colonel Charles Ballou of the Twenty-Fourth Infantry over the more senior Lieutenant Colonel Charles Young to preside over and motivate these dedicated race warriors was a disappointment to many in the black community. Ballou would go onto be promoted to brigadier general in the American Expeditionary Force and lead a campaign of disinformation against the black officers of the Ninety-Second Division. The fact that in May 1917 the Selective Service Act passed and temporarily halted the enlistment of black volunteers because the quota for African Americans was reached highlights Wilson's lack of interest in addressing the dysfunctional race relations in the country. The outcry from the black and white community over the limiting of African American volunteers forced the administration to reconsider its original allotment for black troops. The claim by Woodrow Wilson that the world needed to be made safe for democracy inflamed many in the African American community, and it was infused into the anti-lynching narrative. Protest signs held during a silent march against lynching said, "Mr. President why not make America safe for democracy?" Yet, despite all of the voices of dissent against America's hypocritical stance in World War I, there was optimism among the young men eagerly signing up to serve. Black communities decided to "close ranks" and support their race patriots.

On his way to Des Moines, William Dyer described his feeling of hope and pride:

> It was a beautiful Sunday afternoon September 24, 1917, that I left my home for what fate I knew not but to proceed to my country's calling. When I arrived at the railway station some three hundred or so of my friends and neighbors had gathered to say to me farewell and bid me Godspeed on my perilous journey. Many photographs were taken of the first colored officer of our town and first one of my race from Lincoln to be officered.

Dyer goes on to describe how he did not realize the gravity of his mission or the sadness in his parents' eyes. African American soldiers supported the war effort in various ways, seeing conflict as an opportunity for racial uplift by demonstrating their manhood on a global stage in order to support the black community at home.[37]

However, the majority of African American soldiers who served did so in labor battalions. This caused great concern within the community because of the 360,000 black troops who served, only 40,000 saw combat. The army's decision to send the majority of black troops to labor battalions is yet another example of how racist policies of the army reflected the racist policies of Jim Crow America, which damaged the Wilson administration's effort to successfully market the war to African Americans.

The Wartime Commission of the Federal Council of Churches initiated the Committee on the Welfare of Negro Troops in September 1917. The committee existed because of the concern over the morale of African American soldiers. Charles H. Williams of the Hampton Institute maintained a dual role during the role as both military intelligence informant and advocate for black soldiers. He toured the country and submitted his reports to the Wartime Commission and the War Department on the morale and conditions of black troops at the training camps. The Fort Des Moines officer school served as a triumph simply because it existed, yet the man chosen to be in charge ensured that it would not fulfill the aspirations held by the men who attended the school. Lieutenant Colonel Charles Ballou, after he was promoted, continued to perpetuate the invisible wall in the U.S. Army that served to bring the morale of African American officers down. Ballou, the former commander of the Twenty-Fourth Infantry, was firmly committed to segregation and believed that black soldiers lacked the mental and moral capacity to lead other black soldiers.[38]

THE "WAR ON THE CRACKERS"

The experiences of each of the black units varied little when they arrived in the South. Each unit encountered Jim Crow racism and incidents where black servicemen openly clashed with white civilians and soldiers. John Castles Jr., a white lieutenant with the Fifteenth New York, recounted how the men had to embark for France quickly after arriving in the South because both the white officers and black soldiers ran into racial problems. Bruce Wright of the Sixth Massachusetts National Guard recalled his unit's arrival at Camp Greene in Charlotte, North Carolina, and his first encounter with southern whites:

> We're the first colored soldiers south of the Mason and Dixon line in full equipment since 1865. The colored people used us just fine and everything went well for an hour or so. One of the crackers insulted one of our boys and the war began right there for us. We got plenty of practice for the "Boche," by fighting these dirty crackers.

Wright goes on to discuss how the mayor of Charlotte asked Captain Pryor to keep Wright and his fellow troops in camp. The captain informed the men and the mayor that he would not keep the men in camp as if they were prisoners. Wright and his fellow troops returned to Charlotte and caused "plenty of disturbances in the tour of Charlotte and several crackers were bumped off." A few days later, Wright and his unit were relocated to Camp Stuart at Newport News, Virginia. But while they were at Camp Greene, number one on Wright's list of interesting events that occurred was the "war on the crackers."[39]

The "war on the crackers" highlights a major shift for the black volunteer units from both the type of publicity and attention the "Mutinous Sixth" Virginia received and the rarity of such bold responses against racist actions during the Spanish-American-Cuban-Filipino conflict. This shift indicates that black soldiers felt much more power and authority in wearing the uniform of the U.S. Army. The fact these men willingly and actively defended themselves and their country only added fuel to the fire for the fight for civil rights, which would be led by the very same assertive and militant servicemen in the aftermath of the war.

ENTERING THE GLOBAL ARENA

The American Expeditionary Forces (AEF) entered World War I without being properly mobilized and equipped. The American military did not have enough men in the regular army to both send across the Atlantic and maintain protection along the borders and in the colonies. The American people during this time did not trust having a large standing army, which also contributed to the lack of men and proper equipment.

The voyage across the Atlantic proved to be as tumultuous and trying as the training and preparation for the war. The Ninety-Second Division was composed entirely of black draftees who could not all properly go through boot camp together because of the fear of armed organized black men in the South. The separate training did not allow the various units to form the necessary bonds needed to create a cohesive unit heading into combat. The companies did not set sail together, which further complicated the infrastructure of the Ninety-Second Division. The pioneer and labor battalions, to which most black troops were assigned, did not provide any real training for the men, so when they encountered danger or were sent to replenish the ranks of the combat divisions, they were far worse off than their white brothers-in-arms. The dangerous trek across the Atlantic would prove the most adventurous part of the war for many of the men in the labor battalions.[40]

Soldiers writing to Du Bois for his World War I project stated that the morale of the black troops disappeared once they boarded the ships. Lieutenant William Dyer and Private Bruce Wright each observed the difficulties the men aboard their ship experienced once they were actually at sea, both physically and psychologically. Wright recalled the night he set sail on March 31 as calm: "The water was smooth and we all took great delight in hanging over the sides of the ship. A lot of the boys began to get seasick. Then the fun began. Everywhere you looked you could see some with a shovel and a broom cleaning up the deck in spots where those unfortunate soldiers had emptied their stomachs."[41]

The bulk of the travel experience for black servicemen proved demeaning and discouraging. Lieutenant Rayford Logan recalled how the white officers would make the black enlistees put on shows and perform for them; he refused to attend the shows. Logan and the First Separate Battalion of the District of Columbia were activated as a National Guard unit in 1916. The unit's treatment and exposure to blatant racism—dated to the regiment's activation—differed from the Fifteenth New York, Eighth Illinois, and Fifth Massachusetts. Logan's regiment experienced prolonged delays in pay and infrastructure issues, which contributed to the frustration and disappointment Logan developed with the U.S. Army.

The Ninety-Second and Ninety-Third combat divisions had the support of Emmett J. Scott, the special assistant to the secretary of war, in pushing for more black commissioned officers trained, but Baker fought against having additional black officers commissioned for these units because he believed the black units performed better under white officers and having another class of black officers was not necessary, in his eyes. Yet, according to John Castles, white officers with the 369th/Fifteenth were ill prepared for fighting in the trenches: "I prefer to go with the French, than the American troops because they are the better-trained army in understanding trench warfare."[42]

General John J. Pershing, the man selected to lead the AEF, reorganized and realigned the U.S. forces because the greatest asset the U.S. could contribute to the Allies was manpower. Pershing wanted U.S. forces "to overpower enemy lines and penetrate their rear position." General Pershing and Woodrow Wilson wanted to demonstrate to the Allies that the AEF would be the savior and most powerful force capable of stopping the Imperial German Army. The Wilson administration, learning from its allies, wanted a citizen army, and so the National Guard units were converted and redesignated. The chief of the Militia Bureau implemented strict guidelines for black servicemen and would not allow all of them to serve in integrated units, as proposed by the Arkansas community and the District of Columbia. Major General A. L. Mills supported the inclusion of black Guard units, but when the acting chief of the Militia Bureau took command in August 1917, he blocked the expansion of black National Guardsmen from serving in coastal battalions or beyond infantry and cavalry.[43]

The Ninety-Third Division consisted of "greenies" who, according to John Castles, "were poorly trained and lacked any real military discipline." The commander of the 369th was a difficult man to serve under, according to Castles, and his observations about the lack of training support similar claims made by various black officers.[44]

Lieutenant George Washington Lee of Memphis felt that there were white officers who wanted the Ninety-Second Division to fail. Major Walter Loving, in a report to the chief of Military Intelligence, shared an editorial from *The Crisis* by Du Bois describing the ineptitude of the Ninety-Second Division's chief of staff, Colonel Allen Greer, who was seen as unqualified to command black soldiers: "Instead of doing everything in his power to uphold the honor and dignity of his division, he deliberately wanted to undermine the morale of his own officers and men." Colonel Greer, in a publicized letter to Senator Kenneth McKellar, a Democrat from Tennessee, "brand[ed] the men of his unit cowards and asked the senator to block any plan that might be offered for additional Negro officers or enlisted men."[45]

The men of the Ninety-Second Division also served under the command of Brigadier General Charles Ballou, the former commander of the Fort Des Moines Colored Officers' Training Camp. Several officers and soldiers of the Ninety-Second, as veterans at a League for Democracy meeting, declared that Ballou "opposed having colored officers from the very beginning." In an article on World War I, Du Bois would cite General Sherburne, the commander of the 167th Field Artillery:

> General Sherburne informed Major Patterson[,] the Division Judge Advocate and a black officer, that there has been a concerted action on the part of white officers throughout France to discredit the work of Colored troops in France, and that everything was being done to advertise those things that would reflect discredit upon the men and officers, to withhold anything that would bring them praise or commendation.

Du Bois elaborated further on these types of actions when he reported a conversation he overheard while traveling on a train to Paris:[46]

> I occupied a compartment with three other American (white) officers and two French officers. As the conversation progressed it developed into a discussion of the colored soldiers of France and America. The French officers stated that they had nothing but the highest of praise for their black soldiers, the Senegalese, and that they loved them for the work that they had done at Verdun, and on all of the other fronts. There was an American officer in the discussion who hailed from Virginia, and he said to the Frenchmen that they had no use for "niggers" in the United States, and were only trying them out in the war; that so far they had proved themselves a bunch of cowards, and that every one of the —— would rape a white woman if he was not held down by the whites.[47]

Despite the efforts of various white officers to demean and discredit the actions of black soldiers, these men still found ways to assert their manhood and participate in the fighting on the front line. When Bruce Wright arrived in Saint-Nazaire, France, on April 14, 1918, he and his company spent the first two weeks working on the railroad tracks. Wright stated, "We couldn't see where in we should handle a pick and shovel as we as infantry came to France to fight. So when they found that we just refused to be made to do stevedores work, [they] gave us orders to be shied to the front." Wright believed that his regiment's refusal to work forced the division commanders to send the Sixth to the front to fight. This was not the only instance where black soldiers collectively asserted resistance to white military authority in France. A black serviceman demonstrated his manhood and inspired race consciousness by refusing to come down from atop a boxcar after being ordered to do so by his white commanding officer. His action inspired his fellow black soldiers to join him on the boxcar, thus collectively rejecting white military authority. According to historian Jennifer Keene, "At times for black soldiers obeying white officers became synonymous with accepting the demeaning positions that military authority, in general, had imposed upon them: therefore challenging white officers became a viable way for them to reassert racial dignity."[48]

The 369th of the Ninety-Third Division was attached to the French Sixteenth Division because the French desperately needed men, and Pershing was glad to send the black troops to the French. The Ninety-Third did not fit into his combat plans for the AEF. Two regiments of the Ninety-Third were sent to the French 157th; therefore they received some of the best training available to them because of the French. Many officers of the 369th were glad to be training with the French. Bruce Wright observed in his diary that the training lasted six weeks and the "polius or frog soldiers . . . were tickled to death at how fast we were and how quick we learnt the different things such as hand grenade throwing, shooting with French guns, French style of bayonet fighting." The four regiments participated in the Meuse-Argonne campaign, suffering a total of 2,502 casualties and 1,826 men killed in action. The Meuse-Argonne battle was the second costliest battle in American history; the death toll reached 26,000 for the Americans. Only the battle at Okinawa proved deadlier.[49]

The success of the Ninety-Third Division was overshadowed by the supposed failures of the Ninety-Second. Yet both units were successful compared to the other American divisions. For example, the Ninety-Second, in spite of the division's racist leaders Brigadier General Ballou and Colonel

Greer, succeeded in completing several missions assigned to them by the French. According to the Ninety-Second's divisional history, the division assumed command of the Marbache sector on October 9, 1918, relieving the Sixty-Ninth French Division, and served as the right flank division of the American First Army. Lieutenant George Washington Lee earned a citation for bravery and a promotion while on patrol in this sector.

Military historians have typically portrayed the men of the Ninety-Second Division somewhat negatively because of the claims by the white officers that the men fled from the front line. For example, historian Robert H. Ferrell in *Unjustly Dishonored: An African American Division in World War I* alternates between blaming the incompetent white officers and the poor training by the French for the failures of the Ninety-Second during various battles and even asserts that "Colonel Allen Greer . . . believed the 368th was the best infantry regiment in the division"—the same Colonel Greer who called all the men of his division cowards and did not believe black men belonged in the military. Greer joined with Ballou in his false claims that black soldiers and officers were unable to perform in high-pressure combat situations. Yet, Ferrell in his study does not delve into the campaign launched by the veterans of the Ninety-Second Division to have Greer court-martialed and removed.[50]

The 368th Infantry of the Ninety-Second Division was attached to the Thirty-Eighth French Corps, and the offensive in the Argonne Forest tarnished the reputation of African American servicemen for decades. In communication with Senator McKellar, Colonel Greer claimed, "We went to the Argonne and in the offensive there on September 26th, the one regiment on the line attached to the 38th French Corp failed. They failed there and in all their missions, laid down and sneaked to the rear, until they were withdrawn." Yet the French commander of the Thirty-Eighth offered nothing but praise for the 368th, and Colonel Greer himself in General Order No. 38 commended the meritorious conduct of Corporal Charles E. Boykin. Boykin volunteered to scout the enemy position in the woods of Argonne Forest because the Germans in that sector had machine guns, and the 368th needed to bypass those guns. Boykin, a telegraph line operator, was killed by the very enemy machine guns he was scouting while trying to move to the enemy's flank. Sergeant Major Wellington Willard of the 368th sent evidence to Du Bois that contradicted the damning accusations made by Colonel Greer to Senator McKellar. Willard's account of the Meuse-Argonne battle, along with those of several other officers such as Captain T. M. Dent and Lieutenant George Washington Lee, contradicts the public claims made by Greer. Lieutenant Lee was cited for bravery and promoted for his scouting of enemy positions while serving with the 368th.[51]

The campaign by black servicemen during and after the war to assert their citizenship and preserve their manhood laid the foundation for the Double V campaign (victory abroad, victory at home) of World War II. Black servicemen experienced what military historians call the "fog and friction of war." Their war experience demonstrates true fortitude to preserve racial pride and manly honor, in spite of the politics of racist white commanders and ineffectual training.[52]

"WE MAKE NO ORDINARY SACRIFICE"

The bulk of black servicemen in World War I were in labor/SOS (Services of Supply) and pioneer units. The duties performed by these soldiers were the backbone of the war effort and important to the Allied forces; despite their not being on the front line, their duties were no less dangerous. Lieutenant Blair T. Hunt of Memphis served as a chaplain with several SOS units and in a hospital for those soldiers wounded bringing supplies to the front. He also served men who eventually died from disease because of the poor conditions in the black camps. In surveys conducted by the Virginia War Commission to commemorate the deeds of the soldiers and sailors from Virginia who participated in the Great War, many of the black soldiers from the SOS units reflected on their service in varying ways. Private Purvis Chesson of Norfolk, Virginia, described the physical effects of camp as beneficial but the mental effects discouraging. Sergeant Romulus Archer, also of Norfolk, indicated that "mentally military service taught him how to read men more carefully and the physical routine helped him in regulating his sleep." Private Samuel Ballard stated on his survey that camp life was difficult for him, and he still suffered physically from the ailments he acquired from camp. But Ballard also asserted that, despite the ailments, military service had made him a man. Lieutenant William Dyer of the 317th Engineers had at least twelve of his men die of disease at various camps. His unit did not do any frontline fighting but rather worked between the infantry and artillery. Sergeant Archer, also of the 317th Engineers, reflected on his service as coming naturally to him because "he was somewhat militarily inclined."[53]

The pioneer, engineer, and labor units had to slog through rat-infested trenches to build boardwalks over the mountains of mud so the frontline troops could be properly supplied. Charles Williams, a representative for the Committee on the Welfare of Negro Troops, completed surveys of all the camps where black soldiers were stationed and noted how some of the men did not have proper shoes, uniforms, or places to sleep: "They plunged through the deep mud of the camp and city, without boots. On the dock, they handled the cool steel and iron without gloves." The placing of black servicemen within labor battalions caused grave concern among African Americans and only increased tension in an already agitated black community. Joel Spingarn, now with the Military Intelligence Division, asked his friend W. E. B. Du Bois to help rally support among blacks for the war. Spingarn even recommended Du Bois be commissioned to convince him to support the war effort. However, Major Walter Loving disagreed with this recommendation and informed the chief of Military Intelligence that it would not be wise to allow a man such as Du Bois to serve as an officer. The secretary of war did call a summit in Washington, D.C., of all the nation's top black editors and requested that they print less inflammatory headlines and articles. The goal of the War Department was to boost the morale of the black troops in the labor and pioneer regiments and to change the narrative on the home front among the African American community.[54]

Du Bois agreed to support his friend and ally Spingarn and wrote the famous pro-war editorial "Close Ranks." He proclaimed to the black community, "Let us not hesitate. Let us, while this war lasts, forget our special grievances and close our ranks shoulder to shoulder with our own white fellow citizens and the allied nations that are fighting for democracy. We make no ordinary sacrifice, but we make it gladly and willingly with our eyes lifted to the hills." This call to "close ranks" would go on to haunt Du Bois for the remainder of his life. His unpublished and in some ways unfinished World War I manuscript "The Black Man in the Wounded World," for which he spent over a decade collecting data and primary sources, stands as a testament to the psychological struggle he endured trying to reconcile his support of the war. Every publisher he sent the manuscript to rejected it, which only added to his conflicted conscience. He attempted a joint publication with Carter G. Woodson, who was also working on a history of African Americans during World War I, but Woodson wanted to work alone in the writing and researching and needed Du Bois only for financial support. A. Philip Randolph and Chandler Owen, then editors of the socialist *Messenger*, and Robert S. Abbot, the editor of the *Chicago Defender*, all anti-war activists, criticized Du Bois and other conservative leaders who supported the war, such as R. R. Moton, Emmett J. Scott, and Kelly Miller.[55]

Du Bois attempted in his manuscript to redeem himself by going into detail about how black soldiers were viewed, used, and abused by the racist white officers and soldiers. He sought out letters and accounts from soldiers stationed at home and abroad because he feared that Emmett J. Scott would quash their grievances. Du Bois, in trying to collect information on the 370th, wrote Dr. Charles Bentley about these fears: "I am afraid Scott may get it, and if he does, the complaints will be suppressed." C. P. Duncan also wrote to Du Bois expressing his concern and frustration with Scott over his lack of transparency regarding how black soldiers were being treated: "Mr. Scott was evidently placed in his position as a medium of approach to the government authorities with complaints coming from the black man. And no doubt, these conditions only affect a certain percentage of those who could be given proper attention." Du Bois's investigation into the true story and experience of African American soldiers during the Great War allowed him to compile boxes of information from soldiers wanting to share their side of the war. "These men were known chiefly as stevedores and labor battalions. Somehow a widely circulated report gained ordinance that they had been gathered indiscriminately, and had been landed on foreign soil, a mere group of servants for the white soldiers," he wrote, interpreting the treatment of the soldiers in the labor and pioneer regiments. The belief that many white officers and soldiers wanted to humiliate and exploit black servicemen was virtually universal among the black community and black soldiers.

Yet these men did not allow white discrimination to affect the pride they took in doing their duty. Du Bois described seeing a colored MP standing calmly and assertively in the middle of a busy intersection directing traffic at the port of Saint-Nazaire. The pride and calmness of his nature impressed Du Bois and his party as bicycles, autobuses, and French civilians zipped past him. In many cases, the soldiers worked without shoes or the proper equipment to load and unload the necessary materials to be used on the front. The work of the stevedores and labor battalions was in many ways the hardest of the war. They toiled nonstop moving coal, laying track, building roads, digging trenches, burying bodies, and transporting goods. But despite the necessity of the work of the labor battalions, the use of only two black combat battalions frustrated the black home front and many of the black servicemen. The glory lay in the sacrifice of life and the killing of the enemy; this was the ultimate exaltation of racial pride and manhood. Yet, the damage from the Houston uprising was too much for the War Department to overcome; it could not ease the panic among white southerners at the possibility of large numbers of combat-ready and trained black men.[56]

A TALE OF TWO RACE MEN

Lieutenant George Washington Lee, while stationed in France, spent a fanciful night with a young Frenchwoman satisfying her curiosity about the nuances of American segregation and Jim Crow laws. The night he met the young lady, Lee was reluctant to even acknowledge her presence when she stood by him in the café because a bulletin issued by the commander of the Ninety-Second ordered black soldiers to have no contact with the white French civilians. The young lady ended up following Lee as he left the café when several white officers entered. She grabbed Lee's arm and asked him back to her apartment. When Lee reluctantly accepted and entered her place, to his surprise and disappointment she only wanted to discuss segregation. She observed, according to Lee, that "the darks went one way and the whites went the other. On asking a white U.S. officer he explained that blacks were peons who lived in holes in the ground, had disease and to be segregated to protect whites. But the following day she observed a Negro soldier speaking and conversing in French." Lee proceeded to explain slavery, the Civil War, and the failure of Reconstruction to the curious young lady.[57]

Lieutenant Rayford Logan, unlike Lee, was not afraid of being in public with a young white Frenchwoman. Logan, who was already feeling angry and frustrated with his military experience, disregarded the bulletin ordering black soldiers to stay away from white civilians and was being tutored in French by a young woman at a café. Several white officers entered the café and tried to run her off and have Logan removed from the café, but the young lady informed the officers she was friends with the mayor and would tell him of their behavior. The white officers backed off from harassing Logan and left the café.[58]

In both of these situations, these black officers in a country fighting to preserve democracy served as symbols of Jim Crow racism. Lee's and Logan's responses to their military service abroad also foretold the various types of activism that were inspired by their service in the war. Lee returned to Memphis, Tennessee, and went into politics. Logan remained in Paris and traveled around Europe for several years. At the behest of W. E. B. Du Bois, he became actively involved in the Pan-African Congress.[59]

George Lee returned to Memphis with the hopes of gaining the patronage of the powerful black Republican Robert Church Jr. Church, one of the wealthiest black men in America and founder of the black Republican organization the Lincoln League, which helped to preserve black voting rights in Memphis, had recently helped establish a chapter of the NAACP in Memphis. The political power that Church was able to enact in Memphis helped to make the city an epicenter of racial pride and progress. However, because Church was a Republican, he had no federal clout with a Democratic administration to secure Lee the permanent position with the military that he wanted. Yet he did have significant local power to make use of Lee as a war hero and an ideas man to help stem the rising tide of racial agitation in Memphis. Church advised the young lieutenant "to forget about serving in the peacetime army and get into the firing line of race progress." Robert Church Jr. and George W. Lee were both race men who believed in the uplift philosophy of racial progress. Lee believed that black activism needed to comprise both political and economic power. Lee's message to the black man was, "Give him something to be proud of, to see his contribution to American folk art and dance. Have the idea that the Negro must own some part of the good American Earth and establish a Negro economy." Lee believed that by building racial pride through both capitalism and political activism, the black community would make real progress.[60]

Upon his discharge from the military, Lieutenant Rayford Logan took a different approach to racial uplift and progress. Logan remained in Europe because he was so disgusted by his treatment in the army and by the exporting of Jim Crow racism by military officials. He became heavily involved in the Pan-African Congress from 1921 to 1927 and would become the chairman for the Committee for the Participation of Negroes in National Defense Programs for the *Pittsburgh Courier* in 1940. Logan's gaze and narrative became international rather than domestic. He and many other African American leaders shifted from fighting for the rights of only African Americans to fighting for all people within the African diaspora. Logan, when he met Du Bois in 1921, was involved in the struggle against military racism. He held negative views of American race culture, which is why he chose to stay in Paris and travel around Europe after the war. He became a part of the "Lost Generation," which included such writers as Ernest Hemingway and E. E. Cummings. To be a member of this generation, one had to be an American who served in the war and was filled with bitterness, rancor, and disgust over the senseless bloodshed during the conflict. Logan, like so many African American expatriates wandering aimlessly throughout Paris and Europe in the 1920s, viewed the prospect of returning to America's apartheid system with abhorrence.[61]

Historian David Reed argues, "Logan's development as a Pan-African thinker began with the activism and scholarship of Du Bois. . . . As a disgruntled World War I veteran one could argue that Logan saw an opportunity to strike back at racism through an organized and intellectual medium."[62]

Logan and Du Bois were not the only ones becoming involved with the Pan-African movement. Marcus Garvey and the Universal Negro Improvement Association based out of Harlem, New York, included many former World War I vets. In fact, Garvey surrounded himself with former black servicemen who helped to shape the ideology propagated by the Universal Negro Improvement Association. Garvey declared in 1922, "The morale of the Negro American soldier in France, the morale of the Negro West Indian in France, the morale of the Negro African soldier in France was unbroken and the morale of the soldiers of the bloody war of 1914 to 1918 is the morale of Negroes throughout the world." The Pan-African movement and the various views on Pan-Africanism were some of the notable results of the post–World War I era. Historian Chad Williams observes, "By reading about the exploits of soldiers from Canada, the Caribbean, and various regions of Africa . . . this broadened internationalism provided a crucial foundation for the development of a more specific diasporic consciousness." Williams goes onto assert, "Interactions between African American soldiers and other soldiers of African descent were key to the development of a new identity shaped by their time in France. The convergence of race and war, more specifically military service, function as the crucial nexus where Africa American diasporic consciousness developed."[63]

The black veteran of World War I arguably helped shape and strengthen the "New Negro" ideology, which took hold after the Great War. Hubert Harrison created the ideology of the "New Negro" in 1916. He shared his philosophy of rejecting the politics of conservative leaders such as R. R. Moton and Emmett Scott with young activists Chandler Owen and A. Philip Randolph, but it was the return of thousands of frustrated and energized black veterans that helped invigorate this new radical movement. Chad Williams observes, "The New Negro movement, rooted in the political consciousness and collective racial identity of black people in communities throughout the United States and the African Diaspora more broadly, was a product of the domestic and global upheavals of World War I and its aftermath."[64]

Black soldiers returned from World War I disillusioned and determined to exact change in the fight for civil and human rights for African Americans. According to Williams, "The black veteran, emerging from the crucible of war with renewed self-determination to enact systemic change, symbolized the development of a masculinist spirit of racial militancy." W. E. B. Du

Bois, in one of his more militant editorials after the war, directly challenged the black veteran to return fighting: "We are cowards and jackasses if now that the war is over we do not marshal every one of our brain and brawn to fight a sterner, longer, more unbending battle against the forces of hell in our own land."[65]

Militant and active they were. No vet took the same path toward fighting for racial pride and rights. George Washington Lee chose local political activism and economic actions; Rayford Logan chose the international stage and the Pan-African movement to fight for racial progress. Others organized domestically, created the League for Democracy, or focused on one particular issue, the removal of Colonel Allen Greer from service for the inflammatory remarks he made referring to black servicemen as cowards. Whatever path these men chose, their activism and militancy helped spark a global shift in the fight for civil and human rights not only for African Americans but also for all people of the African diaspora.

So far, we have examined African American soldiers and their interactions with the black community in wars and conflicts since the 1870s. We will now shift our focus and switch to exploring the effect of community interaction in the careers of two black officers, Henry Ossian Flipper and Charles Young, contemporaries of one another who became military celebrities in the African American community. One was destined to obscurity because he did not uphold for the black community the models of manhood and citizenship expected of him. He was not a race man. The other became a celebrated leader in the black community because he fulfilled that model.

Corporal Isaiah Mays
with his Medal of Honor.
*Library of Congress, Prints
and Photographs Division,
W. E. B. Du Bois Photo-
graphic Collection; reproduction no. LC-USZ62–11855.*

"De jubilee am come"—Fourth of July, 1876 / W. H. Redding, South Carolina; drawn by Sol Eytinge. *Library of Congress, Prints and Photographs Division;
reproduction no. LC-USZ62–96103.*

Black soldiers returning home from the Civil War, drawn by Alfred Rudolph Waud. *Library of Congress, Prints and Photographs Division, Civil War Photographs; reproduction no. LC-DIG-ppmsca-21005.*

Tenth Cavalry at Camp Verde. *Library of Congress, Prints and Photographs Division.*

Buffalo soldier with his daughter in Deadwood, Dakota Territory. *Library of Congress, Prints and Photographs Division.*

Chaplain Allen Allensworth. *Schomburg Center for Research in Black Culture, Jean Blackwell Hutson Research and Reference Division, New York Public Library, New York Public Library Digital Collections.*

Chaplain T. G. Steward. *C. M. Bell, photographer; Library of Congress, Prints and Photographs Division.*

Sergeant William Carney
with his Medal of Honor.
*Library of Congress, Prints
and Photographs Division,
W. E. B. Du Bois Photo-
graphic Collection; reproduction no. LC-USZ62-118558.*

Buffalo soldiers of Troop A, Ninth U.S. Cavalry—famous Indian fighters.
*Library of Congress, Prints and Photographs Division; reproduction no. LC-DIG-
ppmsca-08997.*

Black troops leaving Salt Lake City for Cuba, circa 1898. *Library of Congress, Prints and Photographs Division.*

"Some of our brave colored boys who helped to free Cuba," circa 1899. *Library of Congress, Prints and Photographs Division; reproduction no. LC-USZ62–41594.*

A group portrait of soldiers in uniform from Company I, Twenty-Fourth Infantry. *Library of Congress, Prints and Photographs Division.*

Black soldiers fighting in Mexico, circa 1916–17. *Schomburg Center for Research in Black Culture, Jean Blackwell Hutson Research and Reference Division, New York Public Library, New York Public Library Digital Collections.*

Men of the Twenty-Fourth Infantry guarding *villista* prisoners, Mexico, 1916. *Library of Congress, Prints and Photographs Division; reproduction no. LC-DIG-ppmsca-35151.*

African American men enlisting at the Colored YMCA for the Colored Officers' Training Camp at Fort Des Moines, Iowa. A. Merrill Willis (*sitting*) was the first to enlist. *National Archives and Records Administration; local identifier, 165-WW-127-121.*

Black men enlisting for active service in the Eighth Illinois Infantry Regiment (Colored), Chicago, 1917. The Eighth Illinois became part of the Ninety-Third (Provisional) Division; the army later redesignated the Eighth as the 370th Infantry Regiment. *National Archives and Records Administration; local identifier, 165-WW-127–122.*

Black soldier reading to other soldiers who could not read, Camp Gordon, Georgia, 1917–18. *E. B. Thompson, Library of Congress, Prints and Photographs Division; reproduction no. LC-USZ62–76432.*

Postcard of Captain Walter H. Loving, director, Philippine Constabulary Band, circa 1909. *Church Family Papers, Special Collections Department, University of Memphis Libraries.*

CAPT. WALTER H. LOVING
RECTOR, PHILIPPINE CONSTABULARY BAND

Black military police officer with hand resting on his pistol. *Library of Congress, Prints and Photographs Division; reproduction no. LC-DIG-ppmsca-51897.*

Henry Ossian Flipper in uniform after graduation from West
Point. *National Archives and Records Administration; local identifier,*
266824.

Major Charles Young. *Library of Congress, Prints and Photographs Division; reproduction no. LC-USZ62-62353.*

PART 2

4.
HENRY OSSIAN FLIPPER
The Lone Warrior

Social equality, as I comprehend it, must be the natural, and perhaps the gradual, outgrowth of a similarity of instincts and qualities in those between whom it exists.   —Henry O. Flipper

On the warm spring day of May 3, 1940, one of America's most enigmatic historical figures died at his brother's home in Atlanta, Georgia. Henry Ossian Flipper in 1877 became the first African American graduate of the U.S. Military Academy at West Point. Flipper was also the first African American officer ever to be court-martialed and discharged from the U.S. Armed Forces. The strange and tumultuous military career of Henry Flipper has for many decades been a long-forgotten and hidden stain within American military history. Yet, from the time of Flipper's court-martial in 1881 and discharge in 1882 until his death in 1940, he fought to restore his manly honor. What is unique about Flipper's fight to clear his name, though, is that he had virtually no support from the African American community.

In this chapter, our journey shifts to another path, one that looks at the strange and solitary life of a man striving to be a member of the American bourgeoisie while being unable to escape his main handicap—his blackness. We will explore why Flipper never fully developed a strong base of support among African Americans. How did this onetime hero to the black community and idol to James Weldon Johnson have the fight of his life without the support of those who helped him gain entrance to the U.S. Military Academy? In 1999, President Bill Clinton finally gave Flipper the full pardon and exoneration he had fought for since the day of his dishonorable discharge. The questions at the heart of this issue are these: Would it have taken as long if he had enjoyed the support of the African American community and major black leaders? And how did Flipper go from being an inspiration and a headline in every black newspaper to a simple footnote?

EARLY YEARS

Henry Ossian Flipper was born a slave on March 31, 1856, in Thomasville, Georgia, the eldest of five brothers. Methodist minister Reverend Reuben H. Lucky owned Flipper and his mother, Isabella Buckhalter. Festus Flipper, Henry's father, was a shoemaker and carriage trimmer and was owned by a successful slave dealer named Ephraim G. Ponder. Flipper in his autobiography, *The Colored Cadet at West Point,* highlights the fact that both of his parents were of mixed racial heritage.[1]

In 1859, Ponder retired and wanted to relocate from Thomasville to Atlanta. Festus Flipper did not want to be separated from his wife and child, who would remain in Thomasville with Reverend Lucky. Ponder allowed Festus to hire himself out and earn his own money, enabling him to loan Ponder enough money to purchase his wife and son from Lucky. When Ponder arrived in Atlanta, he purchased twenty-five acres of land and erected a "superb mansion for his own family, a number of substantial frame dwellings for his slaves, and three large buildings for manufacturing purposes."[2]

According to Flipper, life on the Ponder plantation was more like a factory than a typical southern plantation. More than sixty-five slaves were living on the Ponder premises. Flipper noted how most of his fellow slaves were mechanics and more often than not were hired out within the city and kept most of the money they earned. Flipper stated, "These bond people were therefore virtually free. They acquired and accumulated wealth, lived happily, and needed but two other things to make them like other human beings, viz., absolute freedom and education."[3]

At the age of eight, Flipper gained one of those two essential things: an education. One of the mechanics on the Ponder plantation convinced the mistress of the house to allow him to start a night school on the property, and he began teaching the children basic reading, writing, and arithmetic. Unfortunately, Flipper's education on the plantation did not last long; he and his family had to flee Atlanta because of the approach of General William T. Sherman and the Union army. The Ponder household, including all slaves, fled to Macon, Georgia, and was spared the wrath of Sherman's fiery march. Yet, Flipper recalled being traumatized by Sherman's invasion and instinctively identified himself with his southern heritage. One particular image of Sherman's "invasion" left an impression on a young Henry Flipper, one that influenced his later decision to become a soldier: "Shocked by the sight of Confederate corpses dangling on tree limbs in the wake of Union Army military executions, he swore a childlike oath to become a soldier and someday avenge those Confederate dead." Despite Flipper's confusion as to who were his liberators and who were his oppressors, this early image inspired Flipper to attend West Point and become a soldier.[4]

In the spring of 1865, Festus Flipper took his wife and sons back to the burned ruins of Atlanta. The Flippers' personal finances and holdings were not damaged, so they were able to move into one of the few houses available in the city. One of the Flippers' new neighbors was an ex-Confederate captain whose wife became the private tutor to the Flipper boys. In March 1866, the American Missionary Association, in association with the Freedmen's Bureau, opened several schools in Atlanta, and the Flipper children enrolled in the famous Storrs' School, which would become Atlanta University. In 1869, the boys began attending Atlanta University's college preparatory program.[5]

Festus Flipper had established himself as a successful shoemaker who attracted both white and black clientele. In his biography, Flipper described his father as sensible, unassuming, and gentlemanly, and he wanted to emulate all of these qualities that his father embodied. It was these characteristics that both men possessed, plus Festus Flipper's wealth and good standing within the community, that helped to win over the white Republicans who would later endorse Flipper's appointment to West Point. Flipper and his family were a part of the black bourgeoisie within Atlanta society, and this also helped him gain his appointment. However, it is the elitist attitude Flipper developed in his early years, as a member of the bourgeoisie, that later alienated him from the majority of the African American community. Flipper took pride in his ultimate goal of monetary success and upward social mobility. He knew that a West Point appointment would be a great opportunity for him to better his position in life. He did not pursue inclusion at West Point to become a symbol of black pride or to uplift the race. In this regard, Flipper's path differed from that of his counterpart James Webster Smith, the first black admitted to West Point, or of Colonel Charles Young, who was one of only three African Americans to graduate from West Point in the nineteenth century. Young, a former slave himself, became a soldier because he wanted to help uplift the race and instill a stronger sense of manly pride within black men. Throughout his entire military career, African Americans saw Young as a beloved hero.[6]

Because of his family's position within Atlanta society, Flipper was able to gain enough support from white Republicans who could influence the newly elected white southern-born Republican congressman J. C. Freeman.

Flipper wrote to Freeman after learning there was a vacancy at the academy. Freeman did not want to recommend Flipper for admittance until he was assured that Flipper would be able to pass the West Point physical examination. So, in April 1873 Dr. Thomas Powell, the family physician, assessed Flipper and assured Freeman that the young man would be able to pass the exam and not embarrass him. Six days after receiving word from Powell, Freeman sent his letter of recommendation to the secretary of war, and then Flipper filled out the appropriate paperwork acknowledging his candidacy.[7]

THE WEST POINT YEARS

When Flipper arrived at West Point in 1873, there was only one other black cadet at the academy, James Webster Smith of South Carolina, who had been admitted in 1870. Five other young black men had also been appointed before Flipper, but only Smith—the first African American admitted to the academy—remained. Observers described Smith as an octoroon and a "troublemaker." Before Flipper's arrival at West Point, Smith sent him a letter warning him of what to expect at the academy. Smith had been admitted in 1870 along with another young man from Mississippi named Michael Howard. Howard had received only one year of formal education before coming to West Point; he unsurprisingly failed all of his initial examinations. Therefore, Smith spent the next three years, before Flipper's arrival in 1873, in almost total isolation. He attempted to force the white cadets to interact with him outside the classroom, but all of his efforts were in vain. Smith's time at the academy was filled with hostility and discrimination; he was spit on and his life was threatened. He then wrote letters to his benefactor David Clark, a Connecticut philanthropist, and Clark frequently published Smith's letters in the press, which brought national attention to West Point. Smith also had the support of General Oliver Otis Howard, who had helped him gain his nomination to the academy. Clark and Howard both found Smith's treatment disgusting. In fact, because of one of Smith's letters, a congressional hearing was held to investigate the treatment he received at the academy.[8]

Smith's frequent confrontational approach to racial discrimination served as a model for Flipper on how *not* to act when he arrived at the academy. Flipper admitted that Smith's private letter helped to mentally prepare him for the treatment he was to receive once he was at the school. Flipper stated, "It was a sad letter. I don't think anything has so affected me or so influenced my conduct at West Point as its melancholy tone." When Flipper arrived at West Point, his reception was similar to Smith's, yet Flipper did not complain to anyone about his treatment, and he did not attempt to force himself socially upon the white cadets as Smith had. In fact, Flipper purposefully isolated himself the entire four years he was at West Point.[9]

Flipper's views about race and social equality were very different from those held by many African American leaders of his day. In particular, his views on social equality were in direct conflict with former West Point roommate James Webster Smith. Flipper argued that racial inequality and prejudice were not problems of color but rather were problems of intellectual and social inferiority among black people, which could only be resolved with proper formal education.

> Social equality, as I comprehend it, must be the natural, and perhaps the gradual, outgrowth of a similarity of instincts and qualities in those between whom it exists. That is to say, there can be no social equality between persons who have nothing in common. . . . Color is of no consequence in considering the question of equality socially. . . . Want of education, want of the proof of equality of intellect, is the obstacle, and not color. And the only way to get this proof is to get an education, and not by "war of races." Equal rights must be a consequence of this proof, and not something existing before it.[10]

Flipper's views on social equality were perhaps more of a coping mechanism to deal with the forced isolation and loneliness he experienced the entire four years he was at West Point. Regarding his solitude, Flipper commented,

> I was the happiest man in the institution, except when I got to brooding over my loneliness. Such moments would come when it would seem nothing would interest me. . . . I learned to hate holidays. I had nowhere to go except to walk the grounds. . . . At these times the barracks would be deserted and I would get so lonely and melancholy I wouldn't know what to do.[11]

Despite sharing a room with Smith, Flipper did not interact very much with him, and after Smith's dismissal for not passing all of his classes, another black cadet eventually took his place. Johnson C. Whittaker was admitted to the academy in 1876, and Flipper treated him the same way he did Smith. Flipper's isolation was by choice so he would not be harassed in the same manner as Smith and Whittaker. When Whittaker first arrived at the academy, a white cadet attacked him. Naturally, Whittaker reported this attack and the cadet responsible received an adequate punishment, but this tarnished Whittaker's chances at the academy with his fellow cadets. Whittaker suffered another attack, but this time he was blamed and court-martialed for purposefully injuring himself; he was then dismissed from West Point. Hazing of first-year cadets was expected, but the type of abuse the black cadets experienced extended far beyond the typical pranks of having one's bed stolen or the requirements of doing the laundry of the upperclassmen.[12]

Flipper viewed Whittaker as weak. Flipper more than likely would not have told if he himself was attacked, which might be why he was able to survive West Point and Smith and Whittaker were forced out. Whittaker's case made national headlines in both the black and white press. His court-martial was overturned by President Chester A. Arthur in 1883 because Whittaker had people such as General William T. Sherman advocating on his behalf. Sherman along with other generals such as Oliver O. Howard criticized the white racist culture cultivated at West Point. Yet Johnson C. Whittaker's dismissal from West Point for failing his philosophy class did not sour him on the military. Two of his sons became officers in the army during World War I. Whittaker and Smith both ended up teaching at South Carolina State College, a black university. Whittaker had the support of the African American community, and his guilty decision ended up being reversed.

Flipper was now thrust into the national limelight for being the new anomaly at the army's military academy. Overnight, he became a celebrity within the African American press and a villain in many major white newspapers. The *Chicago Tribune,* for example, predicted that Flipper would never be allowed to graduate. The black press held a very different image of Flipper. The *Atlanta Herald* described Flipper as being above reproach: "Among colored men we know of none more honorable or more deserving than Flipper. . . . Young Flipper is to make his mark as no other colored youth in the country." The *Herald* was correct in its prediction; on June 15, 1877, Flipper became the first African American to graduate from the West Point military academy. One month after graduating, Flipper accepted a commission as a second lieutenant assigned to the Tenth United States Cavalry.[13]

THE FIRST BLACK OFFICER

At the time of Flipper's graduation from West Point, there were four black regiments in the regular army. His entry into the army as an officer meant that for the first time in American history, a black officer was to command black soldiers in the regular army. There was a prevailing myth within the American military that black soldiers could not be trusted unless they were under the command of a white officer. Flipper's commission as an officer meant that an African American would have a chance to dispel that misguided and unfounded notion. Henry Ossian Flipper's success as an officer not only would determine his destiny but would be intertwined with that of all African Americans who followed his example.

The celebrity status that Flipper received by becoming the first and only black officer in the army at that time attracted much attention that was oftentimes unwanted. The *Charleston News and Courier* reported that once Flipper had served his obligatory two years in the U.S. military, he was going to become the general and commander in chief of the Liberian army. This outraged Flipper because he was opposed to the whole idea of African Americans relocating to Liberia and never considered abandoning the position that he had fought so hard to receive, after serving only two years. He was also dismayed at the fact that many black Georgia residents were persuaded to go to Liberia after learning that he was to become the new Liberian general. Flipper responded to the rumor by writing a letter to the editor of the *News and Courier*:

> I shall consider it no small favor if you will state that there is no law requiring me to serve two years, that I never authorized any such statement as here made, that I have no sympathy whatever for the "Liberian Exodus" movement, that I give it neither countenance nor support, but will oppose it whenever I feel that the occasion requires it. I am not at all disposed to flee from one shadow to grasp at another—from the supposed error of Hayes's Southern policy to the prospective glory of commanding Liberia's Army.[14]

Flipper's response to the Liberian offer not only was published in the black press but also was published in the *Army and Navy Journal* so that when he arrived at his new post in Texas, there would be no question of Flipper's loyalty. However, in his quest to solidify his position in the army, he alienated many African Americans who not only respected the Liberian exodus movement but supported the idea that there was no place for blacks in America and Liberia was their best chance for living in dignity. The Liberian exodus movement did not gain a massive audience until the late nineteenth century under the leadership of Bishop Henry McNeal Turner, but Flipper's dismissal of the exodus movement more than likely upset many African Americans who sympathized with the cause. Flipper unknowingly hurt his standing within the African American community by allowing his letter to be published within the white and African American press and by saying that the end of Reconstruction and the beginning of Jim Crow segregation were not horrible. Many blacks felt unsatisfied with the ending of Reconstruction, but Flipper referred to it as "the supposed error of Hayes's Southern policy."

ON THE FRONTIER

In 1878, Lieutenant Flipper arrived at Fort Sill, Oklahoma, with no fanfare and had a peaceful introduction to army life. The commander of the Tenth Cavalry was Colonel Benjamin Grierson. Flipper was assigned to Company A and served under the command of Captain Nicholas Nolan. He and Flipper became fast friends. Flipper's assignment at Fort Sill was as a signal officer; duties included "night signaling with torches, telegraphy, and establishing and opening communications between two points." Captain Nolan, aged fifty and a widower with two children, quickly married twenty-one-year-old Annie Dwyer of San Antonio soon after the company arrived at Fort Sill. Annie and her sister, Mollie, also became friends with the young Lieutenant Flipper; in fact, "he and Mollie used to go horseback riding together." Flipper boarded with the newlyweds at the insistence of Captain Nolan, and because of this close relationship, he was able to achieve a certain level of respect among the other officers in his company. In many ways, Flipper began to view himself as accepted by his white peers and as their social equal.[15]

When it became common knowledge that Flipper was staying at Captain Nolan's residence with two young white women and that he often would go riding with one of these ladies, it caused a stir at the fort. Nolan wrote a letter to the *Army and Navy Journal* defending his decision for allowing Flipper to board with him and praising the young lieutenant's character. In his second autobiography, *The Negro Frontiersman*, Flipper asserted that his downfall began after he started taking rides with Mollie Dwyer. According to Flipper, before he arrived at the fort, Mollie was taking rides with Lieutenant Charles Nordstrom. He implied that Nordstrom became jealous of his budding relationship with Mollie. Perhaps at Nordstrom's urging, the other officers' attitudes toward Flipper turned sour. Flipper once again became isolated, similar to the way he had been isolated at West Point.[16] In his closing remarks, Flipper's attorney at his court-martial described the isolation that Flipper experienced while serving in the army:

> The isolation to which he has been subjected by nearly every person
> in the profession with whom he has come in contact since he set

foot on the parade ground at West Point, must necessarily have occasioned in him a feeling of insecurity in his position and caused him to regard himself a marked man by those who avoided association with him.[17]

Most of the books and articles written about Henry Flipper and his court-martial go into extensive detail about the isolation and ostracism he faced from his fellow white officers. However, none of these studies explored how Flipper interacted with his fellow African American soldiers. Flipper was not the only black face at his fort. Why did he not seek camaraderie and companionship with any of the black men in his regiment? Flipper's isolation from the white soldiers was beyond his control, but his isolation from the black soldiers was by choice. As mentioned earlier, Flipper's bourgeois and elitist attitudes hurt him. Flipper believed that only the socially equal and properly educated should interact with each other, and those of poor manners and education deserved to be treated as inferior; this, of course, did not help his situation as the only black officer in the army. This attitude is something he continued in his civilian career, once he decided to serve as a spy and consultant to Senator Albert Fall of New Mexico, who was appointed secretary of the interior by Warren G. Harding. As a result, Flipper found himself in "no-man's-land"; in spite of his education and character, most white peers wanted nothing to do with him, and because of his attitude regarding social equality, he had little to do with his black peers.

In the spring of 1880, Flipper served with distinction in the Victorio War. By then his regiment had transferred to Fort Davis, Texas, and Flipper had been promoted to the positions of acting assistant quartermaster, post quartermaster, and acting commissary of subsistence. Unfortunately, Flipper's career as quartermaster was short-lived because, in March 1881, Colonel William R. Shafter became the new post commander. According to one author, Shafter was "coarse, profane, and afflicted with a barely concealed racism." Yet despite these flaws, Shafter effectively led African American soldiers into battle and established himself as a bona fide "Indian fighter." He earned the nickname "Pecos Bill."[18]

Shafter's adjutant was First Lieutenant Louis Wilhemi. Wilhemi was a West Point washout, forced to resign from the school for medical reasons in December 1873. He received his commission in the regular army in October 1875. Wilhemi proved to be Flipper's new worst enemy. In fact, Flipper contended throughout his trial that it was Wilhemi, Shafter, and Nordstrom who were at the heart of the conspiracy to have him removed from the army.

THE COURT-MARTIAL OF LIEUTENANT FLIPPER

Once Shafter and Wilhemi assumed command of the post, things went downhill for Flipper. Shafter immediately removed Flipper from the position of acting commissary officer, although it took over five months to find a suitable replacement. Shafter then ordered Flipper to immediately transfer funds from the "quartermaster's safe" to Flipper's private residence. In Flipper's appeal to Congress in 1898, he highlighted this fact and emphasized his belief that there was a "nefarious scheme" to get him dismissed from the army. Flipper stated, "On reflection, I saw clearly that I was not sufficiently removed from the excitement and prejudices of the time." However, at the time Flipper thought because of his position and education he was immune to these prejudices, prompting his ambivalence to Shafter's motives for requesting him to transfer the funds to his private residence.[19]

Flipper did as Shafter ordered and moved the commissary funds to his private residence. This is the point at which Flipper's real troubles began. On May 2, 1881, Major M. P. Small, chief commissary of subsistence for the Department of Texas, notified all commissaries of his impending absence from headquarters for the month of May and ordered them not to send any cash until June. Unfortunately, Small remained absent from headquarters much longer than a month, and in fact Flipper did not receive word from headquarters until August requesting the immediate transfer of all funds for the entire fiscal year. Flipper also stopped submitting weekly statements for the present fiscal year, which was brought to the attention of Shafter by Small.[20]

In July, Shafter ordered Flipper to transfer all funds to Small, and it was then that Flipper noticed a deficiency of $1,440.43. Flipper was not alarmed by this deficit. He believed he could submit a check from his own account to cover the missing funds because he expected a substantial royalty check—$5,000—from the sale of the first 5,000 copies of his first autobiography. However, this never came to fruition, and Flipper received a check for only $74 from the publisher, Homer Lee and Company. The situation upset him greatly, and unfortunately for Flipper, by the end of July, the shortfall had increased to $3,791.77. Small notified Shafter that he never received the transfer from Flipper. Once Shafter found this out, he immediately relieved Flipper of his duties and replaced him with Lieutenant Frank H. Edmunds, Flipper's former French teacher at West Point. Shafter claimed that he did not become suspicious of Flipper until it was feared that he would flee to Mexico with the stolen money. During the trial, Shafter testified about his suspicions:[21]

Lieutenant Flipper's horse [was] standing in front of the Sender & Sienenborn store in town with saddle bags and saddle, [and] I knew that he had something like over two thousand dollars in money and it occurred to me right then and there that if there was anything wrong he would have an opportunity of getting away if he saw fit. . . . I was very nervous about the matter as I could not conceive what had become of it.[22]

Shafter then ordered Flipper's residence to be searched by Edmunds and Wilhemi. During the course of the search, they discovered the missing weekly financial statements and $300 in transmittal checks. Wilhemi noticed that Flipper's maid, Lucy Smith, was in the room, and when they searched his trunk, they saw that her belongings were mixed in with Flipper's. This raised the question of whether Lucy Smith might know where the missing checks were. Smith was ordered back to Shafter's office, where she was searched, and stuffed inside her dress were found checks totaling $2,853.56. Smith was immediately arrested and charged with theft of government property. The checks found on Lucy Smith were the checks that Flipper had told Shafter had been mailed on July 9. Shafter put Flipper under immediate arrest and confined him to a tiny cell in the post guardhouse. Word was then sent to department headquarters notifying the commanding general of the situation. When Brigadier General Christopher C. Augur learned that Flipper was confined to the guardhouse, both Secretary of War Robert Todd Lincoln and General of the Army William T. Sherman ordered Shafter to have Flipper removed from the guardhouse. In a telegram sent to General Augur, both men stated, "This officer must have the same treatment as though he were white." Flipper was later confined to his own quarters for the duration of the trial with the back door and window barred.[23]

Flipper's arrest for embezzlement and subsequent trial did not receive the same kind of media attention and publicity frenzy as had his graduation from West Point because earlier in the summer, on July 2, 1881, President James A. Garfield's assassination and lingering death dominated the headlines. He eventually died from the infections caused by his gunshot wounds on September 19, 1881. After that, Flipper's trial and the trial of assassin Charles J. Guiteau took place simultaneously, and Flipper's trial received less media attention. None of this mattered to Flipper as he prepared to mount his defense. The trial was set to start on September 17, 1881, but Flipper had not been successful in acquiring adequate counsel. He was granted a delay until November 1, 1881. In an ironic twist, the man who had conspicuously avoided being a part of community uplift now sought help from the black community. Unlike Johnson C. Whittaker in 1880, who had unlimited support from his lawyers and positive press coverage in the black press during his court-martial, Flipper, after countless letters to the leading African Americans in New York, Boston, Philadelphia, and Washington, D.C., was not able to raise enough money to pay a civilian attorney or even get any positive press coverage. Flipper felt completely dejected and depressed and concluded that he would have to fight yet another battle alone. Fortunately for him, this would not be Flipper's fate; Captain Merritt Barber of the Sixteenth Infantry came forward and volunteered to be Flipper's attorney.[24]

The lack of support from the African American community for Flipper and his legal defense could have been the result of several different dynamics, the first being Flipper's arrogant and aloof personality. In his first autobiography, *The Colored Cadet at West Point*, Flipper's cryptic and often bourgeois attitudes about education, social equality, and the other black cadets who attended the academy (James Webster Smith and Johnson C. Whittaker in particular) presented him as a man who did not want to uplift the race. In the book, Flipper also took a very critical position of the Liberian exodus movement and scoffed at the idea of his teaching and training young black men at one of the black colleges or universities. When an army official suggested that Flipper take an appointment at one of these schools, he responded by stating, "He is of the opinion it would be best for me. I could not agree with him. Personally, I would rather remain with my company. I have no taste and no tact for teaching. I would decline any such appointment."[25]

In contrast, Flipper's counterpart Charles Young took an appointment at Wilberforce University after his graduation from West Point. Young was to be in charge of the military affairs department for the school. He accepted the position after the other black West Point graduate, John Hanks Alexander, already on staff at the university, died unexpectedly. Young's decision to train young black men at Wilberforce, his alma mater, emerged from his ultimate goal to serve his country and uplift his race. Compared to these other two African American graduates, Flipper's stance was unusual and striking. And after his dismissal from the academy, James Webster Smith took control of the military affairs department at a black college in South Carolina. Johnson C. Whittaker took a teaching position in South Carolina as well, and in fact two of his sons went on to become officers during World War I. Therefore, it was not surprising that several of the black newspapers printed stories supporting Flipper's appointment to one of these schools, yet

Flipper dismissed these suggestions. In fact, throughout his autobiography, Flipper made it no secret that he had a disdain for the opinions of the black press. True to form, when his trial began he did not make any appeals in the black press proclaiming his innocence. Yet it would have been almost impossible for Flipper to galvanize the black community behind him without the support of the black press.

Another factor that could have contributed to his lack of support from the black military community locally stemmed from his prior relationships with Mollie Dwyer and Lucy Smith. African Americans during the nineteenth century were a cautious group, and Flipper's initial interest in a white woman could have possibly alienated him further from the black soldiers and their families who were stationed with him at Fort Davis. The revelation that Lucy Smith's personal belongings were found mixed in with his and that the missing checks were found hidden in her pocket gave the appearance that she was more than a maid to Flipper. A romantic relationship between a black man and white woman, whether true or not, was a social taboo in nineteenth-century America and was the alleged basis for vigilante violence such as lynching against black men.

The other dynamic that could explain the lack of support for Flipper was the image he allowed others to paint of him of having little to nothing in common with other African Americans. Flipper's stoic personality and convoluted views about not associating with people whose education did not match his made him unapproachable to the majority of the black noncommissioned officers and soldiers. He had no base of support locally or nationally within the black community at large, or within the even smaller black community within the military. William Faxon, an official speaking on Flipper's behalf before Congress, declared Flipper as "having little in common with his race by reason of talents, attainments, and education." During the trial, his attorney, in his closing argument, described Flipper as an anomaly and subject to envy and jealousy from other African Americans.[26] Merritt Barber stated,

> Being the only colored officer in the service and the only colored man who has ever passed the ordeal of either of our national schools, his position in the Army is an anomalous one, just as his whole life has been an anomaly.... Every success in life, which his resolution and perseverance have achieved, every obstacle, which his career has surmounted, has been by himself alone.... [He] has ... had to grapple every obstacle with which one of white birth has to contend,

every feature of poverty, the envy of his own color at his success, and the active prejudice of ours at his presumption.[27]

Flipper wholeheartedly embraced the image of achieving all of his success without the help of others despite the fact that he was born a slave. Flipper's appointment to West Point came from the connections his father had made within the African American community.

Barber brilliantly argued to the court that Flipper's actions were more careless than criminal and could have been prevented if Shafter had been more observant. Nevertheless, Flipper's fate was sealed on December 7, 1881, when, after seven hours of deliberation, the military tribunal found Lieutenant Flipper not guilty of embezzlement but guilty of conduct unbecoming an officer and a gentleman. Flipper's punishment was immediate dismissal from service and a dishonorable discharge. Flipper's last chance for redemption could come only from the president. Under the standards of military justice, no officer can be dismissed in peacetime without the president's approval. Flipper did have two allies in President Chester A. Arthur's cabinet in Secretary of War Robert Todd Lincoln and Judge Advocate General David G. Swaim. Lincoln and Swaim did not support the court's decision to dismiss Flipper, and Lincoln recommended that President Arthur support a lesser degree of punishment. However, their objections were to no avail, and on June 14, 1882, Arthur confirmed the court's ruling. Flipper was dismissed from service.[28]

FLIPPER'S APPEAL

After his dismissal from the army, Henry Flipper went on to have a very successful civilian career. He spent much of the 1890s in southern Arizona, where he surveyed land and edited a local newspaper. Flipper worked as a mining engineer in Mexico and throughout much of the U.S. southwest. He also worked as a special agent for the Department of Justice, in the Court of Private Land Claims. Flipper received a certain level of notoriety in Arizona after saving 700,000 acres of land from unscrupulous speculators. While a special agent for the Department of Justice, Flipper became a recognized authority on Spanish and Mexican land law. His civilian career spanned three decades and made him a very wealthy man, for a brief period of time. But, with the market crash of 1929, he lost his fortune and returned to his brother's doorstep penniless and bitter. Yet despite all of his success, Flipper wanted to clear his name. He waited sixteen years before submitting his first appeal in the spring of 1898.[29]

Flipper's motives for coming forward were related to America's war with Spain. President William McKinley declared war on Spain in April, and in that same month Flipper submitted his official appeal to Congress. He understood that it would take an act of Congress to clear his name and have him reinstated. Flipper met Barney McKay while in D.C. for business. McKay (discussed in chapter 1) had been denied reenlistment in 1897 after sixteen years of service, so when he heard Flipper's story he urged him to seek vindication. Flipper's relationship with McKay was unusual because of his "loner" personality, but Flipper appreciated McKay's support. He stated,

> I took a liking to him instantly. I hadn't done anything at the time, although I was preparing to move in the matter [of reinstatement]. He came to urge me to move and he had the first bill introduced by a Congressman from Wisconsin [Michael Griffin]. He worked like a Trojan, held interviews with Congressmen, took me to call on Congressmen.[30]

In another surprising turn, Flipper also sought help from one of the most influential black leaders of the late nineteenth century: Booker T. Washington. In his letter to Washington, Flipper took a completely different tone from his autobiography and trial, where he claimed his shame as solely his own, and argued that his dishonor was the shame of the entire race:

> In the interest of the Race, to right the wrong done me and through me every member of the Race . . . a flood of letters of this character, carefully prepared after reading my Brief, will show more strongly than anything else how our people resent any wrong done to a single one of its individuals and its determination to have that wrong righted.[31]

Later in the same letter, Flipper impressed upon Washington the futility of agitation in the press. His reasoning for not wanting to use the black press was simply because of all the retired military personnel in the D.C. area—he did not want to antagonize them because it might affect his appeal. In another letter to Washington, asking him to put pressure on McKinley, Flipper voiced his utter disgust at the behavior of an infamous regiment of volunteer black soldiers and officers. The Sixth Virginia Militia had made national headlines because they destroyed a tree in Macon, Georgia, that was used to hang a black man. Flipper viewed this behavior as disgraceful.

He made no secret of his disdain for any type of black volunteer or militia regiments. In fact, the *Cleveland Gazette*, a black newspaper, suggested that Flipper and Lieutenant Charles Young should take charge of their own volunteer regiment, which would allow for more black officers and soldiers. Flipper quickly responded by stating that it was out of the question and he was not interested in serving in any volunteer regiment. In his letter to Washington, Flipper discussed his disgust over these volunteer soldiers: "These soldiers have come to think that because they wore the government's uniform they were at liberty to avenge all wrongs they conceive the white people of the South have ever done them."[32]

Flipper's attitude toward the press and now the black volunteer regiments did not help him garner support from the African American community. Yet, how were the masses of the race going to rise up in protest and anger if they were not made aware of the situation? Flipper never made a public appeal to the African American community, and it is uncertain whether or not it would have made a difference because the Tuskegee Wizard could not convince President McKinley to put pressure on Congress. Consequently, Flipper's bill died in the House Military Affairs Committee. Flipper tried two more times to get Congress to clear his name. His last effort came in 1921, while he was working as a translator for Secretary of Interior Albert Fall. Fall wrote a letter to the Military Affairs Committee on Flipper's behalf, but it was to no avail. Flipper retired and went to live with his brother, Bishop Joseph Flipper, at his home in Atlanta, Georgia, in 1930.

UNWEPT, UNHONORED, UNSUNG

Henry Ossian Flipper lived to be eighty-four years old. He died on May 3, 1940, the same day that the first African American was promoted to brigadier general in the U.S. Army, Benjamin O. Davis Sr. When Flipper died, a *New York Times* headline read, "Ex-Slave, Graduate of West Point Dies," and the *Journal of Negro History* wrote a very short obituary of Flipper's life, only mentioning his court-martial and nothing of his post-military accomplishments. Flipper's passing was not celebrated in the black community. There was no holiday proclaimed in his name, and the only shouts for vindication came from his friends. It would take Flipper's niece and a schoolteacher named Ray O. MacColl of Valdosta, Georgia, to finally succeed in gaining Henry Flipper the exoneration he so desperately wanted in life through their appeals. On November 17, 1976, the Army Board of Corrections cleared Flipper's name. The boarded concluded "that in view of the foregoing findings and conclusions, giving consideration to the circumstances of his service, and the nature of the offense involved, the continuance of the stigma from dismissal, which characterizes the entire service as dishonorable, is unduly harsh, and therefore unjust."[33]

The board's decision ended the ninety-four-year fight to clear his name. In the aftermath of Flipper's vindication, several books and articles emerged in the 1970s and 1980s rescuing him from the shadows of history. In 1978, Flipper's remains were removed from Atlanta, and he was reburied in his hometown of Thomasville, Georgia, with full military honors. The U.S. Military Academy now gives an award in his name to the graduating cadet who demonstrates the highest levels of leadership, self-discipline, and perseverance. The first award was given to the grandson of Mrs. Irsle King, Flipper's niece. Then fifty-nine years after Flipper's death, President Bill Clinton granted Henry Ossian Flipper a presidential pardon. The ceremony was held on February 19, 1999, and was attended by retired general Colin Powell, who kept a picture of Flipper on his desk. Clinton said of Flipper, "This good man now has completely recovered his good name."[34]

Henry Flipper's fight to clear his name had a happy ending. Nevertheless, would it have taken as long if Flipper had not been his own worst enemy? At the time of his graduation from West Point, Flipper's popularity in the African American community was unparalleled. Yet, when he had the fight of his life, he stood alone. His bourgeois upbringing and attitudes distorted views about freedom and race. His sympathy toward the Confederacy as a boy may have influenced his views as an adult. Flipper in many ways accepted the Horatio Alger myth of "rags to riches," and he based his masculine identity on individual merit. He did not embrace the notion of helping the entirety of the race. He did not see his military service as belonging to anyone but himself.

Flipper's rejection of African Americans' notions of collective freedom and masculine identity can best be seen by his rejection of serving as a military science professor or in the militia or in the Liberian army. Compared to every other black officer who served in the militias or Liberia or taught military science at various black colleges and universities, Flipper was not able to forge a bond with other black servicemen, and his court-martial appeal did not get him the vindication he needed until long after his death. Flipper was at fault for his lack of support from the black community. He made no serious political reflections about Reconstruction or the state of blacks during that era. He was a trailblazer in many of his endeavors, yet he died as a sidenote in African American history rather than as a hero or role model.

5.
CHARLES YOUNG

The Diplomatic Warrior

Give us Charlie Young and we'll bring back the Kaiser!
—popular slogan from World War I
as quoted by Lerone Bennett Jr.

Lieutenant Colonel Charles Young, astride his faithful horse Dolly, galloped down a lonely Ohio road, leaving behind the loss and uncertainty of his forced early retirement and heading toward a new destiny filled with promise and hope. He recalled the last words he spoke to his wife before he left: "It's time for my people—my brethren—to know I am physically fit." Young, aged fifty-four, made the nearly 495-mile trek from Xenia, Ohio, to D.C., carrying the mantle of his people on his back. He knew he was not just riding for himself but making this momentous journey for race and country. Charles Young—the first African American to achieve the rank of colonel in the U.S. Army and the third African American to graduate from West Point—was more than just a soldier; Young took great pride in being a "race man."[1]

Charles Young is one of the most important figures in the history of the American military. His multifaceted talent and determination had a tremendous impact on the U.S. Army, on higher education, and on foreign affairs. Young was a leader, a teacher, and a statesman at various stages of his career. His psycho-military study, *Military Morale of Nations and Races*, introduces Colonel Charles Young as not just a soldier but also a military intellectual, civil rights leader, and vocal advocate for social equality for African Americans. Young's monograph was a study of the various race and ethnic militaries throughout the world and served as a direct challenge to the doctrine of white scientific racism that was thriving during the early twentieth century. He used an interdisciplinary approach to demonstrate that supposedly servile races could display military virtue and prowess. Colonel Charles Young was the most celebrated African American soldier at the turn of the twentieth century. He helped to shape and mentor countless young men, such as Benjamin O. Davis Sr., the army's first black general; Major Walter Loving, the famous bandleader of the Philippine Constabulary Band; Paul Laurence Dunbar; and countless less famous young men.

In 1917, Charles Young reluctantly ended his military career after he was found unfit to serve. The campaign to reinstate Young, after he was retired early and against his will, was supported by almost every black leader in the country. It caused President Woodrow Wilson and his administration so much concern and fear of losing the support of the African American community that within a year of his retirement, Young was reinstated at the rank of full bird colonel. The campaign to reinstate Young made him so popular among the African American community that when he died rather suddenly while on a special assignment for Liberia in Nigeria in 1922, most African Americans considered it a tragedy that they were not able to properly mourn him; it took almost a year to get his body back to the United States. His funeral at Arlington Cemetery Amphitheatre in June 1923 was the largest in the cemetery's history. Over 100,000 people lined the streets of Washington, D.C., and New York to watch Colonel Young's funeral processions. Yet, Young is largely absent from the discourse on turn-of-the-century African American leaders today.

Young served in the military for race and country. He spoke out actively against the possibility of European colonization of Liberia. He grew to understand the importance of Liberian independence and incorporated Pan-Africanism into his fight for racial uplift. He also stood up against the Tuskegee Machine and its ideals of industrial education, as advocated by Booker T. Washington. This chapter elaborates on the life of this soldier who helped sustain military educational institutions at Wilberforce University, marked uncharted territory by creating the university's military science program, and helped implement the visions of some of the African American giants of the early twentieth century. In addition, we will examine how Young, who lived on the social fissures dividing America, was a true "race man," dedicated to education and racial uplift.

THE WONDER YEARS

Charles Young was born on March 12, 1864. His parents, Armita Baer and Gabriel Young, were both slaves in Helena, Kentucky, at that time; therefore, he was born a slave. Within a year of his son's birth, Gabriel Young liberated himself and his family and moved to Ripley, Ohio. On February 12, 1865, Gabriel Young joined the Union army and served one year with Company F of the Fifth U.S. Colored Heavy Artillery. Ripley is only twenty-one miles from Helena, but it had a settlement of freed blacks living there, so it was no surprise that Gabriel Young settled his family in that town. Young's childhood was very different from Henry Flipper's. As noted in the previous chapter, Flipper grew up in a family of some financial means and within social networks of other well-to-do black families. Young's father wanted to actively serve and fight for his freedom and did not have the type of financial stability that the Flipper family had during and after the Civil War.[2]

Growing up, Charles Young had a very close relationship with his mother. Armita was literate, and she taught Charles to read, write, and value education. She encouraged him to pursue his love of languages and music and made up for some of the things that Charles's father lacked, though both parents had a strong influence on the boy.

Gabriel was illiterate, but he modeled his life on service and citizenship. Young's father instilled within him that he was not a second-class citizen and that loyalty to race and country were important. Gabriel Young was possibly influenced by Frederick Douglass's declaration "Men of Color to Arms," where Douglass stated that military service offered "a general opportunity to achieve first class citizenship." Young, unlike Flipper, did not grow up among the black bourgeoisie. However, as a boy he was raised in a loving network of black families not far removed from the memories and legacies of bondage. Young's friend William Tweed later stated, "Everything Young did in his life was to show people what African Americans could accomplish." He grew up understanding the need for racial pride. The values instilled in him by his parents helped Young to appreciate his self-worth and allowed him to be willing to tread down paths usually forbidden to African Americans.[3]

Early in Young's life, he began opening doors normally closed to blacks. For example, while in high school, he integrated the foreign language classes. Young loved languages, which would become be a huge asset in his military career. One of Young's white classmates from high school described him as possessing "a good deal of pluck and the backing of the school board" and noted that "Young persevered despite the horrendous treatment of his classmates." Therefore, it is no surprise that later Young was able to survive the harsh treatment he faced at West Point and in the military with a type of ease with which he was uniquely gifted.[4]

After Henry Flipper graduated from West Point in 1877, Young followed Flipper's career closely. He thought that one day he too might be able to attend the military academy. Young graduated from high school with honors in 1881 and went on to teach at a middle school for African American children in his hometown of Ripley. Young shared his monthly salary of thirty-five dollars a month with his mother, givingher twelve dollars out of every paycheck so she would not have to work. However, the opportunity for him to pursue his dream came in 1883 when it was announced that the West Point competitive examination would take place in Hillsboro, Ohio. Young scored perfectly on the written exam and ranked second among all the others competing, eventually replacing the young man who had finished first but decided to withdraw. Therefore, Congressman Alphonso Hart nominated Charles Young for the academy. He left for West Point on June 2, 1884, becoming only the ninth African American ever appointed to the school. David Kilroy, Young's biographer, described his experience at West Point simply as "entering the lion's den and emerging bloodied, but alive."[5]

ENTERING THE LION'S DEN: THE WEST POINT YEARS

When Charles Young spoke of his years at West Point, he did not reflect on them with a fond sense of nostalgia. He was twenty years old when he entered, and he carried the mantle of his race on his shoulders. Luckily for Young, he was not the only black face at West Point; John Hanks Alexander of Ohio had entered the academy in 1883. Normally it was not the policy of the academy to allow upperclassmen and plebes to share rooms. However, because of the unspoken code of silence directed toward black cadets, an exception was made to allow Alexander and Young to be roommates. This helped to ease the difficulties they each faced at the academy.[6]

Young was hazed without mercy while at West Point. He would go days without another cadet speaking to him and received demerits for the most minor of infractions. His nickname was "load of coal" because of his dark skin. Young differed from Flipper and Alexander in this regard because both Alexander and Flipper were fair-skinned. W. E. B. Du Bois, one of Young's closest friends later in life, stated during his eulogy of Young that "no one ever knew the truth about the hell he went through at West Point. He seldom even mentioned it. The pain was too great. When a white southern pigmy at West Point protested at taking food from a dish passed to Young, Young passed it to him first and afterward to himself." It was at West Point that Young learned the discipline and brutality of silence. There were times when he could speak only to his professors, while his classmates treated him as if he was a man without a country. Yet, Young endured because for him it was his duty to persevere and survive. Young stated, "I hold doing my duty as my sole aim in life."[7]

The education Young received at West Point helped prepare him to serve in an imperial army. The course curriculum of West Point focused on engineering and on the European models of battle and taught future officers how to suppress Native American and indigenous uprisings. It could also be argued that the academy indoctrinated Young to believe in the ideology his friend Du Bois would label as the "Talented Tenth." Du Bois believed that it would be a select group of "superior men who would advance and give character to the masses. Du Bois and Young also shared the ideological belief that human history was a chronicle of innovations of a small group of people, not the masses." West Point's pedagogy focused on reinforcing the ideology of exceptionalism, which taught Young and his fellow cadets that they were the small innovative group of people who would shape the course of history.[8]

Young's experience at West Point was far more trying than his high school integration experience. Yet he took something positive from his ordeal: the importance of honor and friendship. He remembered the few white cadets who showed him kindness while at the academy. Even as late as 1915, Young wrote one of his former classmates, Colonel Dehmane Skerrett, and stated,

> You know for me the academy has, even to this day caused me a great many heart aches, in spite of the many advantages I derived there. The sole bright thoughts that come to my heart are the friendship and sympathy from men like you. . . . I could never forget that and have tried to pass along to others the kindness of you all, in America, the Philippines, the West Indies, and Africa. So you can see you cannot always tell the wide reaching influence a word of cheer to even a black man. God knows how many white men I have helped because you all helped me.[9]

Because Young had to repeat his mathematics classes over the summer of 1889, he ended up not graduating with the rest of the classmates he came in with. He finished last in his class of forty-nine students. But Young overcame the many obstacles he faced at West Point because he was able to maintain focus, determination, and strength of character. He would go on to train young black men and encouraged them to keep the same focus, determination, and strength of character in spite of the daily racist attacks they would face in Jim Crow America. Young lived his life as a soldier and leader by the motto of West Point, which is "duty, honor, and country."[10]

A ROCKY START AND THE SHAPING OF YOUNG MINDS

Second Lieutenant Charles Young left West Point and entered the army at the tail end of the Indian Wars. Young joined the Tenth Cavalry in August 1889. He was temporarily transferred to the Twenty-Fourth Infantry but was not happy about being in any other unit than cavalry, so he petitioned and officially joined the Ninth Cavalry with his former classmate and roommate, John Hanks Alexander, and the first black regular army chaplain, Henry V. Plummer.

Young's transition to the Ninth did not sit well with many in his new unit. In fact a few white officers wrote to the *Army and Navy Journal* that they were opposed to having three black officers in the same unit. One officer stated, "Why can't the other three regiments have a share of the colored officers?" Another declared that "white officers will be reluctant to serve with the ninth" if three black officers were in a single unit. Alexander and Young were the only two black line officers in the entire military, and to have them in the same unit was too much for some. The adjutant general of the army wrote in a no-nonsense response, "To have a vacancy fall to him in a white regiment at any moment is to be avoided. . . . As Young had already purchased a cavalry uniform and wanted cavalry, he was transferred to the first vacancy in a colored regiment which happened to be the Ninth and he has now been confirmed by the Senate and commissioned in the Ninth." The army for all of its segregationist policies did not tolerate insubordination from any officer, white or black. In fact, in some ways the army was more progressive in how it dealt with blacks than the civilian world was, quickly and effectively shutting down white objections to having more than a single black officer in one unit.[11]

Young, after his difficult years at West Point, was more than likely eager to serve with Alexander. If he, as an officer, had been placed in any of the other black units, he would not have been able to socialize with the non-commissioned officers and, because of racial segregationist etiquette, would have remained separated from the white officers. He wanted to avoid the isolation of West Point again and got his wish. Young demonstrated early in his career, by protesting being put in an infantry unit, that he would not simply abide the bureaucracy of the military and was willing to fight for what he felt was just. As a duty-bound soldier, Young was reluctant to risk insubordination, so he was careful about the fights that he chose.[12]

While stationed at Fort Robinson, Young and Alexander kept to themselves. Alexander helped Young adjust to garrison life by living by a simple philosophy: "No man can force himself into society anywhere. I have gained the respect of my associate officers by keeping in the background and not intruding myself where I possibly might not be wanted." Young abided by this philosophy throughout his military career.[13]

Lieutenant Young did not remain stationed in the West for long. In 1894, Lieutenant John Hanks Alexander died suddenly while he was getting his hair cut in Wilberforce, Ohio, where he was the military science instructor for Wilberforce University. The Ohio National Guard escorted his body, because regardless of color, Alexander was a West Point graduate and deserved to be escorted with full military honors. Young took the loss of his friend hard, and years after Alexander's death, in a letter to another friend, he fondly mentioned how much he missed his brother-in-arms and wished he was still there.

With Alexander's death and Flipper's dishonorable discharge in 1883, Young was the only black line officer in the army. The president of Wilberforce University wanted Young to replace Alexander as military science instructor. However, the adjutant general was reluctant to allow the transfer, because in 1893 Congress had passed a law requiring all officers to serve at least five years in the field before getting detached service. Yet Young was indeed granted a leave of absence and was given the detail of professor of military science at Wilberforce beginning September 1, 1894.[14]

Charles Young's return to Ohio was in many ways bittersweet. It was a tremendous opportunity for him to assume the duty of professor of military science at Wilberforce, but he was replacing his dear friend and in many ways his brother. Nevertheless, Young arrived at Wilberforce and continued his duty to racially uplift the hearts and minds of young black men. During his first year at Wilberforce, Young formed a lifelong friendship with another new arrival to the university, a young professor of Latin and Greek who would go on to alter the course of history and forever change both their lives, W. E. B. Du Bois.[15]

Du Bois arrived at Wilberforce fresh out of Harvard with his PhD. Young's responsibilities also included teaching mathematics and French, while Du Bois taught English, German, and history. According to one of Du Bois's biographers, David Levering Lewis, "Young was the first genuine male friendship in Du Bois' life." They bonded over their love of languages and their disdain over the hyper-religious atmosphere that surrounded Wilberforce. Neither would attend the annual revival held at the university, which according to Du Bois was more of an interruption than a celebration. Young and Du Bois shared in the belief of the "Talented Tenth" and worked for the remainder of their lives toward the racial uplift of African Americans.[16]

While teaching and training young men and women at Wilberforce, Young was able to focus on the social uplift of his students. He served as a mentor to many young black men who would later become officers in the all-black battalion of the Ohio National Guard. Lieutenant Young encouraged his students always to strive to be good citizens. Young considered himself an enlightened thinker and had his own conceptualization of race. He argued in his book, *Military Morale of Nations and Races*, that "a good citizen should be involved in the political process, education, a voter, and a homeowner." In instilling these ideals into both the men he trained and the students he taught, Young demonstrated his devotion to race and country. He was a dedicated educator and distinguished himself from other African American leaders of the day by promoting a liberal or classical education over the industrial model of education advocated by Booker T. Washington and his supporters. He was able to match wits with Du Bois and share poetry with Paul Laurence Dunbar when he visited his home in Ohio.[17]

The constant bombardment upon the self-esteem of young blacks by Jim Crow America motivated Young to empower young black men through military service, education, and training. It was black soldiers who in many ways were able to express their full rights as citizens because of their ability to serve in the military. Charles Young understood all of this and incorporated it into his pedagogy to ensure that his students knew that their service, whether it be public or private, was a reflection on both race and country.[18]

"MR. DYNAMITE"

The outbreak of the Spanish-American-Cuban War energized those in the African American community to volunteer and support their men in uniform. Young, at Wilberforce at the start of war in 1898, was anxious to rejoin his unit, the Ninth Cavalry, but he was asked to take command of the Ninth Ohio Battalion of the Ohio National Guard by Governor Asa Bushnell. Young would be commissioned as a major and would be in charge of appointing all personnel for the entire unit. Young accepted the position and assigned many of his former students as officers in this new unit.

When Young took command of the all-black unit, he received national attention from both the black and white press. The *Cleveland Gazette* followed Young's service closely and reported almost daily on the unit's activities. In fact, it was the *Gazette* that reported Young's nickname of "Mr. Dynamite," given by his men. However, not all the reports about Major Young were positive. One soldier, T. Miles Dewey, complained to the *Gazette*, "Major Young drills them to death. . . . For white visitors he puts on a good show, but he does not do the same for black visitors." Young's response to those who criticized him for being too harsh was, "We are trying to make soldiers out of these boys; and the Yellow journals are trying to turn them into tin soldiers." The Ninth Ohio was visited by Major Charles Douglass, the son of Frederick Douglass; President McKinley; and the Governor Bushnell. In some ways, the position might have been a high-water mark for Young, given the attention from politicians and the press. It is also worth noting that this would be the only time in his career that Young would command an entire battalion of black soldiers and officers.[19]

The Ninth Ohio never saw action during the fighting in Cuba and Puerto Rico and was mustered out in 1899. Several black newspapers campaigned to possibly appoint Henry O. Flipper to one of the other black National Guard units with Young. However, Flipper completely rejected the idea publicly and in a letter to Booker T. Washington went on to talk rather negatively about the black militia units. Young, unlike Flipper, eagerly embraced serving with the black Ohio Guard, and it was the position as battalion commander that propelled him into the national discourse of the African American press. Flipper, at the same time, was trying to get fully reinstated and rejected all offers to serve in militia units. Flipper's continued refusal of various positions within the African American community, such as possibly teaching at one of the black colleges or universities, helps to further explain why there was never any national campaign to reinstate him in the army or clear his name during his lifetime. Flipper in many ways made a secret covenant to keep black America at arm's length, and black America reciprocated. In contrast, African Americans eagerly supported Young, and in turn the major relished his status as a role model. The way he embraced his role in the National Guard and his teaching position at Wilberforce demonstrated Young's dedication to supporting his race by turning young men into soldiers and leaders. He took his duty seriously, and this helped to further define him as a race man.[20]

After his service with the Ninth Ohio was over, Major Young was transferred to the Seventh South Carolina National Guard unit stationed at Camp Algers. Several white officers there refused to salute Major Young. However, when the camp commandant found out about this situation, he brought

Young and one of the known white insubordinates into his office. He asked Major Young to remove his jacket and place it on the chair. The commander then made the white soldier salute the chair. He next instructed Young to put the jacket back on, and the white soldier was told to salute the major. While at Camp Algers, Young did not have that problem again. The military prides itself on order and structure, the hierarchy of the military must be respected, and whether or not you respect the man, you will respect the uniform—that is what the Camp Algers commander was trying to illustrate. The respect that black men in uniform commanded is one of the reasons Young and other leaders within the African American community encouraged young black men to serve and wear the uniform proudly.[21]

THE CULTURED GENTLEMAN

When Young finished his service with the Ninth Ohio National Guard and his unit was mustered out in 1899, the U.S. became intertwined in open conflict with the Filipino rebels after the terms of the Treaty of Paris were revealed. Lieutenant William P. Colonel Duvall of the Twenty-Sixth Volunteer Infantry asked Young to join his all-black unit as a captain. His greater rank as major in the Ninth was only temporary in the National Guard. Young, however, asserted himself as a true race man and responded to the colonel's offer by simply stating, "I think I must decline anything less than a field officer's position in an organization where my people would expect me to be Colonel or at least Lieutenant Colonel and the considerations of seven million of a race of people is not ignored by me." Young's racial awareness and his respect for the attention he received from the African American community demonstrated his acceptance of his role as a symbol of racial pride. President McKinley even wanted Young to take this position because of the mounting pressure from the black press's "no officers, no fight campaign." Yet, the adjutant general conceded to Young's request to rejoin his unit, the Ninth Cavalry.[22]

Young resumed his duties as a first lieutenant in the Ninth Cavalry. He did have a difficult time initially adjusting to being a lieutenant after serving as battalion commander with the rank of major. He was also disappointed at not being able to lead his troops of the Ohio unit into battle. Despite not fighting in the trenches with a battalion he trained, he ensured his men were capable of fighting if the need ever arose again. Some of those men did go on to serve in Negro Volunteer Units as officers in the Philippines. First Sergeant W. H. Nicholas described Young as an officer who expected the best of his troops:

Captain Young used horseflesh to its fullest capacity, with no abuse to either horse nor man. He was one of us. He was always fair and just, particularly void of pettiness and prejudice. When it came to duty, he was positive and firm never using dogmatic commands or ideas. He was kind and polite, respected all men regardless of race or color for their knowledge and worth to mankind, and at all times, a cultured gentleman.[23]

When Young arrived in the Philippines in April 1901, he was promoted to the rank of captain. He was commander of Troop I and would finally lead troops in combat in the jungles of the Philippines. His troops nick-named him "Follow Me" because he demonstrated fearlessness in battle. His unfaltering nature in battle helped further secure his place as a man to be respected by African Americans.[24]

Young's reputation was gaining him national recognition from leaders such as Booker T. Washington and T. Thomas Fortune. He was a close friend of Du Bois, so it is not surprising that he was willing to become involved in the national discourse between Washington and Du Bois. In fact, after returning to the states following his service in the Philippines, Young gave a speech in 1903 at Stanford University titled "The Ideals of the Negroes in the United States." In it Young was very clear in his criticism of the Tuskegee model of education. When he gave the speech he was the highest-ranking African American officer in the regular army. The fact that he chose to chime in on the validity of industrial education solving the "Negro problem" was unique, because other African American officers essentially remained silent about the debate. It is a sign of Young's confidence in his popularity, as well as of his own fortitude, that he supported Du Bois's vision and risked retaliation from whites and the Tuskegee Machine. Young demonstrated his willingness to fight for the cause of all his people, and his philosophy of racial equality was not one of accommodation. Young asserted his frus-trations with the white discourse on the "Negro problem":

> You have given a few thousands of dollars to Booker T. Washington in order to solve this problem. You have put this money into the slot machine to have the problem solved while you wait. This is not a solution by itself. For when the Negro is given industrial training he is often refused work. We have been told to give up altogether the hope of higher education. But even Tuskegee itself would not exist without the existence of the higher educated Negro and this

advice is offered to us in the hopes of triumphs in painting a picture in the Salon of Paris, poetry of Dunbar, the sculpting of Lewis, and our national instinct for music which is greater than any other race. We are between the devil, which would bid us give up hope, and the deep blue sea of our ambitions that are surging in our hearts.[25]

Young's audience was predominantly white, and he advocated for equality and an education that went beyond simply being trained to serve. Young went on to say,

We know what it is to eat our own hearts. We know what it is to stifle our aspirations, to have our efforts derided, the finger of scorn pointed at us because we fail to reach the level of the white man. ... This feeling is not the result of higher education of the Negro, but it is the result of the American Negro manhood.

Young's bold statement at this time highlighted the importance of raising the self-esteem of young blacks during the tumultuous Jim Crow era.[26] Young closed his speech with this declaration:

In every man, it is said there is a tiger, a pig, an ass and a nightingale. I do not know as to the white race, but I do know that my race has something of the ferocity of the tiger, the selfishness, which the pig represents, the patience of the ass. I do believe that you all have the spirit of the nightingale, representing those things that rise and soar and go upward. ... I do come to demand that as you love your country you will not disgrace its escutcheon by oppression.[27]

The sentiments expressed in this speech place Young within the discourse of the major race leaders at the turn of the century. For a military officer to be so outspoken in favor of civil rights was rare at that (or any other) time in American history, and he set the mold for other officers who followed.

IN THE LAND OF REVOLUTION AND COCKROACHES

By the turn of the twentieth century, Charles Young had firmly established himself as a trailblazer within the military. In 1904, he set yet another precedent for African American soldiers, serving as a park ranger. Young and the Ninth Cavalry were detached to protect the newly established Sequoia National Park in California. Not long after Young gave his Stanford speech and had finished a successful stint as the superintendent of the Sequoia National Park, he was appointed military attaché to Hispaniola, the island comprised of Haiti and the Dominican Republic.

The United States, at the very end of the nineteenth century, was attempting to assert itself as a global power, and with the addition of the Roosevelt Corollary to the Monroe Doctrine, the U.S. even more directly sought dominance throughout the Western Hemisphere. Young was thus one of twenty military attachés sent around the world by the U.S. military and the State Department. In Hispaniola, he was charged with mapping the island and gathering information about the military strengths of both countries. Ironically, when the U.S. later invaded Haiti and occupied the island from 1915 to 1932, the military work of this committed "race man" undermined black self-determination; Young's maps and intelligence helped greatly with the U.S. Marine invasion and occupation.[28]

Captain Young had a number of qualities that led to his selection: his West Point background, his language skills, his training and experience in the Philippines, his time spent with the cavalry on the western frontier, and, of course, the color of his skin. Young learned Haitian Creole and made a detailed manual of the language for the U.S. military. He easily navigated around the island because he was able to blend in fairly easily. Young's service in Haiti also provided the opportunity for him to a write a play about the revolutionary life of Toussaint L'Ouverture, who was a national hero to Haitians and African Americans. And it was while he was in Haiti that he decided to write *Military Morale of Nations and Races*.

The purpose of this book was to provide psychological evidence that directly challenged the racist ideology claiming African Americans were inferior to whites. It was also an analysis and discussion of the military capacities of various nations and races and an examination of the effects of European imperialism and colonialism on the modern and developing world. Young stated, "The intent of this study is to show how the spirit of the man can be fortified, the loins of his courage girded up, and his soul and body give themselves in willing effort if need be, for the triumph of the best interests and ideals of his country." He then opened the book with a discussion of the famous Fort Wagner charge and with a discussion and definition of the word "morale," addressing the psychological warfare being committed against the black community. The book was published in 1912, during the rapid expansion of the American eugenics movement.

Throughout *Military Morale*, Young discussed his philosophies of various nations and the morale of men fighting in different parts of the world and considered who made the best soldiers. According to Young, soldiers of African descent were not the cowards and animals described in the white press. He asserted,

> As a soldier, in Africa, in the English army and in America, the Negro has been a success, measured by the white man's standards and as penned by the historians and testified by his white officers. In spite of the disadvantages of prejudice to which they are at times subjugated, their trainability, military pride, good nature, obedient spirit, and heroism in the hottest fight have won them the highest encomiums from even their enemies.

Young, however, did espouse a Eurocentric view of Liberia and other West African nations: "With exception of the small independent republic of Liberia on the West coast, the other African peoples should be classed as tribes. Some of these are barbarous and very little lifted above the animal in the scale of humanity and others are progressive, displaying an aptitude for agriculture, commerce, and even government." Young demonstrated that despite his progressive views on social and racial uplift, he was still a product of an Americanized view of the world.[29]

Haiti's political instability concerned American interests in the Caribbean. A state department official stated, "Captain Young is probably a precautionary measure adopted because of the chaotic conditions and political affairs in that country." Young also viewed the conditions in Haiti—which he described as "the land of revolution, surprises, and cockroaches"—as chaotic and fully supported U.S. military occupation. He even asserted that Haiti's democratic government was more autocratic by nature because the Haitian people preferred that type of political structure. In fact, in his reports to the War Department, he stated that U.S. occupation would probably be necessary in order to provide stability on the island. It was perhaps these sentiments that led to Young's tumultuous relationship with the Haitian government.[30]

He served for over two years, by which time the Haitians had grown suspicious of Young. The Haitian government did not like how easily Young blended in with the general population, and they grew even more mistrustful because of all the sketches of the island Young had in his possession. Young's clerk, Charles Stephens, broke into his office one weekend while Young was away, stole classified documents out of his desk, and sold them to the Haitian government for $600. By 1907, Young's relationship with the

Haitian government had deteriorated. The Haitian press presented Young as an American spy sent to undermine their government. In order to defuse the situation, the State Department recalled Young.[31]

After his service in Haiti, Young reunited with the Ninth Cavalry in 1908 and was detailed to the Philippines. While there, Young continued his push for expanding education for the Filipino population. He aided Ben Davis Sr. in preparing for his lieutenant's exam and helped him to be promoted from the ranks of the enlisted. He also encouraged the continued use of the Philippine Constabulary Band. Young's love of music and his push for music education within the regiments helped to firmly integrate the regimental bands. It should be noted that it was the U.S. Army's black regimental bands that first introduced jazz to the world during the World War I.[32]

Captain Young returned to the U.S. and was stationed briefly at Fort D. A. Russell in Wyoming before being chosen to serve as military attaché to Liberia. The army admittedly struggled to find a place for Young. He was due for another promotion, but since there were still white officers who did not want to work with a black officer who outranked them, Young was sent overseas to help the Liberian Frontier Force (LFF).[33]

IN LIBERIA

"Ex-president G. W. Gibson Chairman of the Liberia Commission to America in 1908 called for the paternal care of the U.S. towards Liberia and the whole of his country looking expectantly to that great country for relief," read the *Washington Bee* on January 22, 1910, highlighting the growing Pan-African vision held by many African Americans at that time. Liberia was facing a territorial crisis from the French and British colonial powers and looked to America for assistance in maintaining its independence. Liberia had a tenuous foundation and had to fend off European imperialism on a consistent basis. The country asked for and received American funding to protect and secure its sovereignty and borders. However, it still had to make serious concessions to the colonial powers. Historian Claude Clegg observes, "Territorial conflicts between Monrovia and European colonial powers date back to the early republic. The Liberian government also had to contend with indigenous African resistance to the expansion of Liberian authority since the arrival of the first black repatriates."[34]

So, it was no surprise when the weary Liberian government asked for assistance from its quasi-colonial ruler, the United States. In 1909, an American commission, comprising Roland Faulkner, George Sale, and Emmett J. Scott, was sent to Liberia. The commission's goal was to investigate whether or not the U.S. should formally assist the Liberian government. Yet, it also wanted to ensure that Liberia could still maintain its own autonomy if it received aid from America. The findings of the commission, among other things, led to Young's assignment in Liberia.

In 1877, upon his graduation from West Point, Henry Flipper had been asked by the Liberian government to take charge of the Liberian militia, but he declined and completely rejected the notion of supporting African American migration to Liberia. This decision by Flipper was yet another major difference between Young and Flipper. Young supported both a free and independent Liberia and those who chose to migrate there. The Pan-African connection was something that was growing stronger within the black community, and Young advocated the strengthening of ties between the United States and Liberia. Therefore, when the commission recommended that the LFF should be reorganized under the command and training of African American officers from the U.S. Army, Charles Young wound up being one of the officers appointed to restructure and organize the LFF.[35]

Lieutenant Benjamin O. Davis Sr., Young's protégé, was the Liberian attaché in 1912. When Davis became ill, Booker T. Washington and Oswald Villard recommended that Young take over for him, an assignment he accepted on May 12, 1912. Davis had attempted to reform the LFF, but he was not particularly effective. Davis viewed the Liberian army negatively and relayed as much to Young before he arrived to take his place, calling it and the militia "worthless." In a detailed letter to Young, Davis explained that the whole political system and structure, not just the military, needed to be reorganized.[36]

Not long after his arrival in Liberia, in August 1912, Young was promoted to major. Young's primary responsibility there was to reorganize the LFF and the Constabulary. However, his responsibilities soon became far more than those of a military attaché. Young made it known that he adamantly opposed any sort of racial segregation and the denial of basic rights and citizenship solely on the premise of race: "Let no American forget that the flag stands for all we were, are, and destined to be; for the freedom, right, justice, and opportunity which must come to all that nobly strive to deserve them."[37]

As a believer in Du Bois's "Talented Tenth" ideology, Young supported the idea of having African American men and women migrate to Liberia in order to help civilize and stabilize the country. One of Young's biographers referred to him as a "civilized soldier." It can be argued that Young was trained at West Point to serve in an imperial army. West Point's institutional structure encouraged notions of national and racial superiority and did not support the belief that change would be best for the proletariat. Young and the three black officers who accompanied him to Liberia—Major Wilson Ballard, Captain Arthur Brown, and Captain Richard Newton, all Wilberforce alums and Young's trainees—were going to help "civilize Liberia." These men took pride in what they were doing; they felt it was their duty to uplift the race at home and abroad. Major Ballard served in the Philippines with Young as well and would be the field commander of the LFF while it was being restructured.

Ballard remained in Liberia after Young was recalled home but left in 1915 to continue his dental practice. In a letter to Liberian president D. E. Howard, Young discussed Ballard's reluctance in leaving Liberia:

> As to the Major's going, it was a matter of casting his lot with the Republic for good and all or of going at the time that he did; one cannot remain from his profession and slump in it. I know he hesitated a long time in making up his mind to go or stay; this is because of his affection for you and the Liberian Idea in general.

Young and Ballard supported the Liberian cause and knew that it would take a lot more time to enact the necessary changes to make the Liberian Republic successful in their minds.[38]

The other two officers, Brown and Newton, were eager to go to Liberia because they would get to serve and be well compensated. Ballard earned $2,000 a year for his service; Brown and Newton, $1,600 a year. Young, the ranking officer, earned even more and was able to send his children to boarding school in Holland and still maintain his home with his mother in Xenia, Ohio. Such salaries helped to establish a precedent to encourage future black officers to serve in Liberia.

The Liberian Frontier Force was supposed to be a standing army, but in 1912 it was in a state of disorganization and near mutiny. Major Young and his unit had their work cut out for them. Many soldiers had not been paid in over three years. Young believed that the Africans, persistently influenced by the corruptive Europeans, allowed an environment of greed, dishonesty, and deceit within their society. Young accepted at face value many pro-Western ideals, yet he remained critical of European colonization and influence over Africa and felt obliged as an African American citizen to help Liberia, whose success in self-government would give courage and hope and whose failure would bring disenchantment and disgrace for the entire African diaspora. Young and his fellow black officers had a very global perspective when approaching the success or failure of a black nation. In fact, there was a very strong possibility of Liberia's failure in 1909. Therefore, it is not surprising that these men and the U.S. government were so willing to secure Liberian independence.

The Field Operations division was successful in getting its program for the LFF in place under the command of Major Ballard. The primary difficulty that both Ballard and Young faced was determining who should be an officer in the LFF. The Americo-Liberians were prejudiced against the indigenous population, and felt it was their right to be officers. Additionally, the LFF was constantly struggling against European imperialists and African rebels. In fact, Young, at the request of the Liberian president, had to embark on a rescue mission into the interior to help relieve Captain Brown. Young's experience in the interior forced him to reevaluate his perception of the indigenous people of Liberia. He found that the Americo-Liberians were guilty of committing atrocities no different from the terrorist tactics used by white southerners against African Americans back in the U.S. Young's interior trip influenced his drafting of a new policy toward the indigenous people that was not so antiquated and oppressive. Young also lobbied the U.S. government for additional military and financial assistance. He asserted that it would be in the best interest of the United States if Liberia remained independent of European control. Another one of Young's contributions to Liberia's military was the establishment of a military academy to properly train soldiers and officers. He encouraged the Liberian government to allow both Americo-Liberians and indigenous men to attend.[39]

However, while Young may have been moved to be more sympathetic to the indigenous population, Major Ballard took the opposite approach. He became known as a tormentor. When Young came down with malaria and Ballard assumed temporary control, many Liberians were worried. Ballard was not the only black officer accused of excessive force and violence. Captain Brown's wife, Rosa Brown, accused her husband of beheadings and committing other atrocities against the indigenous population. Yet Young made it very clear to his American officers that he did not approve of these tactics, and one of the key components of Young's reform of the LFF was to limit abuses by officers who were exercising excessive brutality in the frontier conflicts. When Young and the other officers were recalled in 1915 after the start of World War I, they left the LFF in far better condition than they found it. According to historian Claude Clegg, "Young and the other African-American military reformers arguably played an important role in recasting the organizational structure of the LFF. From eliminating the much abused tradition of fusing military and civilian authorities, the officers had an impact that was quite significant."[40]

It can be argued it was the persistence and commitment of these black American officers that allowed Liberia to successfully continue as an independent nation and not become subject to European colonial rule. Young was able to establish a military training academy and to exercise a certain level of power and authority within the Liberian government that superseded the authority initially assigned to him. Young not only acted as an officer but also assumed the role of a diplomat, carefully navigating between the Liberian and American governments to help ensure the longevity of this nation. Among his many accomplishments, Young petitioned the U.S. government to issues loans and send the U.S. Navy to help protect the Liberian border and advocated for human and civil rights within Liberia as well as in the United States. He shaped America's policies in Liberia like no other American diplomat and helped to restructure in some ways America's foreign policy toward Africa. Young's insistence in his reports to the State Department that Liberia needed to remain independent facilitated financial support for Liberia. And he informed the American government about the anti-American propaganda being spread along the West Coast of Africa by both the British and the French. It could be argued that, prior to Liberia asking for assistance, the U.S. did not include Africa within its sphere of foreign policy. Young helped to lay the foundation for the U.S. to intervene on behalf of the Liberians during World War I by sending the Navy to secure Liberian ports and to support its military in its defense and suppression of indigenous rebellions.

Young's service in Liberia was considered such a success that he would go on to win the NAACP's Spingarn Medal for his service there. Secretary of State Robert Lansing wrote of Young's service, "Due to Maj. Young's watchful efforts, much good has been accomplished in patrolling the British and French boundaries, in the construction of roads, and, to a great extent, in preventing uprisings of native Liberian tribes. . . . Maj. Young has been found most valuable." When Major Charles Young returned to the U.S., he was the highest-ranking black line officer in the army and the first African American to achieve field grade rank.[41]

THE MEXICAN EXPEDITION

After Young's service in Liberia, he was sent right back into the field and was posted with the Tenth Cavalry at Fort Huachuca, Texas. This was the first time Young served with the regiment, yet there were many familiar faces in it from his time with the Ninth Cavalry. He arrived at Fort Huachuca on February 28, 1916. The fort was located along the U.S.–Mexico border, where tensions had been high since 1911. The power struggle in Mexico culminated with the dictator President Porfiò Diaz being replaced by Francesco Madero. General Victoriano Huerta eventually overthrew Madero, but President Woodrow Wilson refused to recognize his government in 1913. So in 1916, the Mexican revolutionary leader Francisco "Pancho" Villa, who controlled much of northern Mexico, began making raids into Texas and New Mexico, killing Americans and destroying property. It is no surprise that Wilson ordered him captured or killed. Major General Frederick Funston ordered Brigadier General John J. Pershing to capture Villa. One of the regular squadrons of Pershing's "Punitive Expedition" was a part of Young's Tenth Cavalry.[42]

Young reunited with his old friend Chaplin George W. Prioleau; they had known each other since they taught at Wilberforce together. Young was appointed second in command of the Second Cavalry Brigade. He was promoted to the rank of lieutenant colonel and led the Second Squadron of the Tenth Cavalry. Young's field promotion and command suggested the strong possibility of his being promoted to the rank of brigadier general. General Pershing was very impressed with Young's performance as a leader and his performance in battle.

Young was proud of his promotion, yet he never forgot about the type of racial climate that African Americans were experiencing at home. He was able to raise $600 from among his troops and sent it to the anti-lynching fund, evidence that Young was concerned and active in the fight for civil rights for African Americans.[43]

His leadership during the Mexican Punitive Expedition caused problems among the white officers who were his subordinates. Colonel Young was put in charge of the Tenth Cavalry after General Pershing was promoted to major general; at this point Young was the first black officer to ever take command of the Tenth Cavalry. His promotion received national attention in the black press, and it brought about negative attention from white southern officers, who in some instances petitioned President Wilson and Secretary of War Newton Baker that they not be made to serve under Young's command.

Lieutenant Albert Dockery of the Tenth Cavalry was one such officer who refused to serve in the same unit as Young and demanded a transfer to an all-white unit. Dockery wrote his father and his father then wrote Mississippi senator John Sharp Williams, who in turn went on to contact

President Wilson. After receiving Senator Williams's letter, Wilson contacted Secretary Baker:

> Albert B. Dockery, First Lieutenant of the Tenth Cavalry now stationed at Fort Huachuca, Arizona, is a southerner and finds it not only distasteful but practically impossible to serve under a colored commander. The Tenth Cavalry is temporarily in the command of Lt. Colonel Charles Young and I am afraid from what I learned that there may be some serious and perhaps even tragic insubordination on Lt. Dockery's part if he is left under Colonel Young, who is a colored man.[44]

Baker discussed with President Wilson how he too received letters from several senators who spoke on behalf of officers who "were under the same embarrassment as Lieutenant Dockery." Baker generally responded to the complaints of these officers by either getting them reassigned to other regiments or reminding them of the oath they took when joining the army.[45]

THE GREAT WAR AND FORCED RETIREMENT

After his service with the Mexican Punitive Expedition, Young had high expectations of being promoted to the rank of full colonel and eventually brigadier general. Young's promotion seemed inevitable; he was the most senior officer up for promotion and Adjutant General Henry P. McCain supported Young's promotion and requested his health evaluation.

Young believed that he would be most useful training black soldiers and officers for the upcoming war in Europe. In fact, while stationed at Fort Huachuca, Young, as a part of the preparedness movement, initiated an officers' training camp in 1917.[46] In a letter between Young and Special Assistant to the War Department Emmett J. Scott, they discussed that Young would be put in charge of the black officers' training camp in Des Moines, Iowa. Scott stated, "I was just as sure as I could be about anything that you would be put in charge of the training for colored officers at Des Moines." It was thus a surprise to Scott and many in the black community that Young was ordered to Presidio, California for a physical examination.[47]

After that exam, Charles Young was forcibly retired on July 30, 1917, almost four months after the U.S. declaration of war on Germany. News of his retirement swept across the black community and ignited a nationwide protest for his reinstatement. The official line was that Young was retired because he suffered from high blood pressure, chronic intestinal nephritis, scrota arties, and hypertrophy of the left ventricle. However, Young's retirement seemed rather suspicious to many, including Young. [48]

Political pressure was on the president and the secretary of war to ensure that Young did not end up in command of white soldiers. Therefore, Young's questionable status of his health and his unwillingness to retire helped start a movement within the black community to have Young reinstated.[49]

The Wilson administration solicited the advice of Arthur Spingarn of the NAACP and Emmett Scott, who both concluded that for the overall morale of the black community, several things needed to happen for them to support the war; one of them was Young's reinstatement. In the "Bill of Particulars," published in various black newspapers, they made fourteen demands on behalf of the African American community; Charles Young's reinstatement and promotion was number eight on the list. Secretary of War Baker informed President Wilson of the growing anxiety and unrest among the black community. The black press played a crucial role in relaying and publicizing the demands of the African American community and applying pressure to the government. Additionally, the Negro Silent Protest was held on August 1, 1917, against racial violence and the continued violation of African American civil rights. The Committee of 100 Colored Citizens at the start of the war had already put pressure on President Wilson about the African American community's frustrations with the constant violations of black civil rights through racial violence and Jim Crow segregation. There was also the growing push for a national anti-lynching legislation. All of this activism was tied to the demands for the reinstatement and promotion of Charles Young to full active duty.[50]

THE LAST RIDE OF CHARLES YOUNG

The unexpected discharge of Lieutenant Colonel Young served as another slap in the face for the black soldier. Young felt it was his personal duty to help "build the self-esteem of young black men and hoped to help them to overcome the strong sense of innate inferiority that so many black men felt in the face of constant and persistent racial propaganda from the white community." Young considered himself a "race warrior out to slay the dragon of racial inferiority." He was very active in the NAACP and eventually served on the executive board. Young was a hero to many African Americans. Many of the headlines in the black press called Young the "Greatest Negro Soldier." Young was on his way to becoming the first black general, but in July 1917 that dream was officially dashed, when Young was declared unfit for duty and discharged from the army. Young had many supporters, including General "Black Jack" Pershing and Theodore Roosevelt. Roosevelt had in fact proposed to Young that they should raise an all-black regiment together to go fight in World War I. He later wrote to Young expressing his disappointment at not being able to join the fight: "We are both in the same boat now, not being needed by our government in a time of war."[51]

In an attempt to prove he was fit for duty in Europe, Young decided he would ride his horse from his home in Ohio to Washington, D.C. In June 1918, he started on his 495-mile journey on horseback. Traveling 31 miles a day, he arrived on June 22, met by a very surprised and excited black press. Young's action had captured the attention of the American people, but it was to no avail; he would not be reinstated. The Wilson administration would not allow Young back into the military on active duty. This was a hard blow to the black community, especially for the soldiers. It seemed that there was a glass ceiling in the military for African Americans, and Charles Young had found it. The race riots of 1919, the rise of the Ku Klux Klan, and the dishonorable treatment of one of black America's most beloved heroes helped to fuel a movement of change within the black community.[52]

Young became very vocal in the press, challenging the prevailing myths about blacks being unfit to serve as officers in the military. Young stated in the *Washington Bee* on July 7, 1917, "The Negro people of the world over more than any other race lends themselves to service and sacrifice for the love of an ideal." In an earlier letter to the *Cleveland Gazette*, dated May 4, 1916, Young vented his frustration with his current status: "When in the world did I ever play politics or seek personal preferences when the welfare of my race or country depended upon my actions?"

Young was reinstated in the Ohio National Guard in 1918 and promoted to the rank of colonel, five days prior to the armistice in Europe. The unit was burdened with administrative problems and would not see any action in the war. In 1919, the State Department sent Young back to Liberia. At the Omega Psi Phi annual conclave right before he left for Liberia, Young gave a final speech in which he stated, "I want to share with you lot for I fear that this will be my last opportunity." He said he heard "the call of the Gods to make these last days his best." Young knew that this was to be his final service to his race and country.[53]

On December 12, 1921, Charles Young, while on a secret mission to Nigeria, entered into the hospital. He died January 8, 1922, of black water fever. Young was buried with full military honors in Lagos, Nigeria, but his family and the African American community wanted his body returned to the United States. A year and a half later, Colonel Charles Young's body arrived in Harlem, New York, on June 2, 1923, and his body was under the escort of the Honor Guard of the New York Fifteenth Infantry, the New York National Guard, a company of Marcus Garvey's Universal Negro Improvement Association Guard, and Boy Scouts and Girl Scouts of America. His remains lay in state for several hours, and his lifelong friend W. E. B. Du Bois gave his eulogy. Du Bois stated angrily, "Young died of a broken heart." His body was then taken to Washington, D.C., so he could be buried at Arlington National Cemetery. Young's service was so large that it was held at Arlington's Amphitheatre, which is rarely used. The day of his burial was made a national holiday for African Americans nationwide, and there were countless memorial services for Young several decades after his death. The African American community gave Colonel Charles Young one of the most notable military funerals the nation's capital has ever seen. Over 100,000 people lined the streets to pay their final respects to the fallen officer. Young was honored in death in the way he deserved to be honored while he had lived.[54]

In the annals of military history, there are very few African American trailblazers. There is Benjamin O. Davis Sr., the first African American general, and Colin Powell, first African American chief of staff. However, before any of these men made their way into history, there was Charles Young. Young set the standard for black officers in the military. He embraced carrying the mantle for both his race and his country. Charles Young was more than just an officer; he was a race leader.

CONCLUSION

> I've had white people tell me, "This is white man's country, white man's country." They don't sing that to the colored man when it comes to war. Then it's all our country, go fight for the country. Go over there and risk his life for the country and come back, he ain't a bit more thought of than before he left.
>
> —Nate Shaw

James Baldwin, in *Notes of a Native Son*, observed that African Americans experienced the rage of the disesteemed. At the end of World War I and during the ensuing violence of the summer of 1919, rage and bitterness filled the hearts and minds of returning soldiers from Europe. Historian Jennifer Keene notes, "The failure of the Great War to deliver its promise of democracy to African Americans emerged as a key theme in several postwar civil rights campaigns." Black soldiers and veterans were going to be at the vanguard of this campaign going forward.[1]

This is why military service mattered so much to the black community. These men were given new tools and training to bring back to the community, which benefited their fight for racial progress. "The Negro race has a right to be proud of the achievements of the colored troops. . . . They were representative of the whole race in conflict," said Edward Johnson, a veteran of the Spanish-American-Cuban-Filipino War. He went on to state, "Let it be said that the black soldier did his duty under the flag, whether that flag protects him or not." Black soldiers' evolution into race men and defiant warriors against white racism allowed these men to exercise their citizenship and manhood. At the end of the Filipino conflict in 1902, they realized it did not matter that they were willing to sacrifice their lives for their country or fight foreign enemies; they would not be seen as equals. They needed to prove to white Americans that they were not going to simply acquiesce to white brutality, which is why the Brownsville uprising of 1906 and the Houston uprising of 1917 occurred.[2]

Scholars of African American soldiers in the post-Vietnam era often present their military service as a kind of paradox and have shifted the narrative of these men away from racial uplift and the long civil rights movement to being tools of American imperial oppression. The antimilitary sentiment within academia continues today. African American soldiers and their activism prior to World War II are often glossed over within the larger narrative of the civil rights movement; yet the Double V campaign would not have happened if not for the activism and organizing of the "no officers, no fight" campaign of the late nineteenth century or the organizing of the African American community of the early twentieth century in pressuring the Wilson administration to commission black officers.

Duty beyond the Battlefield demonstrates that the discourse on these men needs to be shifted toward the actions they performed and roles they held in their communities as soldiers/agents of the federal government. T. G. Steward asserted at the turn of the twentieth century that black soldiers would never accept and had grown impatient with the discriminatory and paternalistic rhetoric of their white officers:

> The colored American soldier, by his own prowess, has won an acknowledged place by the side of the best trained fighters with arms. In the fullness of his manhood he has no rejoicing in patronizing paean, "the colored troops fought nobly," nor does he glow at all when told of his "faithfulness" and "devotion" to his white officers, qualities accentuated to the point where they might well fit an affectionate dog.[3]

It was the vocal objection of black soldiers and the African American community that got Ben Davis Sr. and John E. Green promoted to officers. Such victories helped catapult the NAACP in its early years to success outside the courtroom.[4]

Within the military, by the 1890s the buffalo soldiers had changed from an emphasis on individual citizenship and manhood to racial citizenship and manhood, and as race warriors, they incorporated racial uplift into their identities as soldiers and men. Military service was a means of exercising citizenship, which had been claimed and proven through the Civil War and was one of the few areas to do so during the era of segregation.

Black soldiers' continued evolution into race men and defiant warriors against white racism took another step after the Spanish-American-Cuban-Filipino War. After mustering out, some decided to remain in the Philippines and build lives and families, while others returned home, determined to make progress in the next war. The "no officers, no fight" campaign evolved into a stronger push for an officer training school for blacks during the preparedness movement prior to World War I. The national campaign for African American officers during this period proved successful and helped garner support in the black community for the war in Europe.

The stories of Henry O. Flipper and Charles Young reveal how the themes of racial uplift and the "race man" ideology played out in the lives of two black officers. Flipper rejected the possibility of serving as a race leader through his determination to refuse leadership positions in all-black militias and National Guard units during the Spanish-American-Cuban War and through his criticisms of the Twenty-Fourth Infantry during the Houston uprising of 1917. He was subsequently forgotten during his lifetime because of his rejections. Charles Young, on the other hand, thrived as a professor of military science at Wilberforce University, accepted leadership in the Ohio National Guard, and went to Liberia to train the Liberian Frontier Force. Additionally, Young served on the board of directors of the NAACP and was supported in the black press and the black community. Young's reinstatement and promotion after being forcibly retired from the army served as a victory for some African American leaders. The funeral of Charles Young ended up being a holiday in the black community, and memorials were celebrated across the country for many years after his death.

Black soldiers were more radicalized and militant in the post–World War I era. Despite the rising tide of racial violence domestically, many of these men expanded their concerns and activism toward a Pan-African vision and advocated for change for the entire African Diaspora. Their overall status as American citizens became more secure because of their participation in the draft and the expansion of ROTC programs on twelve black colleges and universities. Rienzi Lemus of the Twenty-Fifth Infantry, for example, would leave the service in 1918 after serving twenty years and go on to help organize the Brotherhood of Dining Car Porters. Lemus successfully led his union in its lobbying effort for the eight-hour workday with the U.S. Railroad Administration in 1920, exemplifying the type of activist soldier who used his position and skills as a soldier to fight for the rights of the oppressed.[5]

In the civilian world, Black Nationalism and rapid urbanization helped to encourage migration. Between 1910 and 1920, nearly 500,000 southern blacks moved from the rural South to several major metropolitan cities throughout the North. By the time the stock market crashed in 1929, nearly 1.25 million blacks had emigrated from the South to the North. The complete disenfranchisement of blacks in the South and rule of mob violence, along with increased opportunities for economic and social betterment in the North, drove these people out of the South. After World War I, white America believed it had crushed the dreams of democracy and equality for black veterans. But if one looks closer at the language and activism by African Americans, one will see clearly that in spite of racists' best efforts, blacks found a way to thrive and force the world to truly see the "New Negro" who emerged during the Jazz Age. The strategy was laid out for the next war so that after World War II the U.S. military desegregated, something unthinkable forty years earlier.[6]

Black veterans returning from service overseas contributed to the growing frustration that African Americans had with the Jim Crow South. The freedom they experienced abroad encouraged their interest in and support of Pan-Africanism and their militancy against not only Jim Crow racism but also the continued segregation within the military. The status of soldiers as leaders in and heroes to the black community laid the groundwork for and was the backbone of the activism and eventual expansion of blacks in the military during World War II, helping to influence the future leaders of the twentieth century civil rights movement. Black soldiers and veterans became living forces who made history not only for their race but also for their country. It is time for us to reclaim the narrative relating to the long civil rights movement and the black military experience in the quest for racial equality.

NOTES

BIBLIOGRAPHY

INDEX

NOTES

INTRODUCTION

1. Adam, *Class and Race in the Frontier Army*, 7; Upton and Ball, "Who Robbed Major Wham?," 99–100.

2. Cox, *Segregated Soldiers*, 12.

3. Hall, "Long Civil Rights Movement," 1233.

4. Gatewood, "Black Americans and the Quest for Empire," 545.

5. Adam, *Class and Race in the Frontier Army*, 9.

6. Dobak and Phillips, *Black Regulars*, 1.

7. Gaines, *Uplifting the Race*, 23.

8. *Indianapolis* Freeman, April 23, 1898.

9. Nelson, "Significance of the Afro-Frontier in American History," 5–6.

10. Willard Gatewood's article "Black Americans and the Quest for Empire" appeared before his book *Black Americans and the White Man's Burden* and is just a preview of his work in this book. He did publish another article before this one about black soldiers while they were stationed in Tampa, Florida, but its argument is very similar to that in his book published in 1975. All of his work is very reflective of the disillusionment of blacks and Americans as a whole with the military during the Vietnam era. He is the most prolific writer of this era of "rediscovery" of the forgotten history of the black soldier. The historiography of African American soldiers never went away; it just was never a part of white American history.

11. Baldwin as quoted in Gatewood, *"Smoked Yankees,"* 3. For more a thorough examination of the inherited settler ideology, see Jackson, *Creole Indigeneity*.

12. Squires, "Rethinking the Black Public Sphere," 446. Squires discusses three types of public spheres: enclave, counter-public, and satellite. I am only using enclave and counter-public in this work.

13. The term "New Negro" when used in this study is defined as a movement started by Hubert Harrison in 1915 as a rejection of the previous generations of African Americans' acceptance of Jim Crow segregation. The New Negro soldier

was militant and politically active. Black Nationalism and the New Negro movement grew out of the same group of young black activists who embraced the color of their skin and their African heritage.

1. BULLETS AND TORCHES: THE MAKING OF THE RACE WARRIOR ON THE WESTERN FRONTIER, 1870–1896

1. Stover, "Chaplain Henry V. Plummer," 30. The *Omaha Bee*, May 4, 1893, reprinted the letter under the title "Threatened by Soldiers!"

2. Schubert, "Violent World of Emmanuel Stance," 217.

3. Gaines, *Uplifting the Race*, 26–27.

4. Bonsal, "Negro Soldier in War and Peace," 322; Black, *Dismantling Black Manhood*, 13; Lindquist, *Race, Social Science and the Crisis of Manhood*, 17; Gaines, *Uplifting the Race*, 23.

5. Pfeifer, *Roots of Rough Justice*, 13; Buckley, *American Patriots*, 110; Clancy and Nelson, *Proceedings of the Republican National Convention*, 26–27.

6. Nalty, *Strength for the Fight*, 43; Fletcher, "Negro Volunteer in Reconstruction," 128.

7. Fletcher, "Negro Volunteer in Reconstruction," 129; Schurz, *Report on the Condition of the South*, 19.

8. Carby, *Race Men*, 2.

9. Bederman, *Manliness and Civilization*, 5; Jackson and Balaji, *Global Masculinities and Manhood*, 13; Leckie, *Buffalo Soldiers*, vii; Kimmel, *Manhood in America*, 6–7.

10. As quoted in Q. Taylor, *In Search of the Racial Frontier*, 164.

11. Astor, *Right to Fight*, 44; Schubert, *Voices of the Buffalo Soldier,* 40.

12. Buckley, *American Patriots,* 118–19; Records of the Colored Troops Division, 1863–94, RG 94.7, Adjutant General Office, General Order No. 56 8/1/1866 and No. 92, U.S. National Archives, Washington, D.C.; Utley, *Indian Frontier*, 12; Leonard, *Men of Color to Arms!*, 34.

13. Schubert, *Voices of the Buffalo Soldier*, 63–64.

14. The Thirty-Eighth and the Forty-First became the Twenty-Fourth, and the Thirty-Ninth and Fortieth became the Twenty-Fifth.

15. Patton, *War and Race*, 5.

16. Keim and Sherman quoted in Utley, *Frontier Regulars*, 80–81.

17. Oder, "Education, 'Race-Adjustment' and the Military," 5–6.

18. Horne, *Black and Brown*, 53.

19. Hawbaker, *Toward the Great War*, 2–3. The Mexican border crisis is explored in more detail in a later chapter.

20. Buecker, "One Soldier's Service," 56.

21. Leonard, *Men of Color to Arms!*, 121; Leiker, *Racial Borders*, 4.

22. A. Fowler, *Black Infantry in the West*, 77.

23. Clark, "Improbable Ambassadors," 287.

24. Adam, *Class and Race in the Frontier Army*, 24.

25. Clark, "Improbable Ambassadors," 288.

26. MacGregor and Nalty, *Blacks in the United States Armed Forces*, 15; Clark, "Improbable Ambassadors," 288–89; Schubert, *Voices of the Buffalo Soldier*, 31.

27. Koelle, "Pedaling on the Periphery," 310.

28. Koelle, 312.

29. A. Fowler, *Black Infantry in the West*, 58.

30. As quoted in A. Miller, *Elevating the Race*, xv.

31. A. Miller, xx.

32. Kenner, *Buffalo Soldiers and Officers of the Ninth Cavalry*, 12; A. Miller, *Elevating the Race*, 120; Stover, *Up from Handymen*, 103.

33. Oder, "Education, 'Race-Adjustment' and the Military," 197–98.

34. Lieutenant George Andrews, "Twenty-Fifth Infantry," in Rodenbough and Haskin, *Army of the United States Historical Sketches*, 291; A. Fowler, *Black Infantry in the West*, 93–94.

35. Lieutenant John Bigelow, "Tenth Cavalry," in Rodenbough and Haskin, *Army of the United States Historical Sketches*, 288; Schubert, *On the Trail of the Buffalo Soldier*, 14–15.

36. Quoted in A. Fowler, *Black Infantry in the West*, 97.

37. A. Fowler, 103.

38. Kenner, *Buffalo Soldiers and Officers of the Ninth Cavalry*, 32–33.

39. Stover, "Chaplain Henry V. Plummer," 21, 24.

40. Kenner, *Buffalo Soldiers and Officers of the Ninth Cavalry*, 332.

41. Chaplain Plummer, Monthly Report to the Adjutant General, March 1892, Adjutant General Office, RG 94, AGO file #7043 and 1356799, U.S. National Archives.

42. Plummer, 349.

43. Stover, "Chaplain Henry V. Plummer," 32.

44. Kenner, *Buffalo Soldiers and Officers of the Ninth Cavalry*, 334; Stover, "Chaplain Henry V. Plummer," 35.

45. Kenner, *Buffalo Soldiers and Officers of the Ninth Cavalry*, 336.

46. Stover, "Chaplain Henry V. Plummer," 39.

47. Kenner, *Buffalo Soldiers and Officers of the Ninth Cavalry*, 342.

48. Quoted in A. Fowler, *Black Infantry in the West*, 104.

49. C. Alexander, *Battles and Victories of Allen Allensworth*, 242–44.

50. C. Alexander, 263.

51. C. Alexander, 264.

52. A. Fowler, *Black Infantry in the West*, 106; *Washington Bee*, August 20, 1887; *St. Paul Appeal*, June 6, 1891; Oder, "Education, 'Race-Adjustment' and the Military," 136; C. Alexander, *Battles and Victories of Allen Allensworth*, 244.

53. C. Alexander, *Battles and Victories of Allen Allensworth*, 265.

54. Steward, *Fifty Years in the Gospel Ministry*, 267–74.

55. Schubert, *Voices of the Buffalo Soldier*, 31.

56. Schubert, 31–34; Kenner, *Buffalo Soldiers and Officers of the Ninth Cavalry*, 90–91.

57. A. Fowler, *Black Infantry in the West*, 26–27.

58. As quoted in F. Schubert, "Suggs Affray," 60.

59. U.S. Congress, Senate, *U.S. Congressional Serial Set*, "Brownsville Affray," 386–87.

60. Schubert, "Black Soldiers on the White Frontier," 411–12; Schubert, "Suggs Affray," 68.

61. Schuyler, *Black and Conservative*, 41–43.

62. *Cleveland Gazette*, February 2, 1884, 22.

63. *Cleveland Gazette*, 28.

2. MY HOME, MY COUNTRY

1. Quoted in Leonard, *Men of Color to Arms!*, 202–3.

2. Glasrud, and Searles, *Buffalo Soldiers in the West*, 140.

3. Morris, Rise of Theodore Roosevelt, 433–34.

4. Hoganson, *Fighting for American Manhood*, 3–4. The U.S. also almost went to war with Spain in 1897.

5. Gatewood, *"Smoked Yankees,"* 5; Fletcher, "Black Volunteers in the Spanish-American War," 48.

6. *Cleveland Gazette*, February 19, 1898; *New York Age*, June 10, 1889; Gatewood, *Black Americans and the White Man's Burden*, ix; *A.M.E. Review* 13 (October 1896). *Plessy v. Ferguson* was the eight-to-one decision that sanctioned and legalized segregation in the South. Justice John Marshall Harlan of Kentucky was the lone justice who dissented. For more on this, see Hine, Hine, and Harold, *African-American Odyssey*, 349.

7. White was a longtime supporter of black officers for black soldiers and helped advocate for the organization of an all-black volunteer regiment, the Third North Carolina Volunteers.

8. *American Citizen* (Kansas City), February 24, 1898.

9. Kimmel, *Gendered Society*, 266–67.

10. *Cleveland Gazette*, May 13, 1898. See also Gatewood, *Black Americans and the White Man's Burden*, for more on the rising tide of Jim Crow racism throughout the South.

11. Quoted in Gatewood, *"Smoked Yankees,"* 25.

12. Cashin, *Under Fire*, 60, 109, 120, 140. McKinley's manhood was constantly being challenged, and he was consistently described as weak and unmanly. It became truly hostile during the *Maine* investigation. McKinley did not want to go to war; on March 30, he burst into tears to a friend exclaiming that Congress was trying to drive the nation to war. He remembered the Civil War as a horrible

conflict and did not want to relive it. For more on this, see Hoganson, *Fighting for American Manhood*, 105; and Emerson, "Negro as a Soldier." Emerson served as a war correspondent and attempted in this article to present a positive image of black soldiers, but it is still very representative of the benevolent racism of the day.

13. Cashin, *Under Fire*, 62; quoted in Kilroy, *For Race and Country*, 4 (an excellent up-to-date biography of Charles Young).

14. *Indianapolis Freeman*, April 23, 1898. See also Hoganson, *Fighting for American Manhood*.

15. Chauncey, *Gay New York*, 113; *Indianapolis Freeman*, August 19, 1905. George Chauncey's study is primarily about the making of a gay subculture, essentially a world within a world, but he does have a discussion about the crisis of the "over-civilization" of men and the need for men to rediscover their moral primal instincts. Bederman gives an excellent description of the crisis of white masculinity at the turn of the twentieth century in *Manliness and Civilization*.

16. Clifford, "Medal of Honor Recipient," 6 Christian Fleetwood served in the Fourth U.S. Colored Infantry during the Civil War, enlisting in 1863 and serving until 1866. Due to Fleetwood's intelligence, he was quickly promoted to sergeant major and later served as a clerk for the War Department from 1881 until 1892. Fleetwood also wrote a pamphlet for the Negro Congress titled "The Negro as a Soldier," published by Howard University, in which he traces the heroic deeds of black soldiers starting in the American Revolution and ending with the Civil War. James Harrison biographical sketch of Christian Fleetwood, 5–8, folder 1, Christian A. Fleetwood Papers, Schomburg Center for Research in Black Culture, New York Public Library.

17. It should be noted that Fleetwood also participated in several musical organizations and served as choirmaster to several choirs. He also lived next to Paul Laurence Dunbar, and Frederick Douglass was a frequent visitor to Fleetwood's home. Fleetwood passed away on September 28, 1914, and was buried with full military honors.

18. *Baltimore Ledger*, June 11, 1898.

19. *Illinois Record* (Springfield), May 21, 1898.

20. *Illinois Record*, June 11, 1898.

21. Cashin, *Under Fire*, xiv.

22. Gatewood, *"Smoked Yankees,"* 41; General Wheeler to Adjutant-General, Fifth Army Corps, July 7, 1898, Records of the Adjutant General's Office, RG 94, document file 1890–1917, U.S. National Archives, Washington, D.C.

23. *Baltimore Ledger*, June 17, 1899; Gatewood, *"Smoked Yankees,"* 55; Curtis, *Black Soldier*, 37; Fletcher, "Black Volunteers in the Spanish-American War," 49. The four immune volunteer regiments were the Seventh, Eighth, Ninth, and Tenth. They were called immune regiments because of the belief that blacks were better suited for tropical climates and were immune to yellow fever. The only

regiment to see active duty was the Ninth in Cuba. See Coston, *Spanish-American War Volunteer*, which includes the muster rolls, biographies, and photographs of the Ninth's experience in Cuba.

24. Steward, *Colored Regulars*, 209. General J. F. Kent to Assistant Adjutant-General, Fifth Army Corps, July 7, 1898, Records of the Adjutant General's Office, Record Group 94. The charge at El Caney and at Kettle were both successful. The army was able to push the Spanish forces back and claim the blockhouse. Excuses were made for the poor performance of the Seventy-First New York, including the claim that most of the men in the National Guard unit had never fired a rifle before and had poor equipment.

25. Steward, *Colored Regulars*, 207. The Twenty-Fourth Infantry received a lot of press and accolades, not because of the troops' performance on the battlefield but because of their actions off the field. A yellow fever epidemic broke out in the army hospital, and the army was short on nurses to help care for the sick. When the request came for forty to fifty soldiers to come and help, the entire regiment volunteered. Also see Bonsal, "Negro Soldier in War and Peace."

26. E. Johnson, *History of Negro Soldiers*, 92. The Sixth Virginia Infantry was organized from the first Colored Battalion of Richmond. John Mitchell Jr. was a major supporter of this regiment. In fact, Mitchell helped organize black Virginians and put pressure on Governor J. Hoge Tyler to place black officers over the black soldiers. Mitchell is credited with coining the phrase "No officers, no fight." Most black newspapers that campaigned for black officers for black troops adopted this.

27. Gatewood, "Virginia's Negro Regiment." The First Battalion of Virginia's "colored infantry" was organized in 1876. It originally had four companies, and the black commander for the regiment was Major William H. Johnson.

28. Gatewood, *"Smoked Yankees,"* 200.

29. General Order No. 21, September 17, 1898, Regimental Records of the Sixth Virginia Infantry (Colored), Records of the Adjutant General's Office, RG 94; Gatewood, "Virginia's Negro Regiment," 204.

30. *Richmond Planet*, December 17, 1898, and March 25, 1899; A. Alexander, *Race Man*, 91–97.

31. James Young's biography is in the *National Encyclopedia of the Colored Race*, 1919; Edmonds, *Negro and Fusion Politics in North Carolina*, 23; the North Carolina State Archives for the James Young historical marker. James Young was heavily involved with creating the Fusion Party in North Carolina and was elected to the state legislature in 1899. Young, considered the Fusionist architect, helped to get Daniel Russell elected governor, and it was Russell who supported Young when he organized an all-black volunteer regiment to serve during the Spanish-American-Cuban conflict.

32. *Regimental Records of the Third North Carolina*. A total of four men were killed from the Third. Three of the four were justifiably explained, while Robert Thomas's death was not.

33. *Regimental Records of the Third North Carolina.*

34. *Indianapolis Freeman*, September 17, 1898; *Colored American* (Washington, D.C.), August 27, 1898. In cities such as New York and Washington, black soldiers were given parades and served as escorts for the president. The official proclamation ending the conflict with Spain was issued on August 12, 1898, by President McKinley to General Miles, Ponce, Puerto Rico; General Merritt, Manila; and General Shafter, Santiago.

35. *Colored American*, December 7, 1898.

36. Gilmore, *Gender and Jim Crow*, 112–16.

37. *Richmond Planet*, November 18, 1898.

38. Gatewood, *"Smoked Yankees,"* 92.

39. Quoted in Schubert, *Voices of the Buffalo Soldier*, 215–16.

40. Schubert, 216.

41. *Broad Ax* (Salt Lake City), October 27, 1900; *Indianapolis Freeman*, December 30, 1899; General Otis to Adjutant-General, Washington, November 13, 1898, Records of the Adjutant General's Office, RG 94, document file 1890–1917. General Otis actually sent a message to the secretary of state that there would be a need to retain the troops in the Philippines because the Filipinos were becoming hostile toward the Americans. Admiral Dewey to Secretary of the Navy, Washington, February 5, 1899, Records of the Adjutant General's Office, RG 94, document file 1890–1917. Dewey's message was that the insurgents had begun attacking the previous night.

42. The Philippines became a colony of the Spanish in the sixteenth century. The first Filipino to become a monk was Kanilli Trujillo in 1585, who became a Franciscan. The $20 million used to purchase the Philippines from Spain was the largest amount the U.S. had ever spent in order to purchase territory. (The U.S. had spent $15 million for the Louisiana Territory in 1803, $6.5 million for Florida in 1819, and $7.2 million for Alaska in 1867.) Emilio Aguinaldo to General Wesley Merritt, Manila, August 27, 1898, and General Otis to Adjutant-General, Washington, February 5, 1899, Records of the Adjutant General's Office, RG 94, document file 1890–1917. *Republican Courier* (New Orleans), January 20, 1900; Guthrie, *Campfires of the Afro-American*, 706–10; Schoonover, *Uncle Sam's War*, 84.

43. The Spaniards introduced Christianity to the Filipinos long before the founding of Jamestown in 1607. Ngozi-Brown, "African American Soldiers and Filipinos," 43; *Richmond Planet*, July 29, 1899. See also Rudyard Kipling's poem "The White Man's Burden."

44. General Orders No. 107 from H. C. Corbin, Adjutant-General, Washington, June 15, 1899, Records of the Adjutant General's Office, RG 94, document file 1890–1917.

45. *Baltimore Ledger*, October 1, 1898.

46. Gatewood, "Black Americans and the Quest for Empire," 558.

47. Guthrie, *Campfires of the Afro-American*, 710.

48. *American Citizen*, July 14, 1899.

49. *Indianapolis Freeman*, November 18, 1899; Gatewood, *Black Americans and the White Man's Burden*, 261; *Savannah Tribune*, March 7, 1900; *Colored American*, March 24, 1900.

50. *Cleveland Gazette*, December 2, 1899.

51. *Richmond Planet*, December 30, 1899; *Cleveland Gazette*, September 29, 1900. The commanding general of the Philippine forces, General E. S. Otis, clearly addresses the issue of claiming "booty" and the appropriate treatment of prisoners in this letter of September 8, 1898, Records of the Adjutant General's Office, RG 94, document file 1890–1917. Chaplain T. G. Steward in his journal noted the treatment of the Filipinos by white soldiers and was disgusted with the level of abuse. He was proud of the men of the Twenty-Fifth for not participating.

52. Ngozi-Brown, "African-American Soldiers and Filipinos," 47–51; quoted in Gatewood, *"Smoked Yankees,"* 303.

53. *Cleveland Gazette*, February 3, 1900. Pogue also states that the pamphlets they found were actually addressed to the Twenty-Fourth Infantry. To see a discussion on the low rate of desertions, see chapter 1.

54. Gatewood, *Black Americans and the White Man's Burden*, 280–82.

55. Gatewood, 283.

56. Nankivell, *History of the Twenty-Fifth Regiment*, 104. Colonel Burt recommended Sergeant James K. Lightfoot for the Medal of Honor because of his performance at O'Donnell. The battle took place on November 17, but the official report was not sent until three days later. General Otis to Adjutant-General, Washington, November 20, 1899, Records of the Adjutant General's Office, RG 94, document file 1890–1917. Jack Foner discusses the Filipino and American losses, which were around four thousand; see *Blacks and the Military in American History*, 89.

57. Roosevelt declared the war in the Philippines over on July 4, 1902. The war was technically already over because General Aguinaldo had been captured the previous year, which sparked the withdrawal of the majority of American forces from the Philippines. General Orders No. 66, from Secretary of War Elihu Root to the Army of the United States, Washington, D.C., July 4, 1902, Records of the Adjutant General's Office, RG 94, document file 1890–1917.

58. *Indianapolis Freedman*, December 14, 1901.

59. Ngozi-Brown, "African-American Soldiers and Filipinos," 48; Adjutant General's Office, RG 94, AGO file #7043 and 1356799, U.S. National Archives, Washington, D.C. Special Order No. 201 was issued on December 3, 1900, and it stated that Calloway would be discharged without honor.

60. Brown, "White Backlash," 170.

61. Boehringer, "Imperial Paranoia and Military Injustice."

62. Ngozi-Brown, "African-American Soldiers and Filipinos," 50.

63. This quote is from Marcus Garvey and is the best definition of black manhood in early twentieth-century black America. The self-made man was key to the Garveyite ideology; quoted in Summers, *Manliness and Its Discontents*, 84; and *Colored American*, March 24, 1900.

64. This was a letter from Sergeant Major T. Clay Smith to the *Savannah Tribune*, November 1, 1902.

65. *Washington Bee*, December 16, 1899.

3. FOR RACE AND COUNTRY, WE NEVER FORGET

1. Beasley, *Negro Trail Blazers of California*, 283.

2. W. E. B. Du Bois speech given in 1951, W. E. B. Du Bois Collection, University of Massachusetts–Amherst Special Collections and Archives (UMA). When I use the term "hegemonic masculinity," I am referring to traditional white male definitions of masculinity and manhood, which is characterized as being superior to African American manhood.

3. Kiesling, "On War without Fog," 325; Leiker, *Racial Borders*, 41; Matthews, *U.S. Army on the Mexican Border*, 53.

4. Matthews, *U.S. Army on the Mexican Border*, 60.

5. Boot, *Savage Wars of Peace*, viii.

6. Boot, 62–63. The Plan of San Diego as described by the University of Houston was meant to cause a race war. "This revolutionary manifesto called for a revolt against the United States to begin on February 20, 1915, and establishment of an independent Mexican American republic on lands seized from Mexico by the United States in 1848. The plan also called for an army consisting of Mexican Americans, blacks, and Japanese to kill all whites over the age of sixteen, the creation of a black republic in six southern states, and the restoration of tribal Indian lands." See "Plan of San Diego."

7. Brinkley, *Unfinished Nation*, 631; quote appears in S. Harris, *Harlem's Hell Fighters*, 28–29.

8. Boot, *Savage Wars of Peace*, 199; Newton Baker to General Pershing, March 11, 1916, Woodrow Wilson Papers, Woodrow Wilson Presidential Library, Staunton, VA, http://www.woodrowwilson.org/library-archives.

9. Boot, *Savage Wars of Peace*, 199; Woodrow Wilson to General Funston, March 13, 1916, Woodrow Wilson Papers.

10. Boot, *Savage Wars of Peace*, 200; Matthews, *U.S. Army on the Mexican Border*, 69–73; "Zimmermann Telegram."

11. Mark Schneider, *"We Return Fighting,"* 219.

12. Buckley, *American Patriots*, 186; Mjagkij, *Loyalty in Time of Trial*, 60–62; Barbeau and Henri, *Unknown Soldiers*, 26–27.

13. Weaver, *Brownsville Raid*, 15–16; Christian, *Black Soldiers in Jim Crow Texas*, 86. In 1973, ex-private Dorsey Williams, after being honorably discharged, stated, "None of us said anything because we didn't have anything to say. It

was a frame up through and through" (Christian, *Black Soldiers in Jim Crow Texas*, 86).

14. Mjagkij, *Loyalty in Time of Trial*, 29; Minton, *Houston Riot*. For more information about the Houston Riot, see Hayne, *Night of Violence*.

15. The report on T. C. Hawkins, Defendant, *United States v. William Nesbit*, Company I, and the Twenty-Fourth Infantry is discussed in detail in Borch, "'Largest Murder Trial in the History of the United States.'"

16. Report to Military Intelligence Headquarters, Walter Loving Papers, Mooreland-Spingarn Research Center, Howard University, Washington, D.C. (hereafter MSRC).

17. Jordan, *Black Newspapers and America's War for Democracy*, 94–95.

18. Borch, "'Largest Murder Trial in the History of the United States,'" 1–2.

19. "Mr. Flipper," *The Crisis*, November 1917, 12; Mark Schneider, "*We Return Fighting*," 226–27.

20. *The Crisis*, October 1917, 284–85. Walter Loving, in a report to the chief of Military Intelligence, discusses the Memphis lynching and requests that something be done to curb the rising tide of racial violence against African Americans in order to maintain their support for the war effort. The race riot of East St. Louis was caused by the insecurities of white workers over the arrival of black southern migrants competing for factory jobs. Walter Loving Papers, MSRC.

21. C. Williams, *Torchbearers of Democracy*, 48, 46; Barbeau and Henri, *Unknown Soldiers*, 26.

22. Kornweibel, "*Investigate Everything*," 235.

23. Keene, "W. E. B. Du Bois and the Wounded World," 142; *Iowa Bystander*, June 29, 1917, 2.

24. Chase, "Struggle for Equality," 297.

25. Chase, 298.

26. NAACP *Branch Bulletin*, March 1917.

27. General Leonard Wood wrote a letter to Joel Spingarn expressing his doubt that he could find enough qualified candidates; see Joel E. Spingarn Papers, MSRC.

28. *The Crisis*, March 18, 1917; Charles Young to Harry Smith, March 23, 1917, Colonel Charles Young Papers, Ohio Historical Society, http://dbs.ohiohistory.org/africanam/html/page6b5b.html?ID=5409.

29. Waldron to Wilson, May 11, 1917, and Baker to Wilson, May 17, 1917, Woodrow Wilson Papers. In this letter to Wilson, Baker expresses his frustration over the barrage of letters he received from John Milton Waldron. The campaign to reinstate Lieutenant Colonel Charles Young is examined in more detail in chapter 6. The "Bill of Particulars" was printed in several black newspapers at various times of the year in 1917 and the "Bill of Particulars" contained fourteen points that addressed the need for democracy at home.

30. Doward, "Determining If the Actions," 24. Emmett Scott to Charles Young, June 1917, Colonel Charles Young Papers. Even Newton Baker in a letter to President Wilson assumed that Young would be in charge of the camp: "I am endeavoring to use Colonel Young in connection with the training of colored officers for the new Army at Des Moines, Iowa." Baker to Wilson, June 27, 1917, Woodrow Wilson Papers.

31. The Ninety-Second was organized in November 1917 from black draftees. It reached full strength in May 1918. The principal units of the division were these: 183rd Infantry Brigade (365th, 366th, 350th Machine Gun Battalions); 184th Infantry Brigade (367th, 368th, 365th Machine Gun Battalions); 167th Field Artillery Brigade (349th, 350th, 351st, 317th Trench-Mortar Batteries); Divisional Troops (348th Machine Gun Battalion, 317th Engineer Regiment, 325th Field Signal Battalion, Headquarters Troop). The Ninety-Third Division was organized in December 1917 from the black National Guard units from the states of New York, Illinois, Connecticut, Maryland, Massachusetts, Ohio, and Tennessee and the District of Columbia and from some draftees from South Carolina. The principal units were the 185th Infantry Brigade (369th Infantry and the 370th Infantry) and 186th Infantry Brigade (371st Infantry and the 372nd Infantry). This regiment never reached its full strength. Chase, "Struggle for Equality," 309.

32. Haywood, *Black Bolshevik*, 110.

33. *The Crisis*, August 1918, 164; Hamburger, *Learning Lessons*, iii.

34. Boot, *Savage Wars of Peace*, viii.

35. Morrow, *Great War*, 33–35; Keene, "W. E. B. Du Bois and the Wounded World," 136–38.

36. Major Walter H. Loving served as the top black undercover intelligence operative for the Military Intelligence Division during World War I, the precursor to the Defense Intelligence Agency. He monitored the actions and investigated reports of treason in the black community and among black soldiers.

37. William H. Dyer Collection, 2, Schomburg Center for Research in Black Culture, New York Public Library.

38. Charles Williams to Walter Loving, Walter Loving Papers, MSRC; Mjagkij, *Loyalty in Time of Trial*, 60.

39. Unpublished diary, 8, John Castles Jr. Collection, U.S. Military Academy, West Point, N.Y.; Spencer, Spencer, and Wright, "World War I as I Saw It," 144.

40. Pioneer units were the labor regiments that worked directly behind the front-line constructing trenches and boardwalks. They also dug the graves and helped maintain the supply train.

41. Anonymous soldier to W. E. B. Du Bois, W. E. B Du Bois Collection, box 14, folder 36, "The Black Man in The Wounded World" manuscript and research materials, Fisk University Special Collections, Nashville, Tenn.; William H. Dyer Collection, 3; Spencer, Spencer, and Wright, "World War I as I Saw It," 145.

42. *Federal Surveillance of Afro-Americans*, reel 19; Emmett Scott to Newton Baker, Woodrow Wilson Papers, Woodrow Wilson Presidential Library, Staunton, Va.

43. Astor, *Right to Fight*, 211.

44. Unpublished diary, 10, John Castles Jr. Collection.

45. Colonel Greer to Senator McKellar, Walter Loving Papers; *The Crisis*, May 6, 1919; George Washington Lee Collection, box 1, folder 23, Memphis Public Library, Special Collections, Memphis, Tenn. Greer's letter to McKellar became a rallying issue for black veterans after the war and caused the leaking of several military documents to Du Bois, which were then reprinted in *The Crisis*. Both Greer and McKellar were from Memphis, which is probably why Greer wrote to the Democratic senator McKellar.

46. Walter Loving Papers. The League for Democracy was organized and created specifically for black veterans in March 1919. Du Bois, "Negro Soldier in Service Abroad," 324.

47. Du Bois, "Negro Soldier in Service Abroad," 325.

48. Spencer, Spencer, and Wright, "World War I as I Saw It" 148; Keene, *Doughboys*, 89.

49. Unpublished diary, 10, John Castles Jr. Collection. Spencer, Spencer, and Wright, "World War I as I Saw It," 149; American Battle Monuments Commission, *93d Division Summary of Operations*, 4, 25. The four regiments were split up and alternated between being attached to the 161st French Division and the 157th French Division.

50. American Battle Monuments Commission, *92d Division Summary of Operations*, 10; Ferrell, *Unjustly Dishonored*, location 365.

51. Willard to Du Bois, May 6, 1919, Du Bois Collection, UMA; American Battle Monuments Commission, *92d Division Summary of Operations*, 24; *Cleveland Advocate*, January 4, 1919.

52. Willard to Du Bois, May 6, 1919, Du Bois Collection, UMA; American Battle Monuments Commission, *92d Division Summary of Operations*, 24; *Cleveland Advocate*, January 4, 1919.

53. Blair T. Hunt to Du Bois, November 22, 1919, Du Bois Collection, UMA; Purvis Chesson Survey, Romulus Archer Survey, Samuel Ballard Survey, Virginia War History Commission Questionnaire (VWHC), Library of Virginia, Richmond; William H. Dyer Collection.

54. Walter Loving to the Office of Military Intelligence, Walter Loving Papers; Spingarn to Du Bois, Joel E. Spingarn Papers; Du Bois to Young, Colonel Charles Young Papers; Charles Williams to Emmett Scott, Emmett J. Scott Papers, MSRC; "The Black Man in the Wounded World" manuscript, 99–100, Du Bois Collection (Fisk).

55. *The Crisis,* May 6, 1919; Astor, *Right to Fight*, 108; Woodson to Du Bois, November 16, 1918, Du Bois Collection, box 14, folder 32 (Fisk). Woodson informed Du

Bois that they were the only two qualified to write the history of African American soldiers in World War I, completely dismissing the book written by Emmett J. Scott.

56. C. P. Duncan to Du Bois, July 16, 1919, Du Bois Collection, box 14, folder 36 (Fisk); "The Black Man in The Wounded World" manuscript, 97–98, Du Bois Collection (Fisk); Arthur Barbeau and Henri, *Unknown Soldiers*, xiii.

57. George Washington Lee Collection, box 1, folder 36.

58. Keene, *Doughboys*, 145.

59. George Washington Lee Papers, box 1, folder 36; Logan, *Historical Aspects of Pan-Africanism*.

60. As quoted in the personal papers found in the George Washington Lee Papers, box 1, folder 36.

61. Meyer, *World Remade*, 483. Ernest Hemingway completely rejected the idea of a so-called Lost Generation, but Logan's pessimism about the African American future led to his decision to define the late nineteenth century as the nadir of the African American experience.

62. Reed, "Rayford W. Logan," 27, 38.

63. C. Williams, "Vanguards of the New Negro," 362; C. Williams, "Torchbearers of Democracy," 157–58.

64. C. Williams, "Vanguards of the New Negro," 348; Onishi, *Transpacific Antiracism*, 15. For more about Hubert Harrison and the origins of the "New Negro" movement, see Jeffrey Perry's biography *Hubert Harrison: The Voice of Harlem Radicalism, 1883–1918*.

65. As quoted in C. Williams, "Vanguards of the New Negro," 348; W. E. B. Du Bois, *The Crisis* 18 (May 1919).

4. HENRY OSSIAN FLIPPER: THE LONE WARRIOR

1. Flipper, *Colored Cadet*, 5–6; Taylor, "Does Anyone Care?," 2.

2. Flipper, *Colored Cadet*, 10.

3. Flipper, 3.

4. Robinson, *Court Martial*, 2; Taylor, "Does Anyone Care?," 8. Flipper made these statements in his autobiography, *Colored Cadet*, 15–16—in which he refers to himself in the third person—but I have not seen any evidence to suggest that Confederate soldiers were murdered in such a fashion.

5. Robinson, *Court Martial*, 2; Taylor, "Does Anyone Care?," 12–13. In March 1865, the Bureau Bill established the Bureau of Refugees, Freedmen, and Abandoned Lands under the authority of the War Department. In the first Bureau Bill of 1865, Congress did not appropriate any money for education (it did not appropriate educational money until July 1866), forcing the bureau to be completely reliant on the funding from benevolent societies. As a result of the financial state of the bureau in 1865, Howard had to appoint commissioners for each state that would work well with the benevolent societies, the American Missionary Association in particular.

6. Flipper, *Colored Cadet*, 14; Meier and Lewis, "History of the Negro Upper Class"; Kilroy, *For Race and Country*, 4.

7. Robinson, *Court Martial*, 3. The other cadets appointed before Flipper all washed out within their first two years.

8. Vaughn, "West Point," 100. James Webster Smith's letter was published in the *Hartford Courant* and within a few weeks of its publication was reprinted nationwide. It drew the attention of General Oliver O. Howard, commissioner of the Freedmen's Bureau, who went on to state that if West Point could not protect Smith from attacks, then the tide of the people might change against the academy. Benjamin Butler and Charles Summer of Massachusetts called for a federal investigation of Smith's treatment.

9. A. Williams, *Black Warriors*, 18–19.

10. Flipper, *Colored Cadet*, 181–84.

11. This quote is from Flipper and is quoted in Shellum, "Silencing of Early Black Cadets," 73.

12. On April 6, 1880, Johnson C. Whittaker was attacked. Due to his injuries—which some school officials believed were self-inflicted—he was unable to attend several classes, which led to Whittaker being found deficient in those classes. After two years of inquiries and a court-martial, Whittaker was convicted of perjuring himself, but his conviction was overturned and he was instead dismissed for failing his philosophy exam.

13. Flipper, *Colored Cadet*, 13–14; Dinges, "Court-Martial," 13.

14. Flipper, *Colored Cadet*, 217.

15. Dinges, "Court-Martial," 13; Robinson, *Court Martial*, 6–7; Taylor, "Does Anyone Care?," 31.

16. Bentz, "Henry Flipper, West Point's First Black Graduate," 56.

17. General Court-Martial of Lieutenant Henry O. Flipper, in Records Relating to the Army Career of Henry Ossian Flipper, 1873–1882, RG 153, Records of the Judge Advocate General, QQ-2952, T-1027, p. 588, U.S. National Archives, Washington, D.C. (hereafter GCM). Closing arguments can also be found in this source (see p. 587).

18. Dinges, "Court-Martial," 14. The Indian Wars west of the Mississippi started in the 1830s and lasted until 1890. The Victorio campaign ended on October 15, 1880. An estimated two thousand soldiers, miners, cowboys, and Mexican troops pursued Victorio in this campaign. Victorio and seventy-eight other warriors were all killed by Mexican soldiers in Chihuahua. Victorio is considered by many historians to be the "greatest warrior in Apache history." Taylor, "Does Anyone Care?," 35.

19. Before the Committee on Military Affairs, House of Representatives, 55th Cong., 2nd Sess., H.R. 9849: In the Matter of the Court-Martial of Henry Ossian Flipper, Statement and Brief for Petitioner, RG 233, U.S. National Archives, Washington, D.C.; Flipper, *Western Memoirs*, 20.

20. Dinges, "Court-Martial," 15.

21. Taylor, "Does Anyone Care?," 46.

22. GCM, 63, 122.

23. Robinson, *Court Martial*, 18.

24. Flipper, *Western Memoirs*, 40; Dinges, "Court-Martial," 16.

25. Flipper, *Colored Cadet*, 222.

26. Before the Committee on Military Affairs, House of Representatives, 55th Cong., 2nd Sess., H.R. 9849: In the Matter of the Court-Martial of Henry Ossian Flipper, Statement and Brief for Petitioner; Flipper, *Western Memoirs* 56.

27. GCM, 63, 587–88.

28. Taylor, "Does Anyone Care?," 65–66; Wilson, "Black Lieutenant in the Ranks," 35.

29. Eppinga, "Henry O. Flipper," 33.

30. Flipper, *Western Memoirs*, 36–37.

31. Henry Ossian Flipper to Booker T. Washington, in *The Booker T. Washington Papers*, 497.

32. Flipper to Washington, 529; *Cleveland Gazette*, May 28, 1898.

33. Taylor, "Does Anyone Care?," 80.

34. As quoted in Taylor, 80–81; Palmer, *Encyclopedia of African-American Culture*, 804.

5. CHARLES YOUNG: THE DIPLOMATIC WARRIOR

1. Bennett, "Old Soldier Who Wouldn't Surrender," 85.

2. Shellum, *Black Cadet in a White Bastion*, 7; Shumaker, *Untold Stories from America's National Parks*, 75.

3. Shellum, *Black Cadet in a White Bastion*, 31–32; Greene, *Charles Young*, 14; Kilroy, *For Race and Country*, 25; Obama, "Presidential Proclamation."

4. Shellum, *Black Cadet in a White Bastion*, 75; Kilroy, *For Race and Country*, 24–27.

5. Kilroy, *For Race and Country*, 18–20.

6. Shellum, *Black Cadet in a White* Bastion, 53.

7. W. E. B. Du Bois, *The Crisis*, February 1922, 155; Greene, *Charles Young*, 23, 32.

8. Clegg, "'Splendid Type of Colored American,'" 53–54.

9. Charles Young to Colonel Dehmane Skerrett, July 23, 1915, Colonel Charles Young Papers.

10. Shellum, *Black Cadet in a White Bastion*, 135; Kilroy, *For Race and Country*, 20.

11. *Army and Navy Journal* 26, no. 50 (August 10, 1889): 1021–22; Adjutant General's office to the commander of the Ninth Cavalry, 1889, Records of the Colored Troops Division, 1863–94, RG 94.7, U.S. National Archives, Washington, D.C.

12. Shellum, *Black Officer in a Buffalo Soldier Regiment*, 21.

13. Shellum, 20.

14. Gatewood, "John Hanks Alexander," 106–10; Greene, *Charles Young*, 54; Young to Harry Smith, March 23, 1917, Colonel Charles Young Papers.

15. Lewis, *W. E. B Du Bois*, 176–78.

16. Greene, *Charles Young*, 62–63; Shellum, *Black Officer in a Buffalo Soldier Regiment*, 37.

17. Young, *Military Morale*, 12. Paul Laurence Dunbar visited Wilberforce frequently, which is how he became fast friends with Young and Du Bois.

18. Cox, *Segregated Soldiers*, 7. At any given time there were 3,600–15,600 black soldiers on active duty during this time in the four black units. The regiment sizes varied as the army began to expand.

19. *Cleveland Gazette*, June 6, 1898; Greene, *Charles Young*, 51; Shellum, *Black Officer in a Buffalo Soldier Regiment*, 90–91.

20. Flipper to Washington, 1898, *Booker T. Washington Papers*, 497; *Washington Bee*, May 1, 1898. After Young's service with the Ninth, Washington offered him a position at Tuskegee as the military science professor; however, Young declined Washington's offer after he found out the students would not be able to use weapons. Washington told Young that it would be too upsetting for southern whites to have these students drill with real weapons.

21. Greene, *Charles Young*, 52.

22. Greene, 52–53. The conditions of the Treaty of Paris allowed for the U.S. to purchase the Philippines from Spain for $20 million and to make it a U.S. territory. The Filipino leaders were led to believe that if they helped the U.S. defeat the Spanish, they would get their independence. Once the terms of the agreement were released, the Filipinos openly rebelled against becoming a U.S. territory.

23. W. H. Nicholas to Ada Young, January 1945, Colonel Charles Young Papers. W. H. Nicholas served with Young for six years, from the rank of private to the rank of first sergeant. Nicholas also served as Young's troop clerk, so he got to know Young quite well. Greene, *Charles Young*, 59; Kilroy, *For Race and Country*, 47; Shumaker, *Untold Stories from America's National Parks*, 79.

24. Young was sent to Fort Duchesne after ending his service with the National Guard. He spent eighteen months settling disputes between white settlers and the Ute Indians. When he was sent to the Philippines in 1901, he spent eighteen months on various islands such as Luzon and Samay. Shumaker, *Untold Stories from America's National Parks*, 79.

25. Young, "Ideals of the Negroes in the United States." The speech Young gave was reprinted in several newspapers and occurred three years after Dubois's 1900 Paris exposition. Du Bois compiled 363 photographs and placed them into albums. These images were to demonstrate "Negro Life." For more detailed information about this photographic project, see Du Bois, "American Negro at Paris." Despite his criticism of industrial education, Young did not lose the support of Booker T. Washington or his supporters.

26. Young, "Ideals of the Negroes in the United States."

27. Young, "Ideals of the Negroes in the United States"; Shumaker, *Untold Stories from America's National Parks*, 80–81.

28. Young and the Ninth Cavalry helped to survey and protect the Sequoia National Park. Young served as the superintendent successfully for eighteen months, leading his men to accomplish more in one summer than had men under any of the previous three officers who served in his post. His service was so successful there was a proposal to have a tree named after him; however, he insisted that the tree be named after Booker T. Washington instead. While in California, Young married Ada Mills, and they would go on to have two children, Charles Noel and Marie. Shellum, *Black Officer in a Buffalo Soldier Regiment*, 160–61; Shumaker, *Untold Stories from America's National Parks*, 81. See Renda, *Taking Haiti*, for more information about the U.S. occupation of Haiti.

29. Young, *Military Morale*, 10.

30. Young, 223.

31. Greene, *Charles Young*, 74–75; Kilroy, *For Race and Country*, 63–65; *Army and Navy Journal* 98, no. 28 (May 7, 1907): 870. It should be noted that there are no surviving documents of Young's reports on Haiti. The War Department had them all destroyed in the 1920s. Young's maps and French Creole handbook were used by the U.S. Marines when they invaded Haiti.

32. Greene, *Charles Young*, 76.

33. Heinl and Heinl, *Written in Blood*, 678; Shumaker, *Untold Stories from America's National Parks*, 93.

34. *Washington Bee*, January 22, 1910. Garret W. Gibson was the fourteenth president of Liberia and was born in Baltimore, Maryland. Clegg, "'Splendid Type of Colored American,'"50. There were several rebellions by the Grelo people as well as the Kru. The Americo-Liberian is defined as a Liberian of African American descent. For more about the Americo-Liberian identity, see Wegmann, "Christian Community and the Development of an Americo-Liberian Identity."

35. Clegg, "'Splendid Type of Colored American,'" 49.

36. Benjamin O. Davis to Charles Young, 1911, Colonel Charles Young Papers.

37. As quoted in Clegg, "'Splendid Type of Colored American,'" 53; Henderson, "Charles Young, Colonel," 4.

38. Charles Young to D. E. Howard, President of Liberia, October 12, 1915, Colonel Charles Young Papers.

39. Greene, *Charles Young*, 90–95.

40. Clegg, "'Splendid Type of Colored American,'" 69–70.

41. "The Feet of the Liberian Young Men," Colonel Charles Young Papers; Bennett, "Old Soldier Who Wouldn't Surrender," 88.

42. Shellum, *Black Officer in a Buffalo Soldier Regiment*, 230.

43. Charles Young to Oscar Villard, 1916, Colonel Charles Young Papers; Shellum, *Black Officer in a Buffalo Soldier Regiment*, 243–44.

44. Woodrow Wilson to Newton Baker, June 25, 1917, Woodrow Wilson Papers.

45. Obama, "Presidential Proclamation"; Buckley, *American Patriots*, 245.

46. Greene, *Charles Young*, 137–38.

47. Emmett Scott to Charles Young, June 18, 1917, Colonel Charles Young Papers.

48. Special Orders No. 119, May 23, 1917, Colonel Charles Young Papers. These orders instructed Young to report to Presidio for a physical examination. Buckley, *American Patriots*, 247.

49. Newton Baker to Woodrow Wilson, June 26, 1917, Woodrow Wilson Papers.

50. Negro Silent Protest Committee to Wilson, August 1, 1917, and John Milton Waldron to Woodrow Wilson, May 11, 1917, Woodrow Wilson Papers; Jordan, *Black Newspapers and America's War for Democracy*, 126–27; Mjagkij, *Loyalty in Time of Trial*, xxiii.

51. Kilroy, *For Race and Country*, 121–25. Young was not the only black officer attempting to be reinstated. Henry O. Flipper, the first black man to graduate from West Point, was dishonorably discharged from the army in 1881 on charges of embezzlement. For the remainder of his life, Flipper attempted to clear his name. There were several small campaigns to have him reinstated by the black community during the Spanish-American War so he could serve with Young in a militia unit. Flipper rejected this idea. See his memoir, *Black Frontiersman*.

52. Kilroy, *For Race and Country*, 130–31.

53. *Washington Bee*, July 7, 1917; *Cleveland Gazette*, August 8, 1917; Greene, *Charles Young*, 177.

54. W. E. B. Du Bois, "Charles Young's Eulogy," *The Crisis*, June 8, 1923.

CONCLUSION

1. Baldwin, *Notes of a Native Son*, 169; Keene quoted in Snell, *Unknown Soldiers*.

2. E. Johnson, *History of Negro Soldiers*, 133–39; Curtis, *Black Soldier*, 56; Schneider, *"We Return Fighting,"* 36.

3. Steward, *Colored Regulars*, 326–27.

4. Patton, *War and Race*, 6–7.

5. Schubert, *On the Trail of the Buffalo Soldier*, 262–63.

6. Schneider, *"We Return Fighting,"* 3.

BIBLIOGRAPHY

MANUSCRIPT AND ARCHIVE COLLECTIONS

Fisk University Special Collections, Nashville, Tenn.
  W. E. B Du Bois Collection (including "The Black Man in the
    Wounded World" manuscript and research materials)
Library of Virginia, Richmond
  Virginia War History Commission Questionnaire (http://www.lva.lib
    .va.us)
Memphis Public Library, Special Collections, Memphis, Tenn.
  George Washington Lee Collection
Moorland-Spingarn Research Center, Howard University, Washington, D.C.
  Walter Loving Papers
  Emmett J. Scott Papers
  Joel E. Spingarn Papers
Nebraska Historical Society, Lincoln
  Henry V. Plummer Collection
Ohio Historical Society, Columbus
  Colonel Charles Young Papers (http://dbs.ohiohistory.org/africanam
    /html/mss/831.html)
Schomburg Center for Research in Black Culture, New York Public Library,
  New York
  Henry Plummer Cheatham Collection
  William H. Dyer Collection
  Christian A. Fleetwood Papers
  Jesse Johnson Collection
  Melvin McGraw Collection
  Theophilus G. Steward Collection
  Booker T. Washington Collection
U.S. Army Military History Institute, Carlisle Barracks, Pa.
  Wilbert Curtis Papers

Richard Johnson Collection
Samuel Jones Papers
Thomas Jordan Papers
Vance Marchbanks Papers
Spanish-American War Project Questionnaire
U.S. Military Academy, West Point, New York
Buffalo Soldiers Collection
John Castles Collection
U.S. National Archives, Washington, D.C.
Adjutant General Office, RG 94, AGO file #7043 and 1356799
Before the Committee on Military Affairs, House of Representatives, 55th Cong., 2nd Sess., H.R. 9849: In the Matter of the Court-Martial of Henry Ossian Flipper, Statement and Brief for Petitioner, RG 233
Federal Surveillance of Afro-Americans, 1917–1925: The First World War, the Red Scare, and the Garvey Movement, edited by Theodore Kornweibel (Frederick: University Publications of America, 1985), RG 86/100, reel 18–25
General Records of Selected Documents Relating to Blacks Nominated for Appointment to the U.S. Military Academy during the 19th Century, 1870–1887, roll 21
Muster Rolls, Ninth Cavalry, 1891–1912
Records of the Adjutant General's Office, RG 94, document file 1890–1917
Records of the American Expeditionary Forces (World War I), RG 120
Records of the Colored Troops Division, 1863–94, RG 94.7
Records Relating to the Army Career of Henry Ossian Flipper, 1873–1882, RG 153, Records of the Judge Advocate General, QQ-2952, T-1027, Washington, D.C., Government Printing Office
Regimental Records, Ninth United States Volunteer Infantry, 1898–99
University of Massachusetts–Amherst Special Collections and Archives
W. E. B. Du Bois Collection (http://credo.library.umass.edu/view /collection/mums312)
University of Memphis, Special Collections, Memphis, Tenn.
Church Papers
Woodrow Wilson Presidential Library, Staunton, Va.
Woodrow Wilson Papers (http://www.woodrowwilson.org/library -archives)

GOVERNMENT PUBLICATIONS
Federal
Adjutant-General of the Army and Military Commanders in the United States, Cuba, Puerto Rico, China, and the Philippine Islands. *Correspondence Relating*

to the War with Spain and Conditions Growing Out of the Same, Including the Insurrection in the Philippine Islands and the China Relief Expedition, from April 15, 1898 to July 30, 1902 in Two Volumes. Washington, D.C., 1902.

Schurz, Carl. Report on the Condition of the South. 39th Cong., Senate. Ex. Doc. 1st Session. No. 2. 1865.

U.S. Congress, Senate. U.S. Congressional Serial Set. "The Brownsville Affray: Report of the Inspector-General of the Army; Order of the President Discharging Enlisted Men of Companies B, C, and D, Twenty-Fifth Infantry; Messages of the President of the Senate; and Majority and Minority Reports of the Senate Committee on Military Affairs." Washington, D.C.: U.S. Government Printing Office, 1908.

U.S. Department of the Interior, Bureau of the Census. Tenth Census of the United States, 1890: Population. Washington, D.C.: U.S. Government Printing Office, 1900.

———. Eleventh Census of the United States, 1900: Population. Washington, D.C.: U.S. Government Printing Office, 1910.

U.S. Department of War. The Annual Reports of the Secretary of War, 1867–1917. Washington, D.C.: U.S. Government Printing Office, 1867–1918.

———. Office of the Adjutant General. General Court-Martial Orders, Adjutant General's Office, 1881. Washington, D.C.: U.S. Government Printing Office, 1882.

———. Office of the Judge Advocate General. Register of the Records for the Proceedings of the U.S. Army General Court-Martial 1809–1890. Vol. 16, 1877–83 QQ. National Archives Microfilm Publication M1105, Roll 7. Washington, D.C.: National Archives and Records Administration.

———. "Records Relating to the Army Career of Henry Ossian Flipper, 1873-1883." National Archives Microfilm Publication T-1027. Washington, D.C.: National Archives and Records Administration, n.d.

State

Regimental Records of the Third North Carolina. Raleigh: Edwards Broughton and E. M. Uzzell, State Printers, 1900.

THESES AND DISSERTATIONS

Doward, Oscar W., Jr. "Determining If the Actions of African American Combat Forces during World War I Positively Affected the Employment of African American Combat Soldiers during World War II." M.A. thesis, U.S. Army Command and General College, 2007.

Nelson, Timothy Eugene. "The Significance of the Afro-Frontier in American History: Blackdom, Barratry, and Bawdyhouses in the Borderlands, 1900–1930." Ph.D. diss., University of Texas, El Paso, 2015.

Oder, Barron Krieg. "Education, 'Race-Adjustment' and the Military: The Life and Work of Chaplain Allen Allensworth, 24th Infantry, US Army." Ph.D. diss., University of New Mexico, 1994.

Taylor, John J. "Does Anyone Care? Henry O. Flipper and the United States Army." M.A. thesis, U.S. Army Command and General College, 1995.

Wegmann, Andrew N. "Christian Community and the Development of an Americo-Liberian Identity, 1822–1878." M.A. thesis, Louisiana State University, 2010.

Williams, Chad L. "Torchbearers of Democracy: The First World War and the Figure of the African American Soldier." Ph.D. diss., Princeton University, 2004.

ARTICLES

Amron, Andrew D. "Reinforcing Manliness: Black State Militias, the Spanish American War, and the Image of the African American Soldier, 1891–1900." *Journal of African American History* 97, no. 4 (Fall 2012): 401–26.

Auxier, George W. "Middle Western Newspapers and the Spanish American War, 1895–1898." *Mississippi Valley Historical Review* 26, no. 4 (March 1940): 523–34.

Baylen, Joseph O., and John Hammond Moore. "Senator John Tyler Morgan and Negro Colonization in the Philippines, 1901–1902." *Phylon* 29, no. 1 (First Quarter 1968): 65–75.

Bennett, Lerone, Jr. "The Old Soldier Who Wouldn't Surrender." *Ebony*, November 1974, 85–95.

Bentz, Donald. "Black Pioneers at the U.S. Military Academies." *Journal of Blacks in Higher Education* 39 (Spring 2003): 12–14.

———. "Henry Flipper: West Point's First Black Graduate." *The West* 15, no. 14 (July 1972): 17–19, 56–58.

Bond, Horace Mann. "The Negro in the Armed Forces of the United States prior to World War I." *Journal of Negro Education* 12, no. 3 (July 1941): 268–87.

Bonsal, Stephen. "The Negro Soldier in War and Peace." *North American Review* 185, no. 616 (June 1907): 321–27.

Bragg, Bea. "Calm under Fire: Henry Ossian Flipper, First Black Graduate of West Point." *Highlights*, February 1999, 3–18.

Brown, Scot. "White Backlash and the Aftermath of Fagen's Rebellion: The Fates of Three African-American Soldiers in the Philippines, 1901–1902." *Contributions in Black Studies* 13, art. 5 (1995): 166–73.

Buecker, Thomas R. "One Soldier's Service: Caleb Benson in the Ninth and Tenth Cavalry, 1875–1908." *Nebraska History* 74 (1993): 54–62.

Chase, Hal J. "The Struggle for Equality: Fort Des Moines Training Camp for Colored Officers, 1917." *Phylon* 39 (Winter 1978): 297–310.

Clark, Michael J. "Improbable Ambassadors: Black Soldiers at Fort Douglas, 1896–1898." *Utah Historical Quarterly* 46, no. 3 (Summer 1978): 285–92.

Clegg, Claude. "'A Splendid Type of Colored American': Charles Young and the

Reorganization of the Liberian Frontier Force." *International Journal of African Historical Studies* 29 (Winter 1996): 47–70.

Clifford, James. "Medal of Honor Recipient: Army Veteran Paves the Way for African Americans in the Military." *Armed Forces Retirement Home Communicator*, January 31, 2008, 1–7.

Dinges, Bruce J. "The Court-Martial of Lieutenant Henry O. Flipper: An Example of Black-White Relationships in the Army, 1881." *American West* 9 (January 1972): 12–17, 59–61.

Du Bois, W. E. B. "The American Negro at Paris." *American Monthly Review of Reviews* 22, no. 5 (November 1900): 130–40.

———. "The Negro Soldier in Service Abroad during the First World War." *Journal of Negro Education* 12, no. 3 (Summer 1943): 324–34.

Emerson, Edwin, Jr. "The Negro as a Soldier." *Collier's Weekly*, October 8, 1898.

Eppinga, Janet. "Henry O. Flipper in the Court of Private Land Claims: The Arizona Career of West Point's First Black Graduate." *Journal of Arizona History* 36 (Spring 1995): 33–54.

Fletcher, Marvin. "The Black Volunteers in the Spanish-American War." *Military Affairs* 38, no. 2 (April 1974): 48–53.

———. "The Negro Volunteer in Reconstruction, 1865–1866." *Military Affairs* 32, no. 3 (December 1968): 124–31.

Garfield, James A. "The Army of the United States." *North American Review* 126, no. 261 (March–April 1878): 193–216.

Gatewood, Willard B., Jr. "Black Americans and the Quest for Empire." *Journal of Southern History* 38, no. 4 (November 1972): 545–66.

———. "An Experiment in Color: The Eighth Illinois Volunteers, 1898–1899." *Journal of the Illinois State Historical Society* 65, no. 3 (Autumn 1972): 293–312.

———. "John Hanks Alexander of Arkansas: Second Black Graduate of West Point." *Arkansas Historical Quarterly* 41, no. 2 (Summer 1982): 103–28.

———. "Negro Soldier Experiment, 1898–1899." *Journal of Negro History* 57, no. 4 (October 1972): 333–51.

———. "Negro Troops in Florida, 1898." *Florida Historical Quarterly* 49, no. 1 (July 1970): 1–15.

———. "Virginia's Negro Regiment in the Spanish-American War: The Sixth Virginia Volunteers." *Virginia Magazine of History and Biography* 80, no. 2 (April 1972): 195–99.

Gianakos, Perry E. "The Spanish-American War and the Double Paradox of the Negro American." *Phylon* 26, no. 1 (First Quarter 1965): 34–49.

Glasrud, Bruce A. "Western Soldiers since the Buffalo Soldiers: A Review of the Literature." *Social Science Journal* 36, no. 2 (1999): 251–70.

Hall, Jacquelyn Dowd. "The Long Civil Rights Movement and the Political Uses of the Past." *Journal of American History* 91, no. 4 (March 2005): 1233–63.

Hansen, Susan D. "The Racial History of the U.S. Military Academies." *Journal of Blacks in Higher Education* 26 (Winter 1999–2000): 111–16.

Keene, Jennifer. "W. E. B. Du Bois and the Wounded World: Seeking Meaning in the First World War for African Americans." *Peace and Change* 26, no. 2 (April 2001): 135–52.

Kiesling, Eugenia. "On War without Fog." *Military Review* 81, no. 5 (September–October 2001): 325–29.

Koelle, Alexandra V. "Pedaling on the Periphery: The African American Twenty-Fifth Infantry Bicycle Corps and the Roads of American Expansion." *Western Historical Quarterly* 41, no. 3 (Autumn 2010): 305–26.

Meier, August, and David Lewis. "History of the Negro Upper Class in Atlanta, Georgia, 1890–1958." *Journal of Negro Education* 28 (Spring 1959): 128–39.

Ngozi-Brown, Scot. "African-American Soldiers and Filipinos: Racial Imperialism, Jim Crow and Social Relations." *Journal of Negro History* 82, no. 1 (Winter 1997): 42–53.

Reddick, L. D. "The Negro Policy of the United States Army, 1775–1945." *Journal of Negro History* 34, no. 1 (January 1949): 9–29.

Reed, David L. "Rayford W. Logan: The Evolution of a Pan-African Protégé, 1921–1927." *Journal of Pan-African Studies* 6, no. 8 (March 2014): 27–53.

Roosevelt, Theodore. "The Rough Riders." *Scribner's Magazine*, April 1899, 420–50.

Schubert, Frank N. "The Black Soldiers on the White Frontier: Some Factors Influencing Race Relations." *Phylon* 32, no. 4 (Winter 1971): 410–15.

———. "The Violent World of Emmanuel Stance, Fort Robinson, 1887." *Nebraska History* 55 (1974): 203–20.

Sears, Louis Martin. "French Opinion of the Spanish-American War." *Hispanic American Historical Review* 7, no. 1 (February 1927): 25–44.

Shellum, Brian G. "The Silencing of Early Black Cadets at West Point." *Journal of Blacks in Higher Education*, no. 51 (Spring 2006): 72–73.

Smith, Steven D. *The African American Soldiers at Fort Huachuca, Arizona, 1892–1946.* U.S. Army and the Center of Expertise for Preservation of Historic Structures and Buildings, U.S. Army Corps of Engineer, Seattle District (February 2001).

Smythe, Donald. "Pershing in the Spanish-American War." *Military Affairs* 30, no. 1 (Spring 1966): 25–33.

Spencer, Tracey Lovette, James E. Spencer Jr., and Bruce G. Wright. "World War I as I Saw It: The Memoir of an African American Soldier." *Massachusetts Historical Review* 9 (2007): 134–65.

Squires, Catherine R. "Rethinking the Black Public Sphere: An Alternative Vocabulary for Multiple Public Spheres." *Communication Theory* 12, no. 4 (2002): 446–68.

Stover, Earl F. "Chaplain Henry V. Plummer, His Ministry and His Court-Martial." *Nebraska History* 56 (1975): 20–50.

Upton, Larry, and Larry D. Ball. "Who Robbed Major Wham? Facts and Folklore behind Arizona's Great Paymaster Robbery." *Journal of Arizona History* 38, no. 2 (1997): 99–100.

Vaughn, William P. "West Point and the First Negro Cadet." *Military Affairs* 35, no. 3 (October 1971): 100–102.

Williams, Chad L. "Vanguards of the New Negro: African American Veterans and Post–World War I Racial Militancy." *Journal of African American History* 92, no. 3 (Summer 2007): 347–70.

Wilson, Steve. "A Black Lieutenant in the Ranks." *American History Illustrated* 8 (December 1983): 31–39.

Young, Charles. "The Ideals of the Negroes in the United States." *Stanford Alumnus*, December 16, 1903.

NEWSPAPERS AND OTHER PERIODICALS

A.M.E. Review

American Citizen (Kansas City)

The Appeal (St. Paul, Minn.)

Army and Navy Journal

The Bee (Washington, D.C.)

The Broad Ax (Salt Lake City and Chicago)

Chicago Defender

Chicago Record

Chicago Tribune

Colored American (Washington, D.C.)

Colored Citizen (Topeka, Kans.)

The Crisis

The Freeman (Indianapolis)

The Gazette (Cleveland, Ohio)

Illinois Record (Springfield)

Iowa Bystander (Des Moines)

The Ledger (Baltimore)

NAACP Bulletin

New York Age

New York Times

Omaha Bee

Republican Courier (New Orleans)

Richmond Planet (Va.)

Savannah Tribune (Ga.)

The Times (London)

Washington Post

BOOKS

Adam, Kevin. *Class, and Race in the Frontier Army: Military Life in the West, 1870–1890*. Norman: University of Oklahoma Press, 2014.

Alexander, Ann Field. *Race Man: The Rise and Fall of the "Fighting Editor," John Mitchell Jr.* Charlottesville: University of Virginia Press, 2002.

Alexander, Charles. *Battles and Victories of Allen Allensworth, A.M., Ph.D., Lieutenant-Colonel, Retired, U.S. Army*. Boston: Sherman, French and Company, 1914.

Astor, Gerald. *Right to Fight: A History of African American Soldiers in the Military*. Cambridge, Mass.: Da Capo Press, 2001.

Baldwin, James. *Notes of a Native Son*. Boston: Beacon, 2012.

Barbeau, Arthur, and Floretta Henri. *Unknown Soldiers: African American Troops in World War I*. Philadelphia: Temple University Press, 1974.

Beasley, Delilah Leotium. *Negro Trail Blazers of California*. Los Angeles: Timers Mirror Printing and Binding House, 1919.

Beard, Charles A., and Mary Beard. *A Basic History of the United States*. Philadelphia: Blakiston, 1944.

Bederman, Gail. *Manliness and Civilization: A Cultural History of Gender and Race in the United States, 1880–1917*. Chicago: University of Chicago Press, 1995.

Bennett, Lerone. *Before the* Mayflower*: A History of Black America*. 5th ed. New York: Penguin Group, 1982.

Berry, Mary Frances, and John W. Blassingame. *Long Memory: The Black Experience in America*. New York: Oxford University Press, 1982.

Black, Daniel P. *Dismantling Black Manhood: An Historical and Literary Analysis of the Legacy of Slavery*. New York: Routledge, 1997.

Boot, Max. *Savage Wars of Peace: Small War and the Rise of American Power*. New York: Basic Books, 2014.

Brinkley, Alan. *The Unfinished Nation: A Concise History of the American People*. 7th ed. New York: McGraw-Hill Education, 2013.

Buckley, Gail. *American Patriots: The Story of Blacks in the Military from the Revolution to Desert Storm*. New York: Random House, 2002.

Carby, Hazel V. *Race Men*. Cambridge, Mass.: Harvard University Press, 2000.

Cashin, Herschel V. *Under Fire with the Tenth United States Cavalry*. New York: Arno Press, 1899.

Chauncey, George. *Gay New York: Gender, Urban Culture, and the Making of the Gay Male World, 1890–1940*. New York: HarperCollins, 1994.

Christian, Garna L. *Black Soldiers in Jim Crow Texas, 1899–1917*. College Station: Texas A&M University Press, 1994.

Clancy, M. A., and William Nelson. *Proceedings of the Republican National Convention, held at Cincinnati, Ohio, Wednesday, Thursday, and Friday, June 14, 15, and 16, 1876*. Concord, N.H., 1876.

Cornish, Dudley Taylor. *The Sable Arm: Black Troops in the Union Army, 1861–1865*. Lawrence: University Press of Kansas, 1987.

Coston, William H. *The Spanish-American War Volunteer*. 2nd ed. Freeport: Books for Libraries Press, 1899.

Cox, Marcus S. *Segregated Soldiers: Military Training at Historically Black Colleges in the Jim Crow South*. Baton Rouge: Louisiana State University Press, 2013.

Curtis, Mary. *The Black Soldier: or, The Colored Boys of the United States Army*. Washington, D.C.: Murray Brothers, 1918.

Dobak, William A., and Thomas D. Phillips. *The Black Regulars, 1866–1898*. Norman: University of Oklahoma Press, 2001.

Donaldson, Gary. *The History of African-Americans in the Military: Double V*. Malabar, Fla.: Krieger, 1991.

Du Bois, W. E. B. *The Souls of Black Folk*. New York: Bantam Books, 1903.

Edmonds, Helen. *The Negro and Fusion Politics in North Carolina, 1894–1901*. Chapel Hill: University of North Carolina Press, 2003.

Edgerton, Robert B. *Hidden Heroism: Black Soldiers in America's Wars*. Boulder: Westview Press, 2001.

Ellis, Mark. *Race, War, and Surveillance: African Americans and the United States Government during World War I*. Bloomington: Indiana University Press, 2001.

Ferrell, Robert H. *Unjustly Dishonored: An African American Division in World War I*. Kindle ed., 2011.

Fletcher, Marvin. *The Black Soldier and Officer in the United States Army: 1891–1917*. Columbia: University of Missouri Press, 1974.

Flipper, Henry Ossian. *Black Frontiersman: The Memoirs of Henry O. Flipper*. Compiled and edited by Theodore D. Harris. Fort Worth: Texas Christian University Press, 1997.

———. *The Colored Cadet at West Point: Autobiography of Lieut. Henry Ossian Flipper, U.S.A., First Graduate of Color from the U.S. Military Academy*. New York: Homer Lee, 1878.

———. *The Western Memoirs of Henry O. Flipper, First Negro Graduate of West Point*. Edited by Theodore D. Harris. El Paso: Texas Western College Press, 1963.

Foner, Jack D. *Blacks and the Military in American History*. New York: Praeger, 1974.

Foner, Philip S. *The Spanish-Cuban-American War and the Birth of American Imperialism, 1895–1902*. New York: Monthly Review Press, 1972.

Fowler, Arlen. *Black Infantry in the West, 1869–1890*. Santa Barbara: Greenwood, 1971.

Fowler, Charles H. *Historical Romance of the American Negro*. Baltimore: Press of Thomas and Evans, 1902.

Franklin, John Hope, and Alfred A. Moss. *From Slavery to Freedom: A History of African Americans*. 7th ed. New York: McGraw-Hill, 1994.

Freidel, Frank. *The Splendid Little War*. Boston: Little, Brown, 1958.

Gaines, Kevin K. *Uplifting the Race: Black Leadership, Politics, and Culture in the Twentieth Century*. Chapel Hill: University of North Carolina Press, 1996.

Gatewood, Willard B., Jr. *Black Americans and the White Man's Burden, 1898–1903*. Urbana: University of Illinois Press, 1975.

———. *"Smoked Yankees" and the Struggle for Empire: Letters from Negro Soldiers, 1898–1902*. Urbana: University of Illinois Press, 1971.

Gilfoyle, Timothy J. *City of Eros: New York City, Prostitution, and the Commercialization of Sex, 1790–1920*. New York: W. W. Norton, 1992.

Gilmore, Glenda Elizabeth. *Gender and Jim Crow: Women and the Politics of White Supremacy in North Carolina, 1896–1920*. Chapel Hill: University of North Carolina Press, 1996.

Glasrud, Bruce, and Michael Searles, eds. *Buffalo Soldiers in the West: A Black Soldiers Anthology*. Albuquerque: University of New Mexico Press, 2007.

Greene, Robert E. *Charles Young: Soldier and Diplomat*. Washington, D.C.: Robert E. Greene, 1985.

Guthrie, J. M. *Campfires of the Afro-American: or, The Colored Man as a Patriot*. Philadelphia: Afro-American Publishing, 1899.

Haller, John, Jr. *Outcasts from Evolution: Scientific Attitudes of Racial Inferiority, 1859–1900*. Chicago: University of Illinois Press, 1971.

Hamburger, Kenneth E. *Learning Lessons in the American Expeditionary Forces*. Washington, D.C.: U.S. Army Center of Military History, 1997.

Harlan, Louis R. *Booker T. Washington: The Making of a Black Leader, 1856–1901*. London: Oxford University Press, 1972.

Harris, Stephen L. *Harlem's Hell Fighters: The African-American 369th Infantry in World War I*. Washington, D.C.: Potomac Books, 2003.

Harris, Theodore D. *Black Frontiersman: The Memoirs of Henry O. Flipper*. Fort Worth: Texas Christian University Press, 1997.

Hawbaker, John J. *Toward the Great War: U.S. Army Operations and Mexico, 1865–1917*. Fort Leavenworth: U.S. Army Command and Staff College, 2011.

Hayne, Robert J. *A Night of Violence: The Houston Riot of 1917*. Baton Rouge: Louisiana State University Press, 1976.

Haywood, Harry. *Black Bolshevik: An Autobiography of an Afro-American Communist*. Chicago: Liberator Press, 1979.

Heinl, Robert Debs, and Nancy Gordon Heinl. *Written in Blood: The Story of the Haitian People, 1492–1995*. Lanham, Md.: University Press of America, 2005.

Hendrickson, Kenneth E., Jr. *The Spanish-American War*. Westport, Conn.: Greenwood Press, 2003.

Higginson, Thomas Wentworth. *Army Life in a Black Regiment and Other Writings*. New York: Penguin Books, 1997.

Hill, Robert A., ed. *The Marcus Garvey and Universal Negro Improvement Association Papers*. Vol. 1, *1826–August 1919*. Berkeley: University of California Press, 1983.

Hine, Darlene Clark, William C. Hine, and Stanley C. Harold. *The African-American Odyssey*. Upper Saddle River, N.J.: Prentice Hall, 2006.

Hine, Darlene Clark, and Earnestine Jenkins. *A Question of Manhood: A Reader in U.S. Black Men's History of Masculinity*. Vols. 1 and 2. Bloomington: Indiana University Press, 2001.

Hirsch, James S. *Riot and Remembrance: The Tulsa Race War and Its Legacy*. Boston: Houghton Mifflin, 2002.

Hoganson, Kristen L. *Fighting for American Manhood: How Gender Politics Provoked the Spanish-American and Philippine-American Wars*. New Haven: Yale University Press, 1998.

Horne, Gerald. *Black and Brown: African Americans and the Mexican Revolution, 1910–1920*. New York: New York University Press, 2005.

Hunton, Addie, and Kathryn M. Johnson. *Two Colored Women with the American Expeditionary Force*. Brooklyn: Brooklyn Eagle Press, 1920.

Jackson, Ronald L., and Murali Balaji, eds. *Global Masculinities and Manhood*. Champaign: University of Illinois Press, 2014.

Jackson, Shona N. *Creole Indigeneity: Between Myth and Nation in the Caribbean*. Minneapolis: University of Minnesota Press, 2012.

James, Jennifer C. *A Freedom Bought with Blood: African American War Literature from the Civil War to World War II*. Chapel Hill: University of North Carolina Press, 2007.

Jensen, Geoffrey W., ed. *The Routledge Handbook of the History of Race and the American Military*. New York: Routledge, 2016.

Johnson, Barry C. *Flipper's Dismissal: The Ruin of Lt. Henry O. Flipper, First Colored Graduate of West Point*. London: Privately printed, 1980.

Johnson, Edward A. *History of Negro Soldiers in the Spanish-American War*. Raleigh: Capital Printing, 1899.

Jordan, William. *Black Newspapers and America's War for Democracy*. Chapel Hill: University of North Carolina Press, 2001.

Keene, Jennifer. *Doughboys, the Great War, and the Remaking of America*. Baltimore: Johns Hopkins University Press, 2001.

Kenner, Charles. *Buffalo Soldiers and Officers of the Ninth Cavalry*. Norman: University of Oklahoma Press, 1999.

Kilroy, David P. *For Race and Country: The Life and Career of Colonel Charles Young*. Westport, Conn.: Praeger, 2003.

Kimmel, Michael. *The Gendered Society*. New York: Oxford University Press, 2004.

———. *Manhood in America: A Cultural History*. New York: Free Press, 1996.

Kornweibel, Theodore, Jr. *"Investigate Everything": Federal Efforts to Ensure Black Loyalty during World War I*. Bloomington: Indiana University Press, 2002.

———. *"Seeing Red": Federal Campaigns against Black Militancy, 1919–1925*. Bloomington: Indiana University Press, 1998.

Lanning, Michael Lee. *The African-American Soldier: From Crispus Attucks to Colin Powell*. Secaucus, N.J.: Birch Lane Press Book, 1997.

Leckie, William H. *The Buffalo Soldiers: A Narrative of the Negro Cavalry in the West*. Norman: University of Oklahoma Press, 1967.

Leiker, James. *Racial Borders: Black Soldiers along the Rio Grande*. College Station: Texas A&M University Press, 2002.

Lentz-Smith, Adriane. *Freedom Struggles: African Americans and World War I*. Cambridge, Mass.: Harvard University Press, 2009.

Leonard, Elizabeth. *Men of Color to Arms! Black Soldiers, Indian Wars, and the Quest for Equality*. New York: W. W. Norton, 2010.

Lewis, David Levering. *W. E. B Du Bois: A Biography of a Race, 1868–1919*. New York: Henry Holt, 1993.

———. *W. E. B. Du Bois: The Fight for Equality and the American Century, 1919–1963*. New York: Henry Holt, 2000.

Lindquist, Malinda Alaine. *Race, Social Science and the Crisis of Manhood, 1890–1970*. New York: Routledge, 2013.

Love, Eric T. *Race over Empire: Racism and U.S. Imperialism, 1865–1900*. Chapel Hill: University of North Carolina Press, 2004.

Lynk, Miles V. *The Black Troopers: Or the Daring Heroism of the Negro Soldiers in the Spanish-American War*. New York: AMS Press, 1899.

MacGregor, Morris J., and Bernard C. Nalty. *Blacks in the United States Armed Forces: Basic Documents*. Vol. 3, *Freedom and Jim Crow, 1865–1917*. Wilmington, Del.: Scholarly Resources, 1977.

———. *Blacks in the Military: Essential Documents*. Wilmington, Del.: Scholarly Resources, 1981.

Marks, George P. *The Black Press Views American Imperialism, 1898–1900*. New York: Arno Press, 1971.

Mather, Frank Lincoln. *Who's Who of the Colored Race: A General Biographical Dictionary of Men and Women of African Descent*. Vol. 1, *1915*. 1915; repr., Ann Arbor: Literary Licensing, 2014.

Matthews, Matt M. *The U.S. Army on the Mexican Border: A Historical Perspective*. Fort Leavenworth: Combat Studies Press, 2005.

McCoy, Alfred W. *Policing America's Empire: The United States, the Philippines, and the Rise of the Surveillance State*. Madison: University of Wisconsin Press, 2009.

McWhirter, Cameron. *Red Summer: The Summer of 1919 and the Awakening of Black America*. New York: Henry Holt, 2011.

Miller, Albert. *Elevating the Race: Theophilus Gould Steward, Black Theology, and the Making of an African American Civil Society, 1865–1924*. Knoxville: University of Tennessee Press, 2003.

Miller, Kelly. *The World War for Human Rights*. Washington, D.C.: Austin Jenkins, 1919.

Minton, John. *The Houston Riot and Court-Martials of 1917.* San Antonio: University of Texas Institute of Texan Cultures, 1995.

Mitchell, Michele. *Righteous Propagation: African Americans and the Politics of Racial Destiny after Reconstruction.* Chapel Hill: University of North Carolina Press, 2004.

Mjagkij, Nina. *Loyalty in Time of Trial: The African Experience during World War I.* Lanham, Md.: Rowan and Littlefield, 2006.

Morris, Edmund. *The Rise of Theodore Roosevelt.* New York: Modern Library, 1979.

Morrow, John H., Jr. *The Great War: An Imperial History.* New York: Routledge, 2005.

Nalty, Bernard C. *Strength for the Fight: A History of Black Americans in the Military.* New York: Free Press, 1986.

Nankivell, John H. *History of the Twenty-Fifth Regiment of the United States Infantry, 1869–1926.* Lincoln: University of Nebraska Press, 1927.

Nash, Gary B., Julie Roy Jeffery, John R. Howe, Peter J. Frederick, Allen F. Davis, and Allan M. Winkler. *The American People: Creating a Nation and a Society.* Vol. 2, *Since 1865.* 4th ed. New York: Longman, 1998.

Onishi, Yuchiro. *Transpacific Antiracism: Afro-Asian Solidarity in 20th-Century Black America, Japan, and Okinawa.* New York: NYU Press, 2013.

Palmer, Colin, ed. *Encyclopedia of African-American Culture and History.* 2nd ed. New York: Macmillan Reference, 2006.

Patton, Gerald W. *War and Race: The Black Officer in the American Military, 1915–1941.* Santa Fe: Greenwood Press, 1981.

Pérez, Louis A., Jr. *The War of 1898: The United States and Cuba in History and Historiography.* Chapel Hill: University of North Carolina Press, 1998.

Perry, Jeffrey B. *Hubert Harrison: The Voice of Harlem Radicalism, 1883–1918.* New York: Columbia University Press, 2011.

Pfeifer, Michael. *Roots of Rough Justice: Origins of Lynching.* Champaign: University of Illinois Press, 2014.

Pipkin, J. J. *The Negro in Revelation, in History, and in Citizenship.* St. Louis: N. D. Thompson, 1902.

Quarles, Benjamin. *The Negro in the Civil War.* Boston: Da Capo Press, 1953.

Renda, Mary. *Taking Haiti: Military Occupation and the Culture of U.S. Imperialism, 1914–1940.* Chapel Hill: University of North Carolina Press, 2001.

Richardson, Richie. *Black Masculinity and the U.S. South: From Uncle Tom to Gangsta.* Athens: University of Georgia Press, 2007.

Robinson, Charles. *The Court Martial of Henry O. Flipper.* El Paso: Texas Western Press, 1994.

Rodenbough, Theophilus Frances, and William L. Haskin, eds. *The Army of the United States Historical Sketches of Staff and Line with Portraits of Generals-in-Chief.* New York: Maynard, Merrell and Co., 1896.

Roosevelt, Theodore. *The Rough Riders*. 1899; repr., New York: Charles Scribner's Sons, 1939.

Rotundo, E. Anthony. *American Manhood: Transformations in Masculinity from the Revolution to the Modern Era*. New York: Basic Books, 1993.

Samito, Christian. *Becoming American under Fire: Irish Americans, African Americans, and the Politics of Citizenship during the Civil War Era*. Ithaca: Cornell University Press, 2009.

Sammons, Jeffrey T., and John H. Morrow Jr. *Harlem's Rattlers and the Great War: The Undaunted 365th Regiment and the African American Quest for Equality*. Lawrence: University of Kansas Press, 2014.

Savage, Kirk. *Standing Soldiers, Kneeling Slaves: Race, War, and Monument in Nineteenth-Century America*. Princeton: Princeton University Press, 1997.

Schneider, Mark Robert. *"We Return Fighting": The Civil Rights Movement in the Jazz Age*. Boston: Northeastern University Press, 2002.

Schoonover, Thomas. *Uncle Sam's War of 1898 and the Origins of Globalization*. Lexington: University Press of Kentucky, 2003.

Schubert, Frank N. *On the Trail of the Buffalo Soldier: Biographies of African Americans in the U.S. Army, 1866–1917*. Wilmington, Del.: Scholarly Resources, 1995.

———. *Voices of the Buffalo Soldier: Records, Reports, and Recollections of Military Life and Service in the West*. Albuquerque: University of New Mexico Press, 2003.

Schuyler, George S. *Black and Conservative: The Autobiography of George S. Schuyler*. New Rochelle, N.Y.: Arlington House, 1966.

Scott, Emmett J. *Emmett Scott's Official History of the American Negro in the Great War*. Chicago: Homewood Press, 1919.

Shellum, Brian G. *Black Cadet in a White Bastion: Charles Young at West Point*. Lincoln: University of Nebraska Press, 2006.

———. *Black Officer in a Buffalo Soldier Regiment: The Military Career of Charles Young*. Lincoln: University of Nebraska Press, 2010.

Snell, Mark A., ed. *Unknown Soldiers: The American Expeditionary Forces in Memory and Remembrance*. Kent: Kent State University Press, 2008.

Steward, T. G. *The Colored Regulars in the United States Army*. Amherst: Humanity Books, 1904.

———. *Fifty Years in the Gospel Ministry from 1864 to 1914; Twenty-Seven Years in the Pastorate; Sixteen Years' Active Service as Chaplain in the U.S. Army; Seven Years Professor in Wilberforce University; Two Trips to Europe; a Trip in Mexico*. Philadelphia: A.M.E. Book Concern, 1921.

Stover, Earl F. *Up from Handymen: The U.S. Army Chaplaincy, 1865–1920*. Honolulu: University Press of the Pacific, 2004.

Summers, Martin. *Manliness and Its Discontents: The Black Middle Class and the Transformation of Masculinity, 1900–1930*. Chapel Hill: University of North Carolina Press, 2004.

Sweeney, Allison W. *History of the American Negro in the Great World War*. New York: Negro Universities Press, 1969.

Talbert, Roy, Jr. *Negative Intelligence: The Army and the American Left, 1917–1941*. Jackson: University of Mississippi Press, 1991.

Taylor, Quintard. *In Search of the Racial Frontier: African Americans in the American West, 1528–1990*. New York: W. W. Norton, 1998.

Washington, Booker T. *Booker T. Washington Papers*. Vol. 4, *1895–98*. Edited by Louis R. Harlan. Urbana: University Illinois Press, 1975.

Weaver, John. *The Brownsville Raid*. College Station: Texas A&M University Press, 1971.

Wheeler, Joseph. *The Santiago Campaign, 1898*. Boston: Lamson, Wolffe, and Company, 1898.

Williams, Albert. *Black Warriors: Unique Units and Individuals*. West Conshohocken, Pa.: Infinity, 2003.

Williams, Chad L. *Torchbearers of Democracy: African American Soldiers in the World War I Era*. Chapel Hill: University of North Carolina Press, 2010.

Williams, Oscar R. *George S. Schuyler: Portrait of a Black Conservative*. Knoxville: University of Tennessee Press, 2007.

Work, Monroe N. *Negro Year Book: An Encyclopedia of the Negro, 1918–1919*. Tuskegee: Negro Year Book Publishing Company, 1919.

Young, Charles. *Military Morale of Nations and Races*. Kansas City, Kans.: Franklin Hudson, 1912.

ONLINE SOURCES

American Battle Monuments Commission. *92d Division Summary of Operations in the World War*. Washington, D.C.: U.S. Government Printing Office, 1944. http://www.history.army.mil/topics/afam/92div.htm (accessed July 7, 2014).

———. *93d Division Summary of Operations in the World War*. Washington, D.C.: U.S. Government Printing Office, 1944. http://www.history.army.mil/topics/afam/93div.htm (accessed July 7, 2014).

Boehringer, Gill H. "Imperial Paranoia and Military Injustice: The Persecution and Redemption of Sergeant Calloway." http://mail.dialogue21.com/vb/showthread.php (accessed October 10, 2013).

Borch, Fred L., III. "'The Largest Murder Trial in the History of the United States': The Houston Riots Court Martial of 1917." *The Army Lawyer*, February 2011, 1–2. https://www.loc.gov/rr/frd/Military–Law/pdf/02-2011.pdf.

Henderson, Franklin J. "Charles Young, Colonel, United States Army, Third Black Graduate, United States Military Academy, West Point NY." www.buffalosoldiers-washington.com/Colonel%20Charles%20Young.doc (accessed June 5, 2014).

Logan, Rayford. *Historical Aspects of Pan-Africanism: A Personal Chronicle.* Freedom Archives. https://www.freedomarchives.org/Documents/Finder /Black%20Liberation%20Disk/Black%20Power!/SugahData/Essays /Logan.S.pdf (accessed August 28, 2014).

Obama, Barack. "Presidential Proclamation—Charles Young Buffalo Soldiers National Monument." The White House, March 25, 2013. https://www. whitehouse.gov/the-press-office/2013/03/25/presidential-proclamation -charles-young-buffalo-soldiers-national-monume (accessed June 3, 2014).

"The Plan of San Diego." 1915. Digital History. http://www.digitalhistory .uh.edu/disp_textbook.cfm?smtID=3&psid=3692 (accessed August 10, 2014).

Shumaker, Susan. *Untold Stories from America's National Parks.* PBS.org . http://www.pbs.org/nationalparks/media/pdfs/tnp-abi-untold-stories -pt-09-wright.pdf (accessed August 2, 2014).

"The Zimmermann Telegram." National Archives. http://www.archives.gov /education/lessons/zimmermann/ (accessed September 7, 2014).

INDEX

Page locators in italics indicate illustrations.

Homer Lee and Company, 118
home rule campaign, 40
Horne, Gerald, 19
Houston, Charles Hamilton, 78
Houston uprising, 71–75
Howard, D. E., 142
Howard, Michael, 112
Howard, Oliver Otis, 112, 114, 169n5, 170n8
Huerta, Victoriano, 145
Hunt, Blair, 88
Huntsville, Alabama, 53

Illinois Record, 45, 46
"immune" regiments, Cuba conflict, 46, 161n23
imperialist ideology, 39, 55–56
Indianapolis Freeman, 43, 53
Indigenous Americans, 7, 14, 20, 34, 39–40
Influence of Sea Power on History (Mahan), 39
insurgent propaganda, Philippines conflict, 59, 164n53
International League of Darker Peoples, 80
International Migration Society, 29

Jackson, Shona, 7
Jackson, Thornton, 21
Jackson, W. H., 57
Jacobi, Joseph C., 25
Jeffers, D. F., 30
Jim Crow racism. *See specific topics, e.g.,* labor units, World War I; officers, black; racial violence/abuse
Johnson, Benton, 80
Johnson, Edward, 151
Johnson, Frank, 73
Johnson, William H., 49, 50, 162n27
Johnson, Wyoming, 36
Johnson County War, 35–36
Jones, Sergeant, 29
Journal of Negro History, 124

Kansas City Times, 29–30
Keene, Jennifer, 86, 151
Keim, Deb. Randolph, 18
Kent, Jacob Ford, 47

Key West, arrivals of black regiments, 42
Kilroy, David, 129
King, Mrs. Irsle, 125
Knoxville, Tennessee, 48–50, 51
Koelle, Alexandra, 23
Ku Klux Klan, 75

labor units, World War I, 81, 83, 86, 88–89, 90, 167n40
Laden, Wyoming, 22
Lake City, South Carolina, 41
Lansing, Robert, 144
Leavenworth penitentiary, 74
Lee, George Washington, 84, 87–88, 91–92
Leiker, James, 20
Lemus, Rienzi, 153
Lewis, David Levering, 132
Lewis, John E., 45–46
Liberia, 115–16, 120, 140–44, 148, 173n34
Lightfoot, James K., 164n56
Lincoln, Robert Todd, 119, 122
Lincoln League, 91–92
literacy education, soldier opportunities, 9, 19, 24–27, 32, 33, *103*
Livety, J. C., 30
Lodge, Henry Cabot, 39
Logan, Rayford, 67, 83–84, 91, 92–93, 169n61
Lost Generation, 92, 169n61
Louisiana Territory, purchase price, 163n42
Louisville, Kentucky, 38
L'Ouverture, Toussaint, 138
Loving, Walter H.: on Du Bois as officer, 89; federal appointment, 67; and Houston uprising, 73; Military Intelligence position, 167n36; portrait of, *104*; report on racial violence, 166n20; report on white officer problem, 84–85; and Simmons' speech tour, 75–76; Young's influence, 127
Lucky, Reuben H., 110
lynchings, 13, 24, 71, 166n20

MacColl, Ray O., 124
Macon, Georgia, 48, 50, 123
Madero, Francesco, 145

Mahan, Alfred Thayer, 39

Maine, USS, 39, 42

manhood themes, overviews: black soldier symbolism, 7–8, 41, 54, 75, 90; citizenship connection, 40; crisis perspective, 43, 161n15; in militarism spirit, 43, 160n12; with military service, 2–3, 4–5; Philippines conflict, 57, 60–61, 63–65; Reconstruction Era, 16–17; role modeling, 45; World War I, 86. *See also specific topics, e.g.,* military service, overviews; western frontier, black soldiers

Manly, Alexander, 53

Marchbanks, Vance Hunter, 13, 38

marriage, Filipinos-black soldiers, 59–60, 62, 63–64

Mason, Patrick, 58

Matthews, Matt, 68

Mays, Isaiah, 1–2, *95*

McCain, Henry P., 146

McComb, Henry, 17

McKay, Barney, 14, 28–29, 123

McKellar, Kenneth, 85, 168n45

McKibbon, Carol, 6

McKinley, William: African American appointments, 41; Cuba conflict, 42, 52, 123, 160n12; Flipper's appeal, 123, 124; Philippines conflict, 55–56; troop reviews, 52, 134; Wilmington riot, 53; Young relationship, 135

McMullan, J. R., 29

Medal of Honor, 1, 17, 43, *95*, *99*, 164n56

Memphis, 71, 91–92, 166n20

"Men of Color to Arms" (Douglass), 128

Merritt, Lt. Col., 34

Meuse-Argonne campaign, 86

Mexicans, prejudice against, 54

Mexico, border conflicts, 9–10, 19–20, 68–71, *101–2*, 145–46, 165n6

Military Morale of Nations and Races (Young), 126–27, 133, 138–39

military service, overviews: and citizenship rights, 2–3, 8, 14, 128; as civil rights activism, 3–5, 78, 151–54; creation of black regiments, 17–18; literature review, 5, 6–7; Reconstruction Era significance, 15–17; statistics, 15, 17. *See also specific topics, e.g.,*

Cuba conflict; Filipino Rebellion; western frontier, black soldiers; Young, Charles

Militia Bureau, black soldier guidelines, 84

Miller, Albert, 24

Mills, A. L., 84

Mills, Ada (later Young), 173n28

Mississippi Plan, 40

Mitchell, John Jr., 32, 49, 56, 162n26

Monroe Doctrine, 20, 138

Montana, 23, 26

Morrow, John Jr., 80

Moss, James, 23, 24

"Mr. Dynamite" nickname, Young's, 134

Mullins, George, 26

Murphy, John H., 73

Murray, Daniel, 44

NAACP, 71, 74, 78, 92, 144, 147, 152

Nash, Ray, 78

Nashville, Tennessee, 42–43

National Education Association, 32

Native Americans, 7, 14, 20, 34, 39–40

The Negro and Fusion Politics in North Carolina (Edmonds), 50–51

Negro life project, Du Bois's, 172n25

Negro Silent Protest, 147

Negro Trail Blazers of California (Beasley), 66

New Negro ideology, 5, 10, 67, 93, 157n13

Newport News, Virginia, 82

newspaper coverage: bicycle expedition, 23; black officer campaign, 78, 162n26; black politics, 51; with black soldier correspondents, 8, 27–28, 37; chaplains, 29–30, 32; Cuba conflict, 47–48, 53, 54, 133–34, 162n25; of Flipper, 114, 115, 120–21, 124; Houston uprising, 73, 74; Philippines conflict, 56, 57, 60, 61; racial violence, 48; Sixth Virginia Infantry conflicts, 48, 49, 50; Washington lynching, 71; World War I, 89; Young's activities, 145, 148

Newton, Richard, 142

New York Age, 40

New York City, 163n34

New York Times, 124

Ngozi-Brown, Scot, 62–63

Nicholas, W. H., 135–36, 172n23

Nigeria, 148–49

Ninety-Second Division, 79, 83–85, 86–87, 91, 167n31

Ninety-Third (Provisional) Division, 79, 84, 86–87, *103*, 167n31

Ninth Cavalry: chaplains for, 25, 27–30; creation of, 18; Cuba conflict, 42, 46; education opportunities, 25; national park assignment, 137–38, 173n28; Philippines conflict, 59, 135–36; photograph, *99*; reenlistments, 22; responses to racial violence, 13–14, 33–34, 35–36; western frontier postings, 21; Young's commissions, 131–32, 135–37

Ninth Ohio Battalion, Cuba conflict, 133–34

Ninth Volunteer Regiment, Cuba conflict, 161n23

Nolan, Nicholas, 116

Nordstrom, Charles, 116

North Carolina, 40, 82

Notes of a Native Son (Baldwin), 151

O'Donnell battle, 60–61, 164n56

officers, black: as civil rights issue, 5; during Civil War, 38, 44; during Cuba conflict, 46, 56; from National Guard units, 79; North Carolina regulation, 53; during Philippines conflict, 52, 56; Sixth Virginia Infantry conflicts, 48–50; training camps, 67, 75, 76–78, 82, 146; on western frontier, 28; White's advocacy for, 160n7; World War I issues, 84, 85. *See also* Flipper, Henry Ossian; Young, Charles

Ohio National Guard, 132, 133–34, 148

Omaha Press, 28

Otis, E. S., 59, 163n41, 164n51

Owen, Chandler, 89

Pan-African movement, 91, 92–93, 140, 141

Panic of 1893, 39

Patterson, Major, 85

Pershing, John "Black Jack," 70, 84, 86, 145, 148

Philippine Constabulary Band, *104*, 127, 140

Philippines: Spanish colonization, 55, 163n42, 163n43; U.S. purchase, 163n42; Young's assignments, 135–36, 140, 172n136. *See also* Filipino Rebellion

Phillips, Thomas, 5

Pierce, Charles C., 25

pioneer battalions, World War I, 83, 88–89, 167n40

Plan of San Diego, 68–69, 165n6

Plessy v. Ferguson, 3–4, 40, 160n6

Plummer, Henry V., 9, 14, 25, 27–30, 131

Pogue, P. C., 59, 164n53

police officers, military, 90, *104*

Ponder, Ephraim G., 110

postmaster killing, 41

Powell, Colin, 125

Powell, Thomas, 112

Prioleau, George, 9, 40, 42, 54, 59, 145

Pryor, Captain, 82

Punitive Expedition, Mexico conflict. *See* Mexico, border conflicts

Quapo Pacific Commercial Company, 62

quartermaster assignment, Flipper's, 117–18

race man, defined, 9

race war plan, 68–69, 165n6

Racial Beachhead (McKibbon), 6

racial uplift motive, overviews: Cuba conflict, 40–41, 43; military service, 4–5, 14–15; in officer training campaign, 76; Philippines conflict, 63, 65; post–World War I activism, 91–92; with role modeling, 43–45, 52; soldier education, 24–25, 26–27; West Point cadets/graduates, 111, 120; World War I service, 81. *See also* Young, Charles

racial violence/abuse: Dakota Territory, 24; Georgia, 48, 50, 52; Louisiana, 16; Nebraska, 13; North Carolina, 53, 82; South Carolina, 41; Southern region

Le'Trice D. Donaldson, an assistant professor of African American and U.S. history at the Texas A&M University–Corpus Christi, is the author of *A Voyage through the African American Experience*.